GAMBLERS' MONEY

The New Force in American Life

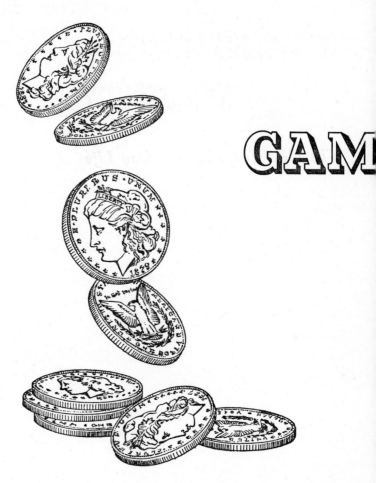

GAM

THE RIVERSIDE PRESS CAMBRIDGE

BLERS'
MONEY

The New Force in American Life

BY WALLACE TURNER

HOUGHTON MIFFLIN COMPANY BOSTON

CONTENTS

GAMBLERS'
MONEY

The New Force in American Life

1

THE LAND OF FUNNY MONEY

LAS VEGAS is an enchanting place, seen first at night with the illusion at its brightest when the thrill of great movement and strong colors and flashing lights can best work their intoxication. There comes a reckoning for this hilarity, a penalty to be paid for defying the laws of emotional stability by soaring in spirit through the neon-lit desert night.

Gambling is legal in Las Vegas, as in all of Nevada, yet many of the casino operators still live the furtive lives of conspirators. They spent so many years in illegal gambling operations in other states that they seem unaware sometimes of their legal status in Nevada. They were schooled in the rackets; their thought patterns are based on those experiences.

The twelve casino hotels provide the heartbeat of Las Vegas, but only one of them is inside the city limits. The others are scattered for four miles on either side of the highway to Los Angeles. This is the Las Vegas Strip. The Strip controls Las Vegas, feeds it, hires it, directs it, owns it, supports it, but resolutely refuses to be a part of it.

Remember this, for it demonstrates a quality about the gambling bosses, the casino owners, that gives them a powerful position in the American economy. They are experts in leverage. With their beachhead at the city limits, they control Las Vegas. With Las Vegas, they have strength in the state capitol in Carson City. This strength in Carson City gives them a strong voice in national politics, for the senators from Nevada speak with exactly the same authority as the senators from New York.

This power in politics is visible. Close examination makes its outlines apparent, for the execution of political aims must sooner or later be done in the open in our open society. But in their effect on the economic life of the United States, the gamblers are able to be more secretive. They are able to exert leverage with their money, for they have rivers of it pouring in from the slot machines and gambling tables. They use it in many ways, for the casinos produce wealth beyond the consumption capacity of their major owners. This pressure has brought about the move into business activity. The ethic of the racket has followed the new investments. This financial power in the hands of some gamblers is a new force in American life, a force for evil.

Powerful through great wealth, these men serve as a transmission belt through which the tactics of the underworld move into legitimate business and economic and sociopolitical structures. They grew up accustomed to extortion and look upon it as a usual business method.

The force is present, and backed by wealth as it moves through the American economy, through the nation's political life, and into our social organizations — even into the religious organizations. Some Las Vegas gamblers revel in the opportunity to subsidize a church and its pastor. The line of their ambition is clear to read: they have money, stacks of it; they have legality in Nevada; now they want respectability; and also they want more money, more power, more control, more legal status. The men who have risen to the top of this gambling operation were born with insatiable hunger for money, for power, for control — for security. They are unsure men. They worry and fret and shy at shadows. This quality comes from their backgrounds in the rackets. We shall examine some of these backgrounds in detail.

For now it suffices to understand that Las Vegas is controlled largely by men who spent their early years as bootleggers during the prohibition era, or as members of the gangs of the 1920's. Others spent many years in illegal casinos in Kentucky, Florida or Chicago before coming to Nevada to operate within the law.

These men and their money constitute the new force in American life — a force fattened on the gambling table profits and motivated by the morals and ethics of the gambling table. This force affects the careers of such public personalities as Frank Sinatra. It feeds on the great pension funds of the Teamsters Union. Robert G. Baker, the former secretary to the United States Senate majority, was in business arrangements with some of the Nevada gamblers including Edward Levinson, the leading figure in the Fremont Hotel. Money from the Nevada gambling tables contributed to a succession of scandals on Wall Street. Latin-American diplomats have been bagmen for the Nevada gamblers, shielding their satchels full of hot money behind the diplomatic immunities of their passports. The criminal conspiracy known as Cosa Nostra has reached a bloodstained hand into the Nevada gambling casinos. Not even the treasury of the federal government itself is immune to the maneuvers of the Nevada gamblers.

The earnings of some of these casinos are immense. Every effort is made by the gamblers to keep these figures secret, for the best of the gambling operators is by nature a secretive man. His is a highly competitive business. Secrecy and conspiracy rule his life. But he must report his gross winnings to the Nevada Gaming Commission for computation of the 5.5 percent tax charged for a casino license. Nevada authorities compiled a list of the earnings of the top thirty places for 1961, intending it for internal use only, but it fell into the hands of some of the Strip gamblers who dribbled out the figures.

It is significant that for 1961 three of the top four money winners were in northern Nevada, not in Las Vegas. In first place was Harrah's Club at Lake Tahoe, at about $20,000,000. Harold's Club in Reno was second with about $13,000,000 in gross winnings, and Harrah's Club in Reno was fourth with about $10,000,000.

William Harrah, sole owner of the places bearing his name, is a man with a passion for restoring old cars, of which he has garages full, and for racing hydroplanes on Lake Tahoe, which he subsidizes at annual costs of hundreds of thousands of dollars. Harold's Club was sold in 1962 by the Smith family which founded it in the 1930's. The Smiths continued to run the place on a leaseback agreement.

It is not unusual for an individual or a group to have more than one casino license, as Harrah does at Lake Tahoe and Reno. The third and fifth spots on this list of the 1961 top money-makers were held by two places on the Las Vegas Strip: the Stardust, third with about $12,000,000 winnings, and Wilbur Clark's Desert Inn, fifth with about $9,000,000. Both are owned by substantially the same group, led by a band of former bootleggers and gamblers from Cleveland and Detroit.

Some observers of the Nevada scene find it remarkable that William Harrah's gambling hall at Lake Tahoe reported earnings twice as large as those of the Desert Inn, one of the leading places on the Las Vegas Strip. Lake Tahoe is in the High Sierra. Deep winter snows cut down the clientele there for several months of the year, while the Desert Inn operates in a year-round climate, thanks to air conditioning. State and federal tax authorities note these peculiarities very carefully. Gambling is susceptible to income concealment. There are no invoices, no checks, no credit cards. The gamblers themselves keep the records. Complicated systems have been devised to prevent this concealment, just as the casino operators have invented intricate ways to insure themselves against theft by their employees. The protection schemes leak, however.

"Top racketeers always deal in cash and there are innumerable ways to conceal cash from the very best investigators," Attorney General Robert F. Kennedy said. "One is the 'skimming' operation, conducted behind barred doors, in which a large percentage of the proceeds of so called legal gambling is skimmed off and then hidden."

Tracing the money hidden from the tax collector is one of the chief problems facing the large groups of investigators combing Las Vegas during the early 1960's. Such hidden money is useful for all sorts of evil purposes — for bribes, for a hired murder, to buy heroin. The uses are governed only by the need and ingenuity of the criminals who have this cash at their disposal. We shall examine this further.

But first, look at Las Vegas and the Strip.

This is the strangest city in America. The list of its peculiarities could be endless. It exists to get money and is said not to recognize any colors but green; yet a Negro in Las Vegas had best be Sammy Davis, Jr., if he wants to stay at one of the casino hotels. Neither he nor his money can expect to be received willingly at any of them. The men who run Las Vegas are white supremists as much as if they came from Johannesburg.

The line of casino hotels stretches along the highway into the desert and looks like nothing else in this land, except for a slight resemblance to the line of hotels that marches up the strand at Miami Beach. But there is a great difference even in this comparison: the main purpose of the Strip hotels is gambling. All other activities are subordinated to the casino. In Miami Beach, the entertainment is sold as a commodity — as a part of the total recreation package of sun, sea and relaxation. But in Las Vegas the entertainment is given away or served up far below cost to entice the suckers near the gambling tables.

The casino promotion expenses are immense. So are the prices paid to top entertainers. Some of them are said to get as much as $40,000 a week on the Strip. A few years ago Wilbur Clark's

Desert Inn, one of the leading casino hotels, was compelled to make public its entertainment and promotion expenses. They amounted to more than $2,500,000, while the reported net earnings for that year were $1,700,000. These promotion and entertainment expenses for the Desert Inn probably are greater now. Remember also that this is but one of a dozen such places in Las Vegas. This multimillion-dollar outpouring has had immense effect on the cost structure of the entertainment business in the United States.

Also, it has had a great effect on the dream images that flit through the mass mind of America. These dollars spent on promotion and advertising, together with other great changes in the nation, have given Las Vegas a place in the national dreamworld comparable to that held by the Hollywood world of fantasy when the star system flourished and Hollywood was at its peak. Where once Clara Bow or Jean Harlow were erotic figures in the world of dreams, an imagined world at Las Vegas now grips many minds. The Las Vegas show girl, the sexual satisfactions felt by the compulsive gambler, and the heady excitements aroused by the Las Vegas atmosphere of immorality fill the dreamworlds of thousands of minds.

Hollywood was a wonderful dream for the depression-tied generation. In a way it was a harmless dream. Hollywood's licentiousness and delicious amorality was closed to all but the members of the club. True enough, the movie industry produced moguls who pranced around among their herds of lovely women like aging stallions; it produced handsome young men to cater to the movie queens whose beauty was fading; it changed the morals of the nation, and probably for the worse. But when it was all added up, Hollywood was an industrial plant, controlled by the men who had money enough to finance the expensive movie-making process. These were bankers and businessmen. They controlled Hollywood. The glorified pimps and whores and racketeers who infested the place did not control it. At the bottom of it all, Hollywood's approach to the dollar was the businessman's approach, based on contracts, options, and court decisions, and then supported in the law.

There are great differences between this and Las Vegas. In the gambling places, the underworld still is king; contract enforcement may be by bullet and muscle, by threat and intimidation. The law is held in low esteem. Moreover, on the Strip, the carnality of a sexual fantasy land is open to anyone willing to pay the price. Big gamblers automatically are members of the club. Money qualifies anyone. One day you can be running a hardware store in Walla Walla and the next be a high roller on the Strip with a beautiful whore assigned to keep you company. The decisions here are made by a different sort of man from those who ran Hollywood. The effect on American life is different, too.

The advertising and publicity promotion from the Strip has a theme all its own. Generally, a thoughtful man can discover what elements of his personality rise to the applied psychology of the advertisement for tires or razor blades or Scotch whisky. But the wise man will shrink from discovering what it is within him that responds to the pitch from the Strip. These campaigns create a twofold impulse: Get to Las Vegas. Take the money. These ads and publicity releases sell a vague and hazy outline of sexuality; they also peddle that universal dream of mankind — something for nothing. There may exist some device for summoning in the sheep for shearing that has been ignored by the Las Vegas casino operators, but it escapes the eye of the neophyte. They buy full-color advertisements in magazines. They achieve frequent mention in columns and in television shows. They distribute thousands upon thousands of brochures, pseudo-personal letters and postcards. To leave a business card in a Las Vegas casino office is to assure receipt for months to come of a steady stream of promotional literature.

The following extracts are from a promotion letter from the Mint, a casino operated at 100 Fremont Street in downtown Las Vegas. Its tone is less elegant than the language of the Strip promotion letters. But it has pulling power:

> The Mint's Fall Fun Festival brings you 14 EXCITING PARTY DAYS you will long remember . . . Be sure to visit us and deposit your drawing ticket . . . If your name is the lucky one drawn, you will approach the gift-laden, colorful Fall Fun Festival Board on the Merri-Mint Stage. At a given signal, you may select your exciting CandyStripe envelope. You are guaranteed a minimum of $100 — but you may win as high as $500. Be sure to be around for the drawings which start at 10 A.M. and run right through the day until midnight. Twice daily, at 3:30 P.M. and 11:30 P.M., we roll out the Golden Wheelbarrow — and if your name is drawn, you get the opportunity to stuff as many Silver Dollars into an airlines travel bag with one hand as is possible in 20 seconds. And — we guarantee each winning contestant a minimum of 300 silver dollars.

In the same envelope was a brochure advertising "Pat Moreno's Artists & Models Revue . . . Downtown's only production show with GIRLS . . . GIRLS . . . GIRLS." The Mint even had a great day planned for those who wanted to spend Thanksgiving Day in the gambling joint. There were to be drawings for eight cash prizes, including three of $1000 each.

The places have different promotion devices. The Las Vegas Hacienda literally marks the end of the line on the Strip — the last outpost before the long trek through the desert to Los Angeles. This place has its own airline, and puts advertisements in newspapers on the Pacific Coast and in the Mountain States offering what amounts to free transportation. Once in the Hacienda's clutches, the visitor is likely to stay. A taxi ride into town and back may cost him as much as an extra night in the low-priced rooms in the casino hotel. So he stays at the Hacienda's gambling tables until he has cashed in the last of the markers of the refund from the price of his package tour. His other resources are soon exhausted. Then they deliver him, baggy-eyed and twitchy-handed, back to the airport and fly him to Los Angeles or San Diego where he must face another Monday morning. After all, he must be delivered home to get some more money to come back and feed the tiger.

The cheaper casinos organize bus trips; the more expensive places encourage the use of regular airlines by paying back a part of the fare. Just how many people these devices entice into the casinos is anyone's guess. But a clue came in the late fall of 1963 when an estimate was made of the traffic through the back country of Northern California into Lake Tahoe. This guess came from the California department of agriculture. It runs inspection stations at the border, stopping all surface traffic. The estimate was two thousand people a day from California into Lake Tahoe. From the more populous areas of Southern California, they pour in much greater numbers into Las Vegas. But the casino operators are unsatisfied working the close-to-home population lodes in the California cities. They encourage the travel agencies to send tours through Las Vegas. The Union Pacific passenger station is at the head of Fremont Street downtown; the honkytonk gambling joints fill the landscape. The airport is mortised in at the edge of the Strip, where the traveler must pass the casino hotels to get into town, in the unlikely event that he has other business in Las Vegas beyond gambling.

The airport, named McCarran Field for the late Senator Pat McCarran, has a fancy terminal building that would appear better suited to a city the size of Seattle than to this 175,000-population desert gambling center. It seems far more spacious than the Washington National Airport. Of course, it was built largely with federal money. The gamblers have talent for getting federal money. It seems fitting that the field should be named for the late Senator McCarran, who was almost a deity to the gamblers. He watched over their interests as if they were his children, which in a sense they were. But the Senator had weaknesses as a statesman. The following quotation is from a letter written by a man who served in the United States Senate with Pat McCarran:

> More than half the bills that went through the Senate originated in the Judiciary Committee, of which McCarran was chairman. He ran the committee with an iron hand and held a pistol at the temple of many a senator. He had absolute power over the so-called "private bills," of great importance to all senators.

This was Senator McCarran and he was the gamblers' senator. When they had trouble, they went to him and he would help if he could.

In a sense, the gamblers really market their "product" on some of the same basic theories that the big grocery stores use. Impulse decides for most people whether to gamble, just as frequently impulse decides which soap to buy. The trick for the gambling operators is to lure potential players into sight and sound of their gambling tables and slot machines.

"Volume!" is their cry, just as it is the grocery store manager's. This is why much of their promotion is directed at the theme: Just come to Las Vegas. The gamblers' great ability to use someone else's money was never better illustrated than in the construction in 1960 of a $6,000,000 convention center a short distance from the Strip. It stands outside the city of Las Vegas, a short cab ride from the line of casino hotels. The existence of this magnificent convention hall has pulled the members of several major national organizations into the orbit of the gambling tables — which of course was the idea. Construction costs were paid by bonds issued by Clark County, Nevada. A small room tax on motels and hotels will retire the bonds. The room tax is paid by the visitors. Thus the gamblers have acquired another gimmick, absolutely free.

They have always enjoyed an affinity with convention crowds, even in the old days when the best they could do was the banquet rooms of their hotels. They particularly enjoyed the visits of those convention crowds where some members had almost unlimited spending money and a desire to gamble it away. Strange things happened to the bookkeeping sometimes. Here's an example:

In the late 1950's, the Western Conference of Teamsters became the object of several investigations, so that the dusty records of past expense accounts were pulled out and examined. As a part of this, Dave Beck, the international president of the Teamsters, went to jail and James R. Hoffa became his successor. But one of the surprising bills discovered in the Teamsters' archives was from the Desert Inn. It was a bill to Frank W. Brewster, the president of the Western Conference of Teamsters in those years. Mr. Brewster and other Teamster officials had attended a "business session" at Las Vegas. Several rooms were billed to Mr. Brewster's account. But one of the fascinating things was the notation that Mr. Brewster had drawn $750 in the casino and charged it to his hotel bill. Then the bill was forwarded to the union offices in Seattle and was paid from union funds. It is highly unlikely that Mr. Brewster was able to leave the casino with any of the $750, or that he won anything with that stake. At any rate, nothing else shows on the record. Apparently, the union paid Brewster's gambling losses.

In the business of manipulating the public's desires, one of the most effective tools is a sweet and friendly piece in a national magazine, illustrated in full color and packed with all the good selling words. The Las Vegas Strip publicity and advertising directors specialize in getting these. They stand ready to play host to a swarm of hungry and thirsty reporters flown in by some airline or on a promotion tour. A few years ago the Strip reaped a great harvest of free newspaper space when interminable delays postponed atomic weapons tests at Frenchman's Flat. This kept the reporters sitting around Las Vegas with nothing to write except feature stories on gambling and entertainment.

In the fall of 1962 *Argosy* magazine carried a classic example of the Las Vegas travel piece. This one extolled the glories of the gambling center in phrases such as these:

"A town blessed by an ideal year-round climate . . . Headquarters for many excellent restaurants . . . A year-round center for major spectator sports events . . . A booming convention city . . . A new dimension of respectability . . . Most accessible . . . Best and most exciting vacation buy."

Now this is gamy stuff, and touches many of the sublimated desires of mankind. But it stands up poorly under analysis. The climate is not ideal unless you trace your ancestry back to the lizards. This is a desert, hot as the hinges of hell in the summer, and always dry. Nothing except cactus and desert shrubs grow there without irrigation. There is so little water that they use the effluent from the sewage treatment plants to irrigate the golf courses.

There are some good restaurants operated as part of the lure in some of the casino hotels. But "headquarters"? The major spectator sports events consist of a golf tournament or so promoted by casino hotels such as the Sahara and Wilbur Clark's Desert Inn, and an occasional big-time fight. The advent of the fights to Las Vegas was caused by the shift from arena gate receipts to the proceeds of nationwide theater television as the promoters' chief reliance. But the gamblers love having the fights in Las Vegas. It brings in all those sporting types who fight their hearts out at the gambling tables before and after the two gladiators thump each other around in the ring.

There is an element of accuracy in describing Las Vegas as a booming convention city, since the public built the big convention center for the gamblers' benefit. But the phrase "a new dimension of respectability" shocks the comprehension. Who can say what it means? Finally, Las Vegas is accessible, but no more so than is Phoenix or San Diego. "Best and most exciting vacation buy" must have been thrown in to satisfy the economy-minded.

None of this language dominated the piece, however. Outshouting everything else was a three-quarter-page color photograph of a Las Vegas show girl in costume: A black top hat, arm-length black gloves, lots of costume jewelry, and a black something-or-other about big enough to make two handkerchiefs. Said the caption: "The scenery is part of action indoors and out for those not busy with the gaming." (Gaming is the euphemism used extensively and officially in Nevada for gambling.)

There you have the elements of the pitch: an all purpose sales job, scatter-gunned to hit any susceptible mind; and a color photo of sex, wild and young and lovely and available at least for looking. But there was more. In fact, this is the clincher:

"There's no law that says you can't win, if you do play. Some of the professional gamblers, like Nick the Greek, as well as thousands of lucky amateurs, have come away with sizable stakes."

This is pure foolishness, of course, for there is such a law, called the law of mathematical probability, and it works for the house, not the customer. But one can visualize this paragraph pushing an otherwise prudent man over the hump of decision. He will, he decides, go to Las Vegas and, like Nick the Greek, earn a fortune at the gambling tables.

Sad and bitter, but preordained events follow. If he has even a modicum of judgment, this fortune hunter will set aside money for his fare home. Otherwise, he faces a grim future. To be a vagrant in Las Vegas is to invite a jail sentence and when all is finished he may get a one-way ticket to the stateline. Everything is against the stranger. The gamblers whose money he wants to win own the tables, the dice, the cards, the slot machines he plays with. They hire the people who control the games — the dealers, pit bosses, even the shills who surround the tables and entice Hiram Hayseed, the fortune hunter, to this crap table or that twenty-one game. The sheriff, the police, the preachers, the social workers — all are friends of the gamblers.

The boss gamblers take every precaution to prevent winning by their customers — winning of any meaningful sums, that is. These gamblers make much of their reputation as being too smart to cheat. They argue that if the word should spread that their games were dishonest, their investments would suffer. The answer to this is simple: the penalty is paid not for cheating, but for getting caught at cheating. They do not get caught. The Nevada Gaming Commission and the State Gaming Control Board have small staffs, with just a few investigators, and they plainly cannot keep track of the operations of all the casinos. But these are the agencies which stand between the gambling public and the ravenous tigers who control the casinos. When a gambler is caught cheating, they probably will take his license. But there are so many things he can do without actually resorting to cheating. (If these all fail, then stern measures can be taken, don't forget.) He can tinker with the odds on his crap table layout cloths. Or he can readjust the slot machines so that they pay out a little less. Or he can send a lovely girl to distract the attention of a high roller in the midst of a long winning streak. All these things change the chance of winning for the player. None is actually cheating. In 1962, Nevada issued a Triennial

Report on gambling in which it recognized these factors' influence on winning and losing.

"In all games," said the report, "the odds may vary slightly among different casinos because of different house rules."

It was in this report that the state printed its famous discussion of the percentages involved in the various gambling games that it licenses. Even though they may actually have only clinical significance, these odds calculated by the state have interest. They cover the five major games played in Nevada casinos: slot machines, craps, twenty-one, roulette and keno. For some reason not immediately apparent, the gamblers who visit the Las Vegas casinos like craps better than any other game, but in the other parts of the state twenty-one is the favorite.

It is important that the statement of odds in gambling as presented by the Nevada authorities be considered in the light of its production. It was worked out through careful studies by mathematicians who screened out all the human elements. This, presumably, is the way it would be if computers gambled with each other. Thus far, except for isolated instances when it was done as a stunt, neither side has used computers at the gambling tables. But the gamblers are sure to install them soon.

In craps, the "passline" and "don't pass line" bets each give the casino an advantage of only 1.4 per cent [says the state report]. Most Nevada casinos also permit the craps shooter to take odds on the line bets. This means the player is allowed, after the point is established on the first roll of the dice, to back up his line bet with an additional bet that the point will or will not be made. This odds bet is paid off at the correct theoretical odds, which are 2-1 for points 4 and 10, 3-2 for points 5 and 9 and 6-5 for points 6 and 8. When the better takes odds, the casino's advantage is reduced to about .7 per cent.

Little has been known about twenty-one until recently,

because there are no theoretical odds as there are in other games of chance. As a result, gambling experts disagree on the advantage held by the house. The game of twenty-one can be played in different ways and the odds shift as the system of play varies. An experienced twenty-one player has a much better chance to win than a novice. Four scientists at Aberdeen Proving Grounds, Md., several years ago concluded from some exhaustive research that a twenty-one player, by following certain prescribed rules of play, can reduce the casino's percentage advantage of .6 per cent. A Massachusetts Institute of Technology scientist more recently concluded that the player could actually tip the game in his favor by following a certain method of play. His method apparently is a refinement of "counting the deck down," a system used by a few gamblers with good memories. In this system the player attempts to remember all the cards that are used during the play so that when only a few cards are left in the deck, he can vary his style of play accordingly. A few players have beaten Nevada casinos out of large sums of money by using this countdown system, but most casinos thwart such a player by simply reshuffling the deck after only half the cards have been used.

Most Nevada roulette wheels have both a single and a double zero, which result in an approximate advantage of 5.26 per cent for the casino. This percentage is only approximate because the percentage is 7.89 for a split bet on five numbers, a bet made very infrequently. Roulette is popular with some gamblers because it is the game which most easily lends itself to system playing. For roulette wheels in perfect mechanical condition, of course, there is no mathematical system possible which will enable the player to beat the wheel.

In Nevada, competition is keen among casinos and none will attract much business from slot machine players if it sets the machines to retain a high percentage of the money played. Consequently, most of Nevada's slot machines retain less than 10 per cent of the dollar played and many machines hold as little as 5 per cent of the money played. However, these mechanical odds are certain and no one can beat the slot machines if he plays them consistently over a long period of time.

Keno is played with 80 numbers, of which the better selects as few as one can or as many as 15. Twenty of the 80 numbers are randomly drawn from a metal cage and the player wins or loses according to how many numbers he selected appear among the 20 drawn. The maximum amount of payoff on a given keno game is $25,000 and it is possible for a better to win this amount for a bet of only 50 cents. Overall, the casino's percentage in keno averages about 20 per cent, the percentage varying somewhat according to different ways in which the tickets are marked.

There you have it: Under the most favorable possible conditions — a fair shake — the player at the crap table stands to lose from .7 percent to 1.4 percent, depending on his skill. At twenty-one, they shuffle the cards to mess up his possibility of winning through superior skill, leaving him with a certainty of .6 percent against him. The roulette player may feel like one of the more rakish Hapsburgs, but still the house has 5.26 percent against him. Roulette system players are looked upon by the state as misguided children and greeted by the casino operators with sly and happy smiles. Keno is just another version of the multi-numbered lottery ticket popularized in West Coast cities by the Chinese decades ago. A 20 percent house advantage should frighten off all the keno players. Either they haven't heard or they don't believe it, for they still line up to mark their tickets for the next drawing.

Beyond all this, the tax collection records of the state of Nevada prove conclusively that the only gamblers who win are those who own the tables. In 1963, the gambling houses reported to the state that they won $248,000,000.

So to assert that "there's no law that says you can't win" is to gloss over the realities of life in the gambling houses. The casinos never miss an opportunity to create the feeling that big winnings are not only possible, but also are probable. A few years ago articles appeared in newspapers across the country about a group of young men who had invented a system for beating slot machines. A great air of mystery was created and followed the journeys of these heroes as they moved across Nevada to trounce the nefarious gambling interests. It had everything, did this tale: The young stalwarts pitted against the evil old ones; a succession of victories for the heroes; a never-solved mystery of the secret of their success; an excellent line of communications to the daily press provided by the publicity agents of the casinos who rushed forth to help chronicle the defeats of their employers.

It was marvelous.

The truth is that it was just a little bit too good to be true. There was a suggestion, even before the valiant young men faded from the news columns, that they were a traveling advertising act. This would have been in an American tradition. In times long gone, when the nation and its frauds were less sophisticated, there was usually an enthusiastic stranger who bought the first bottle of snake oil at the traveling medicine shows. But who can calculate how many persons were persuaded to do battle with the inhuman slot machine, convinced that its automatic, cogwheeled brain could be deceived? The slot machine does what its keeper orders. Here's a story that shows it. The fellow who told it had been a business visitor to a Las Vegas casino, and was talking with one of the chief owners about his losses of silver dollars in the slot machines.

"He pointed to one over in the corner and told me to try it. I did. I got about $150 and won everytime, until he pulled me off of it. I said I'd be back in the morning.

" 'You have to find your own machine tomorrow,' he told me."

Of all the advertising pitches made by the Strip gambling casinos, the greatest attention is paid to creating the hint of sexuality, possibly because this is the one that is most compelling for many customers. Whether this advertising device is conscious or subconscious on the part of the casino management is an open question. Some psychiatrists have argued that all compulsive gamblers are sexually motivated. However it may be, the casinos place heavy emphasis on sex in their advertising and entertainment.

Each of those on the Strip has a big theater-dining room built into it. This is where the high-priced entertainers present their acts. These acts must be so constructed that the permanent chorus line can be worked in. So every night these lovely, long-legged dancers appear on stage, contributing to the vision of Las Vegas that the casino owners hope is burning at the mind of mankind across the continent. The dancers certainly contribute to the general air of suppressed excitement that the gambling operators seek to create. Are there prostitutes among them? Las Vegas being what it is, undoubtedly some of the girls sell themselves for money on occasions. Some of the men who run the casinos and hotels that employ the chorus girls move among the most unscrupulous hoodlums the United States has produced. To some of these, sex is just another commodity and they would insist that it be sold.

But prostitution in Las Vegas has changed in the past few years. There are no houses where prostitutes live together, as they once did. There are no streetwalkers. But there are many call girls, and frequently they do business only through the staff of one or more of the casinos. Some may share their fees with the casino employees who refer them. Others may be called directly by the casino management to deal with a heavy winner and distract him, or at the least keep him in town until the pendulum of the percentages swings again to the house and he is relieved of his winnings.

Las Vegas has many bitter people living in it. Here is a part of what one of those wrote about his town's sexual morality: "This city has more trash peddlers, per capita, than any city three times its size, more broken homes, more prostitutes, and more so-called common law marriages than any city five times its size."

The big-name shows that play to the supper-club crowds in the casinos have contributed a lot to the American image of Las Vegas. An erroneous assumption grew up, built on the flood of propaganda about how reasonable the prices are in Las Vegas. This caused first-time visitors to expect to hear Frank Sinatra or Jack Benny for free, just by wandering into the casino. It doesn't work that way. These shows — which at one time or another have featured the top entertainment talent of the world — are put on in the combination dining room-theater during and after dinner. Two persons can get by on as little as $12, or it can run to more, much more. The tables are crowded together, and one ends up eating with total strangers. Registered guests of the hotel get priority in that hotel's dinner theater. During the slow times, reservations may be had easily by those from other places, or sometimes it is possible to get in without a reservation. The food and services vary widely among the twelve Las Vegas casino hotels. As a general statement, both are better than adequate. The show will vary sharply, depending on the general tone of the place. For example, three places have turned to permanent shows built around almost nude women, while others have such top-drawer entertainers as Harry Belafonte or Eddie Fisher or Jerry Colonna. The shows are short and the food service fast. It must be remembered that all of this entertainment exists only to pull the potential gambler to within sound and sight of the dice and cards and whirling slot machine reels.

"Feed 'em. Give 'em a show. Put 'em out there gambling."

This is the motto of all the supper clubs. But there are other restaurants within all the casinos, too, and the variance in quality of these is very wide. One of the finest is in the Tropicana, a casino hotel in which Frank Costello, the notorious underworld leader, is said to have once had an interest. It has an absolutely luxurious dining room, staffed with an impeccable set of captains, waiters and busboys. Outside, beyond a 150-foot curved wall of glass, a set of fountains changes continually, and it all seems to be an oasis of calm and quiet. But as dusk comes, lights begin to play on the fountains. The colors are of the most vibrant reds. The calm and quiet disappear. The prices are epicurean.

Some people are able to go to Las Vegas, check into a low-priced room and enjoy the sun, the shows, and the activity, but stay away from the gambling.

"As soon as we arrive, we put $10 in the slot machines and that's it — not another dime," one iron-willed visitor explained.

But every motivation supplied to the visitor edges him toward the tables, and shoves his hand toward his wallet. If he stops to watch, soon an employee is elbowing him aside. The place is for gamblers; if you don't gamble, go somewhere else. Thus many of those who go to Las Vegas to sit in the sun and swim in the great pools and play golf and rest find themselves suddenly in the casinos, unaware whether the sun shines or the moon is out, not knowing the time, their stomachs shrunken from the psychological pressures of the gambling table, their minds benumbed by the free drinks served to them at the tables.

One of the maxims of the gambler, carried over to Las Vegas from the days when he ran an illegal joint in an alley in Chicago or New York or Miami, is this — give them something to drink and to eat and they'll stay right there until you have all their money. So pretty girls in scanty costumes carry free drinks to the gamblers and others bring them sandwiches.

The cocktail waitresses fight for these jobs; the opportunities

But it is said that these security guards also serve other purposes. They are a tough, hard crowd and it has been charged in the past that many of their number have extensive police records.

The lounge is on the right, against the wall toward the highway. In there a quartet of cowboy singers moaned through "Tumbling Tumbleweed." One of them said he helped write the song. The bar had a small crowd in it. There were a few couples; a few pairs of women with the look of package tourists spending the allotted hours on "Las Vegas glamorous Strip"; a few men alone; and one woman alone, sleek and lovely and filled with life's elemental purposes just as is a hungry tiger shark.

The lounge was paneled in fine woods, with the main bar running in front of the turntable stage. The cowboy singers waved goodbye as the turning stage brought on a new act. This was a harmonica chorus. It includes a midget and featured crude sight gags.

There were two other liquor service bars, one on each side of the room, and from these the cocktail waitresses moved in and out. The sound system in the lounge brought on the music and dialogue clearly, but not too loudly. Across a low screen, the murmur of the gamblers and the rattle of the chips, the low calls of the croupiers are audible in the lounge. Beyond the tables and banks of slot machines, the voice of Eddie Fisher occasionally escaped from the dining room-theater. When the theater emptied, the crowd of gamblers thickened and the pace of the waitresses to the liquor service bar quickened.

The gamblers were edgy and unhappy, as they usually are. The slot machine players were a little more splendid than those of the Casino Center places downtown on Fremont Street, but still they lacked the éclat of the roulette crowd. The faces around the crap tables were intent, drawn and unsmiling. There was small talk at some of the twenty-one tables. But nobody ever seemed to have a belly laugh.

Outside, the moonlight gave the Desert Inn an undeserved beauty. A gray-haired couple, finished with Eddie Fisher at the supper club and with the gambling in the casino, came out into the patio, took a turn around the swimming pool, and walked through the big arch that towers over it. Then, holding hands, they strolled down the gentle slope toward the hotel's high rent district, leaving behind the turmoil of the gambling hell that supports this moon-struck paradise.

By 1 A.M. the crowd was thinning inside, so that the anxious and compulsive were more obvious, as were the young girls with middle-aged men, the frantic talkers to the dice and the gambling pit boss who was trying to make time with one of the dancers from the chorus line. His approach seemed typical of Las Vegas. He had her play with a blackjack dealer who had no customers, then looked at the dealer's cards before advising her whether she should draw more cards. Of course she won.

This byplay has little to do with the serious gambling, or with the elaborate systems the casinos set up to prevent their employees from stealing, or those the state and federal governments use to try to get all the winnings into taxable accounts. One of the big problems of the casino owners arises from the ease with which their own employees could enter into agreements with confederates to rig the games so that the friends would win big sums. Bluntly, this threat is met in large part by intimidation. A dealer who cheats the house seriously may count on being severely beaten. It is widely believed around Las Vegas that a few dealers who cheated the house were murdered and their bodies buried in the desert. From the point of view of diminishing the natural acquisitive instincts of the dealers, it matters not whether this is true: that the dealers believe it is enough.

But in addition to intimidation, the watchful eyes of the pit bosses tend to keep the dealers in line. Just as some of the pit bosses have eyes that can melt steel welds, some of the dealers can make a deck of cards do almost anything. For those who love to watch the grace of any professional in action, the way some of the Las Vegas dealers handle cards is pure poetry. The pasteboards seem to be extensions of their fingers, appear to move and riffle themselves, seem to slide independently off the pack and into piles before the players. In Las Vegas there are no women dealers, for this is an affectation of Reno which the Las Vegas crowd shuns and abhors — particularly the men who have jobs as dealers. Women work in various positions in the casinos — as payoff girls for the slot machines, as cocktail waitresses, and cashiers. But none deals.

In their years outside the law, the casino operators have learned all the tricks that crooked dealers can use. If these are to be used in the Strip casinos, the system is set up for them to be used for the house, not against it. The process by which a dealer and his confederates steal the house bankroll is so common in the illegal places that it even has a name: The Takeoff. A dealer who participated in a Takeoff on the Strip would never be able to spend his share in peace.

The gamblers assume an outward congratulatory attitude toward winners like that of an insurance adjuster who has paid a claim. Inwardly, there is good reason to believe, they burn at the thought of any of their money being carried out by a winner. It's serious enough to consider the guy taking out the money he brought in the door. To think of him taking out the house's money is horrible.

The casino management feels this same way toward the tax collector. The same ingenuity that sets traps for the employees is brought to bear on the problem of successfully cheating on taxes. The state of Nevada charges 5.5 percent of the gross winnings as its fee for a casino license. The federal government wants 48 percent of 1965 corporation profits as its share. So if a gambling operator can hide $100,000 of his 1965 winnings, he really has saved himself $52,500.

This concealment of income is accomplished in many ways. The simplest is just to fail to record some of the winnings each day. This is the process called "skimming" and since it is the most readily imagined, it is the one most carefully guarded against. The risk of this sort of concealment is high for the casino operator, as can be realized from this description of the process of counting the winnings as it was done in one Las Vegas casino:

The casinos run on a three-shift basis. The shifts begin at noon, at 8 P.M. and 4 A.M. The money and chips on each table are counted at the shift change. Dealers alternate during the eight hours so no dealer is responsible for an individual table. But the shift boss, a shrewd and experienced gambler, is responsible for the entire casino bankroll during his shift. This ensures that the money and chips are well counted at the beginning of each shift.

Three kinds of exchange are used in the gambling casinos — silver dollars, chips and currency. The currency never passes from the house to the players at a table. It moves only from the player to the house. It must go immediately into a slot that leads from the tabletop into a locked box fastened to the bottom of each gambling table. The dealer is even required to shove it into the slot by use of a transparent bit of celluloid. This prevents the palming of the currency by these men whose marvelous dexterity is their livelihood.

There may be $10,000 or more in silver and chips on each crap table at the beginning of the shift. The half dozen or so blackjack tables and the two or three roulette wheels will have stakes of $2000 or more. If a run of luck against the house pulls down these table stakes, a "fill" is ordered and a record kept of the increased stakes for this table. A "draw" or "overage" is used to remove some of the silver and chips if the table wins more than the racks can conveniently hold.

State law requires that a record be kept of each individual table, and of each slot machine, on a shift basis. So at the end of each shift a complete balance of the earning record of each table must be made. The count of chips and silver by the incoming shift boss provides some of the necessary elements for that balance, and a ritual known as "The Count" provides the other element — the sums of money in currency in the locked boxes attached to the bottoms of the gambling tables.

As the shift changes, the special deputies go around to the tables with keys that unlock the fittings that hold the boxes to the tables, and with carts that hold empty boxes for the new shift. The exchange is made, and the boxes trundled into the counting room. Entrance into this room is past an armed guard who seems to need special signals of assurance beyond verbal ones, such as a touch of the hand or a slap on the back or a special word order said slowly and carefully to demonstrate that the person being conveyed has not coerced his guide with a threat or a gun in the ribs.

Inside the counting room, three women employees from the casino's office staff open the boxes and count the currency. They count it several different ways, and unanimous agreement on the counts is required. They enter the figures on the tally sheets so that each table's earnings record will be available to the state auditors, who may be present if they desire. However, the casino operators — forced by state law to admit the state auditors — have refused consistently to admit agents of the Federal Internal Revenue Service.

On the shift that the women were counting, a blackjack table lost about $100; a crap table won about $500. The count of currency ran to about $10,000. This was during a period when activity was slow. Not all of this was winnings, but most of it was.

The currency is just a part of the money to be counted. The slot machines produce a river of coins every day and this must be counted, wrapped, tallied and trucked back to the change booths for resale to people who want to spend the hours of their lives standing and poking money into a slot, then pulling a handle, and occasionally feeling the thrill of hearing the buzzer sound to signal a jackpot. These coins continually circulate through the machines, and an analogy to a bloodstream circulating through the lungs to pick up oxygen is inescapable — with the lungs in this analogy being the change booths where rolls of coins are traded by the casino for folding money.

In the coin-counting room of this casino there are separate machines to count different sized coins. Records must be kept for each machine. Other machines recount the coins, and yet another machine packs them into rolls which are counted again. The various tallies must check. From this total, the day's slot machine profit is established by subtracting the total of the jackpots paid out by men and women who patrol the banks of machines on the floor.

The walls of the coin-counting room are lined with crude plywood cupboards in need of another coat of paint. To call this a vault is to insult those cathedrals of polished steel and brass in the basements of banks. Yet inside these cupboards was $168,250 on this day, all in rolls of coins.

This is how it is in the gambling houses: The flow of coins through the slot machines really is a river of wealth on which the greenbacks float; the counting job is left to other machines. But the stacks of currency produced by the gambling tables are treated with great caution, surrounded by counting procedures and devices to insure honesty. The state and federal governments watch like hungry hawks.

Yet the trickery goes on.

A few years ago the state worked up a case showing that the proprietors of El Rancho Vegas had skimmed off about $400,000.

The gamblers paid a stiff fine and continued in business until their place burned down. A man who worked for a different casino remembers having been sent by his boss to "bring me what's in my steel box in the safe." The employee thoughtfully counted it — $325,000.

The question of "skim" haunts everyone connected with gambling in Nevada. Edward A. Olsen, the chairman of the State Gaming Control Board at Carson City, was asked if he had knowledge or indication or belief that the major casinos were failing to report all their earnings.

"I can't arrive at any honest conclusions at this time," Mr. Olsen said. "We have a plan which we've been using for two and a half years, to try to check. We have some results. But they are not conclusive."

A different estimate of the situation places at "about 5 percent of the gross take" the sum skimmed off before the formal reports are made. Still another view of the problem comes from William V. Sinnot, a former agent of the Federal Bureau of Investigation. He was one of Mr. Olsen's predecessors as head of the control board. Mr. Sinnot thinks there is no question but that untaxed money is taken out of some of the casinos, but he also believes the problem of proof is insurmountable.

Persons in the management of the casinos usually answer a direct question about "skim" by insisting on their own honesty while seldom defending the integrity of their competitors.

"I don't know what they do someplace else," said Sam Lichter, of the Mint Casino on Fremont Street. "But around here we don't do it that way. We report it all."

The answer of M. B. (Moe) Dalitz of Wilbur Clark's Desert Inn was similar if less direct:

"Our costs of operating and cost of entertainment and high wage rates make us glad to make expenses, much less take money off the top."

2

THE NOBLE EXPERIMENT, NEVADA STYLE

GAMBLING became legal in Nevada in the spring of 1931; the reasons have become less obvious in the passage of more than three decades. True enough, the columns of the Reno *Evening Gazette*, which then served a city of 18,000, reflect lists of arguments for and against the idea. But which of these were controlling? Which really made no difference? From this distance no one can say, not even those who were around when the change was proposed, discussed and voted. They remember clearly, however, that it actually was a slight change, for gambling had run wide open and full throttle in Nevada for many years. The effect of legalization was to change the pattern of operation, but not the basic fact that a man with a desire to gamble could find a crap table or a card game.

Gambling had been legal in Nevada during the gold camp days and up to 1910 when a reform swept through the state. New laws put an end to the wide-open gambling hells that had taken the miners' and cowboys' money since men first began to scratch a living from the rocks and mountains and barren, arid valleys. The fact that the Nevada gambling prohibition had to be enforced along with the national liquor prohibition did not do much good in Nevada for either law enforcement program. The speakeasies had gambling tables and slot machines. The people who wanted only to gamble or only to drink felt a brotherhood. Both groups, of course, were outnumbered by that mass who wanted to both drink and gamble. One of the by-products of all this was the creation of a lawlessness in attitude for a whole generation of Americans; and a class of dishonest law enforcement officers and public officeholders such as the nation had never known before.

Perhaps in the final analysis revulsion against the system that had produced these conditions prepared the public mind in Nevada to accept the bold experiment in control of gambling. Governor F. B. Balzar said privately before the legislative session opened in Carson City in January 1931 that he would not try to control what happened with the gambling legalization bill that everyone expected to see introduced. Besides, he understood that the only place the bill was much under discussion was in Las Vegas. But the proposition was discussed widely, despite what the governor said. In those days Las Vegas was a desert trading center in southern Nevada. The 1930 population was 5165. There was no Boulder Dam, except on drawing paper filed in Washington, D.C.; most of the men who were in later years to rule that town as it grew to the 1960 population of 64,405 were then running gambling houses or directing bootlegging operations in the big cities of the eastern United States. It would be eye-catching to say that no one then envisioned the sort of places that legalized gambling would produce — the sort of places that now glitter on the Las Vegas Strip. But these places were predicted, precisely, as we shall see.

A great opposition had built up to gambling. This was among the middle- and upper-class women of Nevada. Before the legislature convened, a meeting was called in Reno by the Democratic and Republican national committeewomen — obviously a joint effort by the two major parties toward blunting any partisan arguments about the coming proposals in the legislature.

The reporter who wrote the account of the meeting that was

held in the Reno Chamber of Commerce on the night of January 8, 1931, had some interesting observations to record. Control of the meeting by the anti-gambling crowd was described as "apparent." A woman speaker said that "Reno should not seek the riffraff of the world."

A Reno lawyer and former Democratic state central committee chairman, H. R. Cooke, delivered one of the arguments that was to be repeated again and again throughout the late winter and early spring until the gambling bill was passed. He spoke of a gambling joint that operated on Center Street in Reno, called it a hellhole, and argued that it was operated only with "the way greased and greased handsomely." He thought that an expensive license system would control things much better than this system of every officeholder for himself and gambling joints running wide open.

The meeting also was graced by a colorful figure known as "Jimmy the Crab," one of the many gambling men who lived in Reno. Said Jimmy, "Reno is known as a wide-open town and there is no reason why gambling should not be thrown wide open and a Monte Carlo established here. It would mean additional revenue." After injecting the bait of lower property taxes through gambling tax revenue, Jimmy left, presumably for the gambling hellhole. The meeting rambled on, and actually contributed little except that it permitted the ladies to say what was in their minds, such as the injunction from one that "we do not legalize murder, highway robbery or other unlawful practices and we should not legalize gambling."

At about this time a district attorney in Nevada put an end to the argument that "you can't keep gambling closed so you should license it and control it." He was in Ely, a small town anywhere else, but an important trading center in Nevada. He ordered law enforcement officers to do their duty and close the joints — or else. Undoubtedly the condition of their consciences led to quick compliance and the gambling places closed quickly. The district attorney replied to criticism by saying that the official grafters had been taking about $5000 a month in his city and county to protect gambling. He objected to this and kept the gambling halls closed until the legislature legalized gambling.

The reporters who covered the Nevada legislature that spring must have felt frustrated. They kept announcing that introduction of the gambling bill was imminent, perhaps tomorrow, and quoted anonymous politicians frequently in such expressions as this: "Generally the members say they will vote for such a measure to stop the practice of local officials taking bribes. The taking of this graft money is so notorious and so vile, most of the members say, that it has become an evil more serious than gambling itself." The bill was still not introduced. The plain fact seems to be that everyone in public life was scared to death to be caught with it. Each hoped that the fellow at the next desk would introduce it. Even the gambling operators — who still flourished in Reno at such notorious places as the Bank Club — were pictured as being in part responsible for the delay because they were not able to decide among themselves just what sort of bill they would accept. It was strange that anyone gave a damn what the gamblers wanted.

There was an amusing incident on February 2, 1931, which showed the legislature's temper on the gambling question. A message had come in from a women's club in Reno. It opposed the gambling legalization bill, no matter what it said or when it was introduced or by whom. This message was not addressed to a particular member, so the speaker ruled that it would not be accepted, that it would go "unreceived." This insistence on protocol was unusual in the rugged Western atmosphere of Carson City, Nevada. In those days, a formal dinner in Carson City was one where all the guests made it a point to be sober when they appeared at the host's home. The letter from the women's club was disregarded officially and for all practical purposes.

Another meeting in Reno at about this time again denounced the gambling bill. After all, Reno had about as much gambling then as it could stand anyway. Stories in the Reno *Evening Gazette* said that two members of the assembly had the bill in their pocket. No one wanted to sponsor it. On February 12, 1931, the *Gazette* printed a copy of the bill, not revealing who wrote it or who was carrying it around, afraid to introduce it.

That did it. On February 13, 1931, a Republican named Phil Tobin introduced a bill which provided for a per table gambling game fee of $75 a month, and a monthly fee of $12.50 a month for each slot machine. The county sheriffs were directed to collect the fees and issue the licenses. The fees were to be divided among the state, the county and the city, if the license were used within a city's limits. The regulations governing the qualifications of a licensed casino operator were simple. He could not be an alien. Any other kind of person could get a license. Even a person in process of getting American citizenship could apply with hope, it seemed from reading the bill. There were other provisions: the applicant was required to say where he intended to use the license; he must pay three months in advance for his permit, with no allowance for transfers or refunds; the sheriff was held responsible financially for collecting the fees; cheating was forbidden, on pain of a fine of $1000 and jail sentence of six months, plus license suspension; landlords were required to be certain that their tenants had a gambling license if gambling was to be conducted on the property; minors were forbidden in the gambling places; but purely social games were not covered in the law and could continue to run.

In the light of how things have developed in Nevada gambling, these provisions are remarkable for the things they do cover. Where is the provision barring ex-convicts? What keeps out gamblers who run illegal games elsewhere? How is the program to be controlled? Who is responsible for seeing that no cheating occurs? The sheriff? Who keeps the sheriff honest? Is there any dollar limit on how much he can take away from gamblers who are caught cheating? Who licenses the dealers? Who sees that the gambling house is financially capable of paying off winners? In short, who is responsible?

The answer: Nobody.

The legislature of Nevada turned loose a group of professional gamblers on its people and on their guests, and then has spent the next three decades trying to control them. Its success in this aim of control has been marginal sometimes, although events of the early years of the 1960's make it appear that the state is getting the upper hand. The truth is that most of the thinking people in the state realized the dangers inherent in what was being done. Either they came out in opposition; or they plainly didn't give a damn. After the provisions of Assemblyman Tobin's bill were published, a slot machine operator — speaking anonymously the way slot machine operators hope always to speak — called the $12.50 a month tax per machine "confiscatory." (Today's slot operators in Nevada wish that was all they had to pay. The federal tax alone is more than $20 a month per machine, and then there are the gross-win taxes to the state and per machine taxes to the counties and cities. But still there are about 20,000 slot machines in Nevada restaurants, grocery stores, bars and casinos.)

There was a continual revival in that winter and spring of 1931 of the argument that the state or the city or the counties would need the revenue from the gambling tax in order to hold down property taxes. A Reno lawyer, Walter Kennedy, directed attention to the fallacy in this. He said the players would have to lose $4,000,000 before taxes would amount to $400,000. However, arguments such as the one advanced by Kennedy had no real weight in the minds of an electorate that was unconcerned and a legislative assembly that was determined. By late February, the arguments that meant anything were over which of the governmental organizations — state, city, county — was to get which portion of the license fees. It was obvious that the gambling bill was going to pass, and there were hints that Governor Balzar was committed to sign it when it did pass.

Meantime, the newspaper columns began to reflect the injection of a new consideration into the discussion. This was the threat of competition for the nation's quick divorce business from such states as Idaho and Arkansas. Divorce had been a Nevada gold mine. Nevada would grant a divorce on ninety days residence, on almost any grounds, and in those days Reno was the most important single divorce market in the country. The Washoe County Courthouse was the scene of the dissolution of many a famous marriage. After the divorce was granted, it was fashionable to walk down Virginia Street from the old courthouse with the funny dome and high ceilings, stop on the bridge across the Truckee River, and toss the wedding ring into the cold mountain stream. One could stand on the bridge for a month nowadays and never see such a ceremony.

However, in 1931, when the legislature met in many of the states, this divorce mill business was threatened. Voters in other states would have liked to get it. They were pressuring their legislators to find something new for the home folks to do to get a little scratch during the Great Depression. Bills had been introduced in Arkansas, Montana, Idaho and other states. The divorce lawyers of Reno, the operators of the dude ranches, the hotel owners — all of these demanded action from Carson City to save the annual migration of dollar-carrying divorce seekers.

The best thing anyone could see was the further liberalization of Nevada divorce law. The proposal was to cut it back to require only six weeks residence. The Reno *Gazette* ran a front-page cartoon which showed the bidding for divorce business between Nevada and Arkansas as the future would develop it under bills then being considered. The Nevada listing was prophetic, for it took into the calculations the possible effect of the gambling law then being considered in the legislature.

Divorce in six weeks.
The details of the legal charges would be kept secret.
Swanky gambling casinos would be built.
Horse-racing tracks would be opened for pari-mutuel betting.
Plush dude ranches would be built.
Swimming and golf facilities would be provided.
There would be winter sports among the mountains.
A gay night life would be possible.
Fine hotels would be constructed.
Theaters would be opened.

All of these were delivered, but not by the divorce business. It would not be accurate to say that the divorce trade has withered away, but it is fair to say that it has less importance in the economy of the state than it had in 1931, or than was visualized then. Nevada still was the place in 1962 where Mary Todhunter Clark Rockefeller would go to divorce the governor of New York. But when Happy Murphy wanted to be free so she could become the governor's second wife, she went to Idaho. The length of residence required was the same.

The legislature of 1931 rocked along, considering many legislative proposals, but it is significant that the gambling law took second place to the consideration of the divorce law change. Eventually, they came to be considered as a package in the closing days, just as the *Evening Gazette's* front-page cartoon had considered them as a package.

On March 6, 1931, the assembly passed the quick divorce law without a dissent and on March 9 the gambling bill was passed 24 to 11. The opposition argument to gambling by this time was built around the propriety of the license laxity — should American citizenship be the only qualification beyond ability to pay the fee three months in advance? The senate passed both bills on March 18, with no reported debate, and the illegal gambling houses located all over Nevada began immediate expansions, getting ready for the flood of customers they expected when gambling became legal. The governor signed the bill immediately and it was all over. On March 21, 1931, after being closed for two and a half months, the gambling joints of Ely, Nevada, reopened. Whatever may have been the lesson demonstrated by the district attorney's closure of them, that lesson was lost.

To place these events in the minds of those old enough to remember: the governor of New York in those days was named Franklin D. Roosevelt and he came from Hyde Park on the Hudson River. The biggest problem before him was whether to stop an investigation of the activities of the mayor of New York. His name was James J. Walker.

The night gambling became legal in Reno was a wild one. The old, illegal places were wide open now but with a difference, banging away under the full and legal protection of the law — no longer under the partial and illegal protection of the policeman. Before, they had been wide open, but there was always a cautious concern that the fix might come apart at any minute.

The speakeasies had a special problem. Now their gambling was legal, but they still had to take care of an official somebody to keep from getting pinched for selling liquor. The Bank Club, where the faro dealer was guarded by a man with a shotgun that helped to keep order, was on the verge of allowing its first women visitors. The place had even barred prostitutes in the old days.

These days Mrs. Marion Welliver works as Assistant to the Director of the Historical Society in the State Building in Reno. But in 1931 she was a reporter and she remembered how it was the night gambling became legal.

"I don't know where they all came from. Maybe from over on

the Coast. Oakland. Sacramento, maybe. San Francisco. They
were the strangest sight I've ever seen. Big fat women had on
cheap evening gowns — and they were wearing sneakers. You
couldn't shove your way into those places. Those women looked
like the wrath of God. They walked the streets all night and slept
in the park. Some of the gambling houses opened and went broke
all in the same day. One thing always puzzled me. Why didn't
they legalize the Chinese lottery, too? They never did."

Mrs. Welliver's husband was the Reno chief of police during
some of those glory years, and she recalled great stories of
things that had happened to Andy Welliver. One of these concerned a celebrated public figure who claimed to have won $25,-
000 in an illegal gambling place and then to have been slugged
and robbed of it.

"I never believed him," Mrs. Welliver murmured.

She also remembered the time a famous Hollywood glamour
queen went to a place at Lake Tahoe.

"I guess she wanted a big fling. She'd been having a time over
in Hollywood, and she came over here. She drank and ate and
gambled and gambled and pretty soon she was in hock for
$25,000 on the crap table and gave them a check. Then she
stopped payment on the check. I remember that one very well
because I broke the story."

Mrs. Welliver's years in Reno also covered the change from
the hit-or-miss operation of the gambling joints in the illegal
years to the smooth operation that has come to the Virginia and
Center Street casinos since.

This is a point that should be understood. Gambling, like
any other business, is run by a different set of business principles when it has a future than when it has the possibility of
being closed out in the next hour. The men who ran it in the
wide-open and illegal days prior to 1931 are generally long gone
from the scene. They either sold out or moved out or went

broke in the first few years of legality. The picture is less complicated in Reno than in Las Vegas, for the big eastern mobs have never had a strong foothold in Reno, nor has the big casino-hotel business flourished much in Reno as it has in Las Vegas at the Strip.

The penny ante types who ran the illegal joints in Reno in the old days were unable to stand up to the pressures of legal gambling. Competition was suddenly almost without limit, whereas in the illegal days the only guys who ran were those who could put in a fix. It all was different. A lot of things made it different. One of these forces was named Raymond I. Smith, an old-time carnival operator, who had sons, daughters-in-law, grandchildren and all of them seemed to have character just like Raymond I. Smith.

The Smiths came to Reno in the 1930's, after Andy Welliver had become chief of police and had instituted close supervision by the city of the licensing of Reno gamblers. Welliver may well be the force that kept the eastern hoodlums out of Reno; and at the least, he contributed to that barrier. Raymond I. Smith got a license for a twenty-one game — and the next day came to Chief Welliver to say he had gone broke and to ask advice. Welliver told him to borrow a stake and try it one more night. This was great advice, for the operation that Smith had was called Harold's Club and it became the most famous of the Reno gambling places in those years of World War II and into the 1950's. What Smith and his sons did was bring the first mass promotion to the Nevada gambling business. It was the supermarket approach to the gambling joint. It is uncertain whether this was a conscious effort, for Smith and his family were much more inclined to be intuitive operators than to give close study of forces involved as a prelude to decision. But whatever moved them, they plastered every available barn wall and roof across the western United States with the slogan "Harold's Club, Reno, or Bust!" My, but this did drag 'em in! They came in on the trains, in buses, in old cars wheezing at the radiator, and even hitchhiking. The Smiths prospered, amassing great mountains of money. They ran all sorts of games, including a thing with live mice and numbered escape chutes.

Spokesmen for the Smith family have said over the years that they started in Reno with $600. In 1962 they cashed it in for $16,675,000 in a sale and leaseback arrangement that may become more popular among the gamblers. The total payoff to the Smith family will come during five years. They sold out to a group of New Yorkers. Several groups over the past decade have tried to buy Harold's Club, but each time some eccentricity of Raymond I. Smith or some shortage in the cash department of the prospective buyers stymied the sale.

The total implications of the Harold's Club sale have not been lost on the others in the gambling business in Nevada. The Desert Inn crowd worked something like it with their properties, as we shall see, but there were aspects to the Smith sale and leaseback that are just hard to beat. It has been obvious since the deal was worked out that the federal tax laws were responsible for the Smiths' decision to sell.

First, the price was ridiculously high for what they had — a group of buildings in downtown Reno, and some speculatively held real estate around the town. Second, there was no disclosure of how much cash the New Yorkers were buying — that is, how much reserve liquid assets the Smiths' corporations had and could not distribute to their owners without ruinous tax bites. The suspicion is that the Smiths sold the money to the new owners who then would have tax advantages that would enable them to use the money. The Smiths would be able to declare their sale proceeds to be capital gains taxable at much lower rates.

Meantime, the Smiths have leases and options that could be extended for twenty-five years. They continue to run the casino.

They will get the $16,675,000 sale price within five years, and the documents indicate that they got $3,250,000 in cash at the time of the sale.

The place where they made all this money is as ugly as sin. Any day one can go there and be shocked by the sight of a full table of old ladies in their seventies, some with eyeshades, some with cigarettes drooping from their lips. They play blackjack with some woman dealer whose red or blond or black hair has the unmistakable sheen of a dye. In contrast to the standard "dyed blonde" in Las Vegas, the hair-coloring jobs in Reno run to various shades, and are not so well done.

Many places have imitated Harold's Club promotion and marketing practices. Beyond the peculiarities of the women who gamble and work in those places, there are other things that would horrify the people who once made the Monte Carlo Casino in Monaco the most famous gambling house in the world. The dignity of Monte Carlo is absolutely missing from the mass gambling joints of Nevada, although the manners tend to be a little more high-toned in some of the places on the Las Vegas Strip.

In the mass places, there are as many different forms of dress as there are customers. But none runs even remotely near to formal. The crowd noise is a steady roar, punctuated by the buzz of signals that mean a slot machine has given up a jackpot. The tone is more folksy here, the customers less sophisticated than those of the money traps on the Las Vegas Strip. To compare the Desert Inn in Las Vegas, for example, with Harold's Club in Reno is to compare the first-class section of a coast-to-coast nonstop jet plane with a cross-country bus.

Of course, these places had entirely different backgrounds in their formation, and they have grown up in different cities. The atmosphere for gambling in Reno is far different from that in Las Vegas. The history of the two areas as to gambling, since the tables and slots became legal, has been vastly different. A picture of the condition of gambling in Las Vegas as of 1950 came out on Wednesday, November 15, 1950, when the Kefauver Committee held hearings there as a part of its famous study of organized crime in interstate commerce. Many things came through that day as the senators polished the windows of history so that the rest of us might peek through.

Take Wilbur Ivern Clark. His name is the most famous of any of the Las Vegas gamblers because he attached it to the place he dreamed of — Wilbur Clark's Desert Inn. The place does not belong to him — in 1964 he sold a minority interest — and did not from the day it opened. It belonged primarily to a group of ex-bootleggers and gamblers who made fortunes in Cleveland and Newport, Kentucky, then took up Clark's invitation that they finance completion of his place. Clark told the Kefauver Committee that he and his friends and relatives put up every dime they could raise to build the Desert Inn. This amounted to about $250,000. They started in May 1947 and ran out of money by 1949. The senators had only slight interest in what Clark's financial problems had been; they were hot on the trail of the Cleveland group and how Clark came to be connected with its members. He explained to the senators this way.

"They are in Reno on a vacation and of course they knew, like everybody in the United States knew, that I was trying to get money. I had set there from 1947 to 1949, was sitting there not finished."

Who did he mean by "they"?

"Well, they are all on record out there. One of them is named Sam Tucker, Moe Dalitz, Morris Kleinman, and Thomas McGinty. And then there is two or three small ones that I don't know whether they have money in it or not. I know they are in the organization."

Clark said that when he brought the Cleveland group into the Desert Inn, he owned it all, but when they gave him about $1,300,-

ooo and finished building the place, he kept 25 percent of the stock, to distribute to his supporters, and they got 74 percent. The remaining 1 percent went to Hank Greenspun, who had been associated with Clark, but left the Desert Inn because of dislike for the Cleveland group. Greenspun later founded and published the Las Vegas *Sun*.

Clark also told of a peculiar arrangement on the gambling. There were two gambling bosses, one for the Cleveland group and one for the Clark group. His statements that he had tried to get money everywhere led to a series of questions about whether he had tried some of the leading gangsters of that day. He said he had not. But he did go to the federal government's Reconstruction Finance Corporation. He was turned down. Clark knew about the gambling and racketeering background of his new associates. He even knew that Morris Kleinman had served a three-year prison sentence for income tax fraud. But he had no criticism of them as partners.

Those questions that were directed to Clark's personal history drew a picture of a small-time gambler who had a great dream, and through good fortune had realized it — the creation of the Desert Inn. He said he had worked in gambling places in Saratoga, New York, in Reno, on the gambling boats that once worked out of harbors near Los Angeles, and in Palm Springs, California. He was a craps dealer, a very humble beginning to prepare him for the grandeur that came with the Desert Inn. He was out of his league, too, with Moe Dalitz and Morris Kleinman. Clark managed to stay on, until the fall of 1964 when the Cleveland group persuaded him to sell his minority interest to them.

Clark was one of the interesting specimens held up and examined that day by the Kefauver Committee. There were others equally fascinating. For example, the first witness that day was William J. Moore, a man trained as an architect. When he testified, he was the gambling operators' representative on the state tax commission which then controlled the gambling licensing and tax collection. There was nothing sub rosa about Moore representing the gamblers, as he explained it to the committee; others represented mining, labor, agriculture, and so forth. Moore owned a piece of the Last Frontier Hotel, and some other gambling interests in Las Vegas.

Moore had two interesting habits of speech. Somewhere in almost every answer, he mentioned that his statement was being given "frankly." Also, as the corners became tighter, he would answer the senators as "fellow." Finally — perhaps it was inevitable — he told Senator Kefauver "Frankly, fellow, the auditor handles that and I cannot answer." He was trying to explain his position in the bitter quarrels over the horse-racing wire, the matters that brought Benjamin (Bugsy) Siegel to Las Vegas.

Siegel showed up just after World War II and began immediately to force the operators of horsebooks to give him a slice of their profits. Siegel — handsome and thoroughly struck by the joys of Hollywood — was a hoodlum with a revolting record. He was in Las Vegas to extend the limits of a wire service operated by the Italian mob in competition to one operated out of Chicago. When the Mob took over the Chicago wire by murdering its proprietor, Siegel then was able to move ahead to his big dream.

Like Wilbur Clark, Bugsy Siegel had a great dream of a plush hotel and fancy gambling joint in the desert, surrounded by green grass and pretty women without many clothes on. The fulfillment of Siegel's dream was the Flamingo Hotel, built far outside Las Vegas in the desert.

No official has ever said for sure what was the cause of Siegel's downfall. Many wild guesses have been offered over the years, with none to contradict because Siegel is dead and the killer is too well-mannered to carry the fight beyond the grave by explaining why he did in handsome Bugsy. Siegel was shot to death as he sat in the parlor of the home of his mistress, Virginia Hill, who was fortunately away just then.

Siegel was shoved aside when Gus Greenbaum showed up at the Flamingo and turned it into a profit-making business establishment, a great change from the Siegel years. It was understood in Las Vegas that Greenbaum had been designated to represent the people who had invested their money in Siegel's gambling joint. These were people who disliked having their names mentioned. Greenbaum did well by these investors, but eventually he left and turned up to manage the Riviera down the road a mile or so, and then another day he turned up in his home in Phoenix — his throat had been cut. So had his wife's.

(Sometimes a great fuss has been raised over the friendship of Senator Barry Goldwater with Gus Greenbaum. Goldwater has said he knew nothing of Greenbaum's life except what appeared on the surface, and that he had no apologies to make for his acquaintance with the gambler. Goldwater also was once friendly with Willie Bioff, a labor extortionist who served time for it. The Senator said he knew Bioff by another name, although he added that Bioff had advised him on labor matters.)

The manager who followed Greenbaum at the Flamingo was little Moe Sedway, a man of great courage and presence who refused to let the senators intimidate him. Sedway was polite when they were polite and not when they weren't. He said he had been in jail. He said he knew almost every big-time hoodlum in the country. Here are some of them: Bugsy Siegel, Meyer Lansky, Jack Lansky, Little Augie Casanno, Frank Costello, Joe Adonis, Nate Rutkin, Frank Erickson, Abner "Longie" Zwillman, James Rutkin, Harry Stomberg, Charles "Lucky" Luciano, Charles Fischetti, Rocco Fischetti, Jack Dragna, Mike Accone, Gene Normile, Tony Corica . . . Little Moe Zedway still knew them when Rudolph Halley, the committee's chief counsel, ran out of names.

In addition, he also said he knew Moe Dalitz and Morrie Kleinman, late of Detroit and Cleveland and Newport, Kentucky, but then — as now — of the Desert Inn. As with the others, Sedway had known Dalitz and Kleinman for about twenty years. He knew them as a matter of course, for they moved about in the circles where he moved.

Bugsy Siegel brought Sedway to Las Vegas. It was part of the bookmaking muscle operation that Siegel used first when he came there. Sedway was perhaps the most important witness for the Kefauver Committee that day. But to understand the events behind the situation that exists today in Nevada, we must follow what was said by another witness, a man who then was lieutenant governor of Nevada — Clifford A. Jones. While he was lieutenant governor, he also was a gambling operator. He had 2½ percent of the Pioneer Club and 1 percent of the Golden Nugget. From the Pioneer Club, his income had been about $5000 a year, and from the Golden Nugget it had been $12,000 a year. He also owned 11 percent of the Thunderbird Hotel and a similar amount of its casino operating company, but how much these interests returned to him was not clear in the record. One of his chief associates in the Thunderbird was the late Marion B. Hicks, and together Jones and Hicks were later to be involved in one of the landmark gambling control conflicts with state authorities. We shall examine that later. In addition to these interests in gambling, the lieutenant governor also was a partner in a law firm. One of the pieces of business that the firm had was the handling of the will of the late Bugsy Siegel.

Jones defended the Nevada practice of giving gambling licenses to ex-convicts. He pointed out that they had had licenses soon after legalization of gambling, and that progressively tighter statutes had always protected their right to continue to hold the licenses, although they might have been unable to get licenses as new applicants. Earlier the state tax commission member for the gambling interests, William J. Moore, had defended the issuance of a license for the then legal Bank Club in Reno, successor to the old "hellhole." The license went to William Graham and James McKay. There was this exchange between Rudolph Halley and Moore:

HALLEY: Did you vote for a license for Graham and McKay?

MOORE: Yes.

HALLEY: Graham and McKay were convicted in the southern district of New York, were they not?

MOORE: That is right.

HALLEY: Of a violation of a federal law.

MOORE: I presume. I have been told that. I have seen the record.

HALLEY: They possessed and then altered and then passed government bonds which had been stolen from the Bank of Manhattan Co.

MOORE: I haven't seen the complete rundown on the case, fellow.

Senator Charles W. Tobey was a member of the committee present that day in Las Vegas, and he asked some questions of Moore.

SENATOR TOBEY: Was that conviction known to the tax commission in Nevada when you voted to give them a license?

MOORE: Yes.

SENATOR TOBEY: How do you reconcile that?

MOORE: To start with, it is an illustration, when a law is passed, we'll say, to protect the people such as the law concerning lawyers, such as the law concerning architects, such as the law concerning engineers, and so forth. There is a certain amount of granddaddy clause in there, isn't there?

SENATOR TOBEY: Of course, I know the Interstate Commerce

Commission has a granddaddy clause, that is the only one I know of.

MOORE: All the other ones have, too, if you read the laws. In other words, there may be attorneys or there may be gamblers, or engineers, at the time that the law goes into effect that are in business in the state. Just because you get the privilege of controlling the thing, is that any reason why you should put the man out of business, if he is operating in the state of Nevada?

SENATOR TOBEY: Yes; I think it is; but you and I might differ about that. I think if you have a man that is crooked and shown to be crooked, and a lawbreaker, I wouldn't give him any privilege at all.

Moore's was a fairly clear-cut statement of the philosophies which high state officials used for guidance in the licensing of gambling operators when the Nevada gambling legalization experiment was almost twenty years old. Another such statement of principle came from Lieutenant Governor Jones in this exchange with Halley:

HALLEY: Since you are lieutenant governor of the state, I am going to presume to ask an overall policy question, which you may or may not see fit to answer.

JONES: All right.

HALLEY: It is definitely a statement of opinion. Wouldn't you say prior to 1949 a great many undesirable characters, with bad police records, were engaged in gambling operations in the state of Nevada, such as Graham and McKay, (Milt) Wertheimer (of the Riverside Hotel in Reno), Bugsy Siegel? I could name a great many more, of course.

JONES: Well, of course.

HALLEY: Moe Sedway?

JONES: Some of those I could very definitely concur with you on that. Some of them are people who have been in the state long before I was here, so I wouldn't presume to pass upon their qualifications to conduct their business.

HALLEY: Well, there had been a lot of people —

JONES: There were some people that you might say had police records and reputations of gambling in other places. But this seems to hold true, that people who came here when the state started to grow, to gamble in the gambling business, they weren't particularly Sunday school teachers or preachers or anything like that from out of the state. They were gamblers. In other words, they came here to gamble.

Between them that day Jones and Moore gave just as clear a picture as has ever been set out of why Nevada gambling is shot through with law violators, former gangsters, ex-bootleggers and trained law violators from all over the country. The gamblers were there as illegal operators before the law was changed in 1931. They were followed in the early years by hoodlums from all over. The people at the top of the government such as Moore and Jones were sympathetic to these hoodlums who were among the earliest legal gamblers in Nevada and would have nothing to do with running them out. The situation has changed somewhat over the years. But the old-time law violators have stayed around as long as they managed to stay out of trouble. There was no real attempt at state control until 1945 when the state tax commission was given the power to make rules and regulations. These powers were included in an act which levied the first gross winnings tax as the price of doing business. It was a modest 1 percent and it produced $100,000.

Those powers to regulate were increased in 1947 and 1949, the era in which Moore and Jones were making apologies for the hoodlums who surrounded them. The taxes were increased to 2 percent on the gross winnings by 1947, and in 1955, a sliding scale of 3 to 5.5 percent was imposed. The state tax commission was left in control of gambling during those years, on the theory that all that was required was to collect taxes. Much more is involved than mere tax collection and in 1955, the legislature took note of this. At that time, when the first real move was taken toward controlling criminal elements within the state's gambling experiment, that experiment was twenty-four years old.

In 1955 the Gaming Control Board was created to act as the enforcement and investigative unit of the tax commission. This worked, but not very well. In 1957, a freshman assemblyman came in from Elko and was assigned to the judiciary committee. His name was Gene Evans, and he was the editor of a small daily newspaper. By meshing his aims with the events that occurred around him, he has had an immense effect on gambling law changes in Nevada. In that session of 1957, Evans' committee received a bill that had been passed by the senate to expand the legal rights of a gambling license holder. Evans studied the bill, decided that he opposed its purpose, and rewrote it reversing the original effect. His rewritten bill was passed eventually, but was vetoed by Governor Charles Russell. In 1959, Evans was back, and with a colleague, Howard McKissick, Jr., a Reno lawyer, he rewrote the state's gambling control laws. Now there is a five-man Nevada Gaming Commission which sets policy and passes regulations. The Gaming Control Board is its enforcement arm. In 1958 the voters elected Grant Sawyer as governor. He was a district attorney and was re-elected in 1962. His program has been to strengthen state control of the gambling operators.

Gene Evans no longer is in the legislature. He left the Elko *Daily Free Press* to become a public relations man in Reno. He directs public relations for William Harrah, presently the king of the Nevada gamblers. More than any of the other big operators, Harrah represents what was desired by the people who in

1931 supported the licensing of the casinos. But they got just one Bill Harrah.

In 1959 Governor Sawyer made public the directions he had given to the Nevada Gaming Commission and the State Gaming Control Board. He told them to keep out "criminal elements, mobs, or syndicates.

"My feeling, to state briefly, is this," summed up the governor. "Get tough and stay tough. A gambling license is a privilege — it is not a right. If you err, err on the side of rigidity rather than laxity. Hang tough and you will be doing a great service to me, to the industry and to the state."

The effects of this policy have been felt. One effect of it was to chase Frank Sinatra out of Nevada gambling because of his association with a much publicized Chicago underworld figure, Sam Giancana. Another effect has been creation of a growing state of tension among the license holders, for the Sinatra case showed conclusively that they have no legal rights to continue as gambling licensees. Any time the state authorities find that a licensee has failed to live up to the responsibilities they have set for him, they can remove his license and he has no recourse.

In the years since 1931, the direct tax revenues deriving from gambling have climbed year after year, and in the late 1940's and through the 1950's, they grew much more rapidly due to increases in the rate of taxation. In 1945, the first gross receipts tax year, the state got $100,792. In 1947, the tax was doubled, and the collections were $518,632. In 1955 they were increased again and the collections were $5,441,327 whch was 19.9 percent of all the state's tax revenues that year. In 1962 the collections were $11,263,463, which was 20.2 percent of the state's tax collections.

(Contrary to popular belief, Nevada does not rely entirely on gambling taxation to support government. As these figures show, about one-fifth of the tax load at the state level is carried by gambling.)

Most of the taxes from gambling come from the gross receipts tax computed on the basis of winnings — the annual sum totals of what is left on each table and inside each slot machine at the end of each shift. No expenses are deductible except checks which cannot be collected. The tax rate is graduated from 3 to 5.5 percent depending on the winnings. Taxes are collected on a quarterly basis. This is the pattern:

GROSS RECEIPTS PER QUARTER

Nothing to $150,000	3 percent
$150,000 to $400,000	4 percent
$400,000 to $1,000,000	5 percent
$1,000,000 and over	5.5 percent

Total winnings include the profits from the slot machines as well as from the gambling tables. The state also collects a table tax on the games being operated. These taxes are collected annually, whether the tables involved run all year or not. The table tax covers craps, twenty-one, roulette, keno and faro. But it does not apply to poker, bridge, and panguingui card games or to slot machines. The annual rates are graduated, with $100 charged for one game and the per game rate climbing until for more than sixteen games the charge is $1000 each for the first sixteen and $200 for each game over sixteen. These taxes were started in 1947, with the state getting the revenue, but in 1957 it was ruled that the money must be divided equally between the seventeen Nevada counties. The counties divided $800,950 in 1962.

One of the peculiarities of Nevada's gambling crowd has been the lack of interest in horse racing and pari-mutuel betting. There is a track at Las Vegas, which has operated a little, but never with any success. The state has never collected any revenue from racing, although the law provides that the state may take 2 percent of the handle for general spending purposes, and another 1 percent to pay the expenses of the Nevada State Racing Commission.

The counties still collect gambling taxes on the same basis that was a part of the original law passed in 1931. The sheriff collects the money, but now he has nothing much to say about licensing, except to recommend against an operator he finds undesirable. Taxes of $600 a year per table are levied against craps, twenty-one, faro, and roulette. Poker, bridge and pan-guingui pay $300 a year per table. Slot machines pay $120 a year each. The state gets 25 percent, the county 25 percent and the city 50 percent of the collections. In places outside a city, the county gets 75 percent.

There are seventeen cities in Nevada, and fifteen of them tax gambling places located within their borders. Gabbs, which has but one casino, does not tax it; Boulder City does not allow gambling. The others tax slot machines from a low of $12 in Lovelock to a high of $120 in Las Vegas. Craps, twenty-one and roulette will pay $1000 a table in Las Vegas, $1050 in Reno, but only $12 in Lovelock. In 1959, the most recent year available for totals on Nevada city gambling tax collections, the take was $1,122,114. Reno, with $442,005, and Las Vegas, with $570,367, between them collected 90 percent of it.

No total figure exists of the tax collections made on gambling by the state, county and city governments of Nevada. But it must be approaching $15,000,000 a year in a state which has about 300,000 people in the middle 1960's. In addition, the federal government puts a big bite of $250 a year on each slot machine and in 1962 this amounted to about $4,480,000, for a grand total of taxation on gambling in Nevada of close to $20,000,000.

The experiment in legalization of gambling has produced tax revenues far beyond the expectations of those who first proposed the system. It also has produced employment. In the summer of 1962, the Nevada Gaming Commission staff took a survey of employment and produced an estimate that 33,615 persons worked at licensed gaming locations. By far the biggest number of these was employed in Clark County, where Las Vegas is the county seat and the Las Vegas Strip flourishes. There were 17,341 jobs in licensed gambling houses in Clark county, compared to 9292 in Washoe County (Reno). There were that summer 1859 licensed places of gambling, of which 1214 had restricted licenses which usually were for slot machines only, while 645 were unrestricted gambling casino licenses. The casino-connected places employed 27,762 persons. These figures do not cover just the gambling jobs; they also include the waitresses, the cooks, the parking lot attendants, and others. In a moment we'll look at the salary scales for people who work around the big casinos, but first consider this table which the state of Nevada compiled. The aim is to show that somehow Nevada is no more in the gambling business than are the states which make great sums from taxes on pari-mutuel betting.

STATE TAX REVENUE FROM GAMBLING — 1961

1.	New York	$96,461,112
2.	California	38,005,566
3.	Florida	26,163,298
4.	New Jersey	25,334,713
5.	Illinois	17,477,867
6.	Massachusetts	14,470,966
7.	NEVADA	10,693,309
8.	Ohio	9,877,668
9.	Maryland	9,209,866
10.	Rhode Island	7,894,040
11.	Michigan	7,804,479
12.	New Hampshire	5,338,512
13.	West Virginia	4,871,804
14.	Delaware	4,350,519
15.	Colorado	2,688,514
16.	Arizona	2,566,766
17.	Louisiana	2,516,669

18. Kentucky	2,315,317
19. Arkansas	1,993,737
20. Oregon	1,396,009
21. Washington	1,342,029
22. Maine	1,048,828
23. Nebraska	753,301
24. South Dakota	133,732
25. New Mexico	130,000

These great sums, which total to $294,838,621, are derived almost entirely from the states' shares of the pari-mutuel betting pools at horse and dog tracks. The exception is Nevada's total, which all comes from slot machines and casino gambling. There is a difference between horse and dog racing, on the one hand, and casino gambling on the other. The moral difference may be slight or even nonexistent; the practical difference is wide. Certainly, the facilitity with which the state collects income from gambling casinos or from dog and horse racing is very different. In pari-mutuel betting, the state and the track will split perhaps 15 percent of the amount bet on each race, deducting this before the amount of winning tickets is calculated. For the gambling casino, taxes are collected purely on the winnings, and at a much lower rate. If the state of Nevada taxed casinos at the rate horse tracks are taxed, Nevada's gambling tax income would be around $100,000,000 a year rather than about $15,000,000 to the state, counties and cities.

No one ever gets rich around a gambling hall except the fellow who owns it. The pay rates are surprisingly low, except in the entertainment scales where they shoot up to astounding heights. Generally, pay rates vary as the skill of the employee. A colorful, pleasing, exciting twenty-one dealer will get more play and win more for the house; therefore, he will be able to get a higher pay rate. Pay is on a per day basis. There are variations between clubs and between cities, but these figures give an idea:

Twenty-one dealer	$16 to $24
Craps and roulette	16 to 26
Coin wrapper	16 to 19
Security guard	17 to 21
Dressing room attendant	14 to 17
Doorman	14 to 17
Keno writers (new)	16 to 22
Keno writers (experienced)	24 to 27
Slots Key carriers	18 to 23
Maintenance man	21 to 24
Parking lot attendants	10 to 13
Parking Lot boss	24 to 27
Telephone operator	16 to 19
Cashier in gaming pit	14 to 17
Porter	15 to 18
Secretaries	19 to 22
Executive secretaries	21 to 24
Slot machine repair man	18 to 27
Slot cashier	18 to 21
Casino cashier	17 to 21
Cocktail waitresses	15 to 18
Bookkeeper	17 to 24
Change girls	15 to 19
Check racker	13 to 16
Food cashier	14 to 18
Keno runner	14 to 17

Those are most of the daily workers in the casino and in the bookkeeping, management offices and restaurants that surround the gambling place. In the entertainment sections, such as the lounge and the supper club showrooms, there are sound technicians who keep the microphones and loudspeakers operational. They get $21 to $25 a day. The stage technicians get $19 to $22 a day. Perhaps the biggest single salary on a daily basis is the pit boss'. He oversees a cluster of craps tables or twenty-one tables and gets perhaps $30 to $50 a day.

Each of the casino hotels which has a showroom where the big talent acts appear also maintains its own chorus line of dancers and show girls. These are paid by the week. The dancers generally get from $125 to $150 a week. A second category within this employment division are the models, or show girls, the tall, leggy beauties who walk around the stage and pose, wearing brief costumes. They get $150 to $175 a week. The top pay for the showgirls is for those featured in some of the places as nudes — bare breasted. They get $175 to $200 a week for standing in niches or posing on the stage.

Almost all the major casinos, whether or not they have supper club showrooms, have entertainment in the cocktail lounges. This runs into big money, although the acts may be second level things compared to the big names playing in the showrooms.

To give an idea of the magnitude of some of these, Frank Sinatra Jr. was singing with the Tommy Dorsey Orchestra in the lounge of Harrah's Tahoe Casino when he was kidnaped in December 1963. The Dorsey Orchestra, a financially successful reincarnation dreamed up by a former Dorsey manager, was just one of the acts playing the casino lounge in rotation in those weeks. There were four others, since the entertainment in the lounge keeps up steadily all night. These acts may consist of a small combo and a couple of girl singers, for a total tab of perhaps $1500 a week; or they may go on up to as much as $10,000 for a show of four or five acts. A total entertainment cost for a casino lounge for a week frequently can come as high as $25,000 and in the bigger places rarely will go much below $15,000.

If the competition gets tough and the casino needs customers badly, it may try to hog the business for a week by going all out for a lounge billing that will include four or five top, high-priced stars. That could cost up to $40,000 or even $50,000.

The management gets back a few dollars on drinks from people who come in to see the lounge shows. Many people just stay outside and look in to hear the acts, not even wanting to buy drinks, which incidentally are reasonably priced at from 60 cents up to $1, depending on the place.

Food and drinks in the showrooms, where the big acts appear before a supper club audience, cost more. Dinner for two there can be as little as $12 or can be much, much higher. This is where Jack Benny, George Jessel, Lena Horne, Harry Belafonte, Eddie Fisher and other headliners appear. The prices paid for them are almost unbelievable. Usually they bring the basic elements of their show with them — a vocalist, straight man, and so forth. In those instances, the casino provides the chorus line and the orchestra, with both groups hired on a regular basis by the club. The orchestra is hired as a unit, the showgirls and dancers as individuals. If the orchestra requires augmentation for different shows, the casino provides it.

A full-blown show brought into Las Vegas by some top entertainer may cost the casino as much as $40,000 a week, and from this the headliner must pay his own staff. The casino will furnish the trimmings like the orchestra and showgirls and dancers. But sometimes an entertainer, usually a standup comedian type, will make a deal only for himself and leave the casino entertainment director the job of building a show around his headline act. The entertainer may get $7500 to $10,000, depending on the strength of his name and position, and the casino can spend an equal or larger amount getting people to appear with him and work around his act.

The main requirement for talent is the ability to draw 'em in.

If the customers aren't interested, neither is the casino. The management also likes the sort of entertainer who draws in customers of a certain outlook — Frank Sinatra draws the gamblers, so the casino owners love to book him. The ideal showroom act would be someone the compulsive gamblers just had to see. If a singer or comedian with that talent ever shows up, he's made — the casino owners will pay him $50,000 a week for the rest of his years, just so long as he can attract the big plungers, the high rollers, so that they have to walk by the house's tables to get in to hear him, and then go past again on the way out.

The casino would make enough to support the tab, and enough more not to have to worry about it.

There is a side to this relationship between the high-priced entertainers and the gamblers that leaks out into public view occasionally, but not often. Many of the top flight old-time comics come from somewhat the same background as the older ownership of the casinos — while the present casino managers were young bootleggers, the present aging comedians were learning their trades in the speakeasies of the prohibition era. Some of these people have known each other for more years than they like to remember. When the Las Vegas booking comes around, past friendships and enmities play a part in deciding which act goes where.

Further, the "book" on the gambling habits of the entertainer is just as important to the casino owners as the "book" on a batting lineup is to a major league manager. After all, you can afford to pay a comedian twice as much if he's going to lose all of it in the casino between his appearances in the showroom.

Just exactly this sort of thing has happened in Las Vegas in times past. At one point, a noted and much beloved comedian actually was in a sort of bondage to a Las Vegas Strip casino hotel. The ownership played on his gambling mania, encouraged it, prodded him more and more to gamble, made credit easy for him, always managed to have him at the tables — and then went out among the other casino owners and laughed and joked about the childlike simplicity of the entertainer. His captors boasted around the Strip about having reduced this talented man to servitude.

Gossip of this situation came to the Nevada authorities, and when they made sure that his continual "extensions" of the tour on the Strip were something beyond what they appeared to be, they ordered the gamblers to set him free. They were told to tear up his markers, bar him from the tables and give him his full salary for a week or so in order that he would have money to live on until he could find another place.

By this time the cognoscenti of the town were laughing behind their hands at the poor man who had been used and duped and almost destroyed by the gamblers. When the gaming control board issued its order to set him free, there was some muted cheering up and down the Strip, too, for while Las Vegas is a cruel, suspicious town, there are many warmhearted people in it.

3

UNDER THE KEFAUVER MICROSCOPE

A DIM, smudged and constantly shifting line divides our society into the ethical and legal, and the unethical and illegal. Some men are on one side, then the other, weaving back and forth; others are on both sides at the same time. These shifts are caused in part by the complex motives of men; and in part by the changes in public tastes and public morality. After all, that dim, smudged line is located by what the legislative majority writes into the law, and by what social leaders persuade their followers to accept as proper manners.

Moreover, there is a pendulum effect in these matters, just as there is in economics and politics and many of the other affairs of life. Once the institution of the lottery was in great favor in the United States. But after a few scandals occurred, it came to be regarded as such an evil that federal statutes were passed forbidding the use of the mails to give information on lottery operations.

Times have changed, too, for the men who run Las Vegas and the casinos there. In Cleveland, Moe Dalitz was a bootlegger; but in Las Vegas he stands as an elder statesman of what they call the "gaming industry." In Detroit, Eddie Levinson paid a $1500 fine for conducting a gambling place; in Las Vegas he is becoming as wealthy as Croesus running two, and his greatest problem is to get the taxes paid. The question is: Have Dalitz and Levinson, picked as random examples, changed that much? The answer is: Nope.

The same is true of their seniors in Las Vegas. The old-timers there are still the same sort of men who once thumped heads in disputes over slot machine locations and the split of the boodle from the illegal gambling joints in Newport and Covington, Kentucky. Or they may have fought over the division of the spoils of an illegal load of liquor that had been ferried across the Great Lakes during the Prohibition Era.

Dalitz and Levinson are symbols of Las Vegas and of the flowering of professional gambling that has come about in Nevada in the three decades since the legislature acted to legalize it. First, consider Dalitz.

He was born in 1899, on Christmas Eve, in Boston, Massachusetts. Dalitz grew up in Detroit, where he attended the Bishop Elementary School and made at least one lifelong friend. He had two arrests for minor charges by the Detroit police department, but at an early age his major criminal interests were concentrated in Cleveland where he became an important factor in that city's violent underworld upheavals that decided control of the rackets. Mr. Dalitz is cool, clever and supremely confident. It was typical of him that when he was finally placed in a position where he had to appear before the Kefauver Committee on February 28, 1951, he was accompanied by a lawyer — not just any lawyer, but one named Charles Carr of Los Angeles.

Said Estes Kefauver after Dalitz had been sworn: "Let the record show that Mr. Charles Carr, attorney at law of Los Angeles, whom the chairman knew back in the Yale Law School some years ago, is representing Mr. Dalitz."

Nothing indicates anywhere that Carr could or would or did exert any influence with Senator Kefauver from their shared recollection of New Haven, Connecticut. But certainly the situation would have pumped up Dalitz's ego, and would have given him the feeling important to the boss gamblers — the feeling that he has the edge on the game, that the odds are for him.

In those days it still was looked upon as somehow inviting investigation to plead the Fifth Amendment, and Dalitz at first would not, for this would have torn the fabric of the respectable life he was trying to weave for himself in the desert at Las Vegas. He answered the questions for a while before he took refuge in constitutional privilege. It must have been one of the most unpleasant afternoons in Dalitz's life.

Immediately he was pinned down as having been known also as Moe Davis. He explained that "Davis became sort of a nickname," because of phonetic confusion with his true name. But it was not treated that way by the committee. Senator Kefauver had a report read that had been made for the committee by Virgil Peterson of the Chicago Crime Commission, one of the most famous of the unofficial tabulators of the underworld's activities. It began on a hard note for Dalitz:

> In the 1930's, according to J. Richard "Dixie" Davis, who was the lawyer for the slain gangster, "Dutch" Schulz, a national syndicate was operated from New York City by Charles "Lucky" Luciano, Benjamin "Bugsy" Siegel, and Meyer Lansky. Dixie Davis who, of course, was in a position to know what he was talking about, stated that Moe Davis became the real power in Cleveland, Ohio, and anyone who would question it would have to deal with Lucky and Meyer and Bugsy.

The report became even more biting. It suggested that Dalitz had some knowledge of the unsolved murder of a Cleveland city councilman, William E. Potter, who was killed in 1931 as he was ready to expose some of the Cleveland underworld.

Dalitz was listed as an associate of Morris Kleinman, Lou Rothkopf, Samuel Tucker, Thomas Jefferson McGinty and others,

who were called the "Mayfield Road gang." After the long statement was read, and Dalitz's alleged involvements with the underworld set forth, Senator Kefauver asked him if he wanted to make
any comment. Dalitz sounded shaken. The most important
thing he could think of to say at first was this: "To start off with
this thing about Dixie Davis, I never saw him in my life, and
wouldn't know him if he was in this room."

He also denied knowledge of Councilman Potter's murder.

There was more, much more, in the time that Estes Kefauver
kept Moe Dalitz on the witness stand and under oath. For example, when the digging went back to the illegal gambling joints
that the Mayfield Road gang had operated in Cleveland and near
Cincinnati, Dalitz resorted to the Fifth Amendment.

The committee had information that Dalitz and his cohorts
had operated places called the Mound Club, the Pettibone Club,
the Jungle Inn, near Youngstown, Ohio, and the Beverly Hills
Club and the Lookout House across the Ohio River from Cincinnati.

These were also the years soon after the invention of the
mechanical rabbit made greyhound racing possible. The Chicago,
Detroit, Cleveland, and Buffalo criminal organizations moved into
this new field with great vigor, exploiting it just as they did
the crap tables and blackjack games in their illegal gambling
houses. They almost finished dog racing, even before it caught
on. The sport was almost wiped out by public awareness of its
crookedness. Gamblers are strange in many ways: The only
poker game in town may be crooked, yet it will be patronized.
But a crooked race is something else again, unless the fix is in for
their benefit.

Moe Dalitz had a dog track at Dayton, Kentucky, and it lasted
thirteen days before the district attorney closed it down. Running an illegal gambling joint is one thing, for this can be done
somewhat quietly. But who can hide the yapping dogs, the

roaring crowd, all the cars and the rest of the trappings of a race track? Not even Moe Dalitz.

The Kefauver Committee also showed that Dalitz had an appetite for legitimate business even in the early years when he was most deeply involved in all sorts of illegal activity. He was born into a family with laundry interests and in the fall of 1963, in an interview with the author, he said proudly: "All these years I been still in the business I was brought up in. I had a piece of a laundry all the time, no matter where I went."

He has had interests in the Michigan Industrial Laundry Company in Detroit and the Pioneer Linen Supply Company in Cleveland. Some of his other interests included holdings in Reliance Steel Company and in Detroit Steel Company. These investments came about through his involvement with the merger of Reliance and Detroit. A friend of Dalitz from the business world became president of the merged companies. Many of his gambling associates put their money into this deal, and they all came out with good profits. There was this exchange:

SENATOR KEFAUVER: You put up how much money, you and your associates?

DALITZ: $66,666, I believe.

SENATOR KEFAUVER: Well, you made something like $230,000 out of the transaction, did you not?

DALITZ: It might have been a little more.

There is a strong possibility that this transaction in corporate finance, merger and stock sales may have given Dalitz and his group an appetite that was to betray them in the mid-1950's. There are some surface similarities to the initial deals that they went into with Alexander L. Guterma in Shawano Corporation. If the Detroit Steel deal was responsible for planting the thought in this gambling crowd's mind that it was capable of feeding off the wolves in Wall Street, they would have been much better off without the money. The Guterma deals almost ruined them all, and did bring disaster to some of Dalitz's associates.

Dalitz tacitly conceded under the gentle but persistent pressure of Senator Kefauver's questions that his money came from bootlegging. It developed this way:

SENATOR KEFAUVER: Now Mr. Dalitz you fellows got your start by rum running, didn't you, back in the old prohibition days? Now is that the way you got your original money to make your original investments?

DALITZ: Well, not all of these investments; no.

SENATOR KEFAUVER: I understand not all of them because some of them are very profitable. As a matter of fact, you had been making a great deal of money in recent years, so I suppose from your profits from one investment you would then go ahead and make another investment. Now, to get your investments started off you did get yourself a pretty good little nest-egg out of rum running didn't you?

DALITZ: Well, I didn't inherit any money, Senator.

Among the gamblers in Las Vegas this answer of Dalitz is remembered with great glee, as if he had somehow vanquished Estes Kefauver. They still recount it, although sometimes so garbled as to be almost unrecognizable, and this demonstrates a peculiarity of the gamblers' attitudes toward those who ask questions about their business, and make criticisms about the casinos. Criticism stings them quickly to response. On those occasions when one of them is able to score with a riposte to some critical questioner, they store up the memory. Sometimes, as in the exchange between the Senator and the bootlegger, they misread the impact of the statement; for Senator Kefauver got what he wanted from Dalitz, a tacit admission that bootlegging was the foundation stone of the great wealth that the Dalitz associates had amassed.

If the senator thought they had money then, he should see them now.

But on that day, Senator Kefauver also got Dalitz to admit that he had gambling interests in Miami and drew from him a series of admissions of his interest in a string of legitimate businesses. These included Milco Sales Company, that was affiliated with the laundry business; the Dalitz Realty Company, which owned land and buildings in Wyandotte, Michigan; Berdeen Realty Company, which built and leased a supermarket in Wyandotte, Michigan; Liberty Ice Cream Company, in Cleveland; heavy investments in the Chicago & Rock Island Railroad Company.

It should be remembered that in all probability Senator Kefauver's questions were based on an analysis of Dalitz's tax return for 1950 and that he had a complete summary of that return in front of him as he asked, "Now generally, since you have obtained these investments, how much does your income run a year, if you don't mind telling us, Mr. Dalitz? Tell us just roughly, if you will?"

> DALITZ: Well, roughly, I would say $70,000 or $80,000 a year.
> SENATOR KEFAUVER: Or $95,000 a year?
> DALITZ: It could be $95,000 a year, yes.

Dalitz came before the Kefauver Committee in Los Angeles a month after it had first sought to question him during the period when hearings were held about underworld activity in Cleveland. During those Cleveland hearings the committee had received a long statement from Alvin Sutton, the director of public safety in Cleveland. Sutton drew an ugly picture of gangster domination of some aspects of the city's life. The main financial support of the gang operation was the income from bootlegging, said Sutton. He added: "At the top of Cleveland's bootleggers were Morris Kleinman, Lou Rothkoph, Moe Dalitz, Sam Tucker and Maxie Diamond. They were at the helm of the board of directors. They had their suppliers of Canadian whisky, and their salesmen and thugs to distribute contraband and to reap the harvest of money . . . Ruthless beatings, unsolved murders and shakedowns, threats and bribery came to this community as a result of gangsters' rise to power."

By the time that Sutton described the situation in Cleveland of the 1930's, the mob had moved on to Las Vegas. He explained why it had left: "Kleinman and others of his ilk weathered the thirteen years of warfare. Only the United States government income tax investigators were able to bring him down."

Among the first business steps that Kleinman took when he came out of jail in 1936 to resume his association with Dalitz and the others was to hire an accountant to help him keep his tax accounts in order. The accountant was the federal tax agent who had worked up the case against Kleinman that put him in jail.

But another reason that the Mayfield Road gang moved out of Cleveland was the appointment of a public safety director who took the job after leaving a federal appointment. He was famous then, but his greatest fame came years later when he was in retirement and near death. A book based on his experiences in the gang days in Chicago attracted the eye of a television producer who made a pair of pilot programs from it and these became a bloody and controversial television series that ran for several years.

His name was Eliot Ness. The program was "The Untouchables."

Kleinman appeared before the Kefauver Committee and took the Fifth Amendment all the way. Sam Tucker followed Dalitz to the witness chair, and in a low voice that was sometimes inaudible made admissions that emphasized the branching out of the bootlegging and gambling racketeers into legitimate business.

To the suggestion from Senator Kefauver that the combination led by Dalitz was a syndicate, Tucker said "they aren't a syndicate. There are some things that I am in on and some that I am not in on." He was unable to say whether a land company in Ohio was legal or illegal. He admitted he had half interest in a real estate company in Cleveland. He made it plain that he owned part of a restaurant in Dayton, Ohio, but refused to answer questions about it because of self-incrimination problems. He also discussed financing he had supplied for a string of theaters.

At the conclusion of the hearings in Los Angeles, Senator Kefauver made a short statement, his voice tired from the grueling effort of questioning witnesses, and his demeanor betraying his fatigue.

"We in our hearings in Cleveland and other places, have shown that there has been a syndicate that has been operating in that part of the country, which follows the usual pattern of having made money during the days of prohibition, rum running and bootlegging, dealing in liquor, and taking the profits that they have made and getting into all kinds of enterprises, both legal and illegal. It will be noted that these men, with this syndicate, apparently have great financial power. The testimony shows that they were sought out by Wilbur Clark, having more than a million dollars available for the purpose of finishing the Desert Inn in Las Vegas. The testimony also disclosed that they had some smaller holdings in Florida.

"Their businesses are very substantial and are among the largest gambling casinos in the United States. The one over across the river in Kentucky where they have been operating for a considerable time, is one of the largest in the country. In the State of Ohio they had various types of gambling enterprises.

"Then you will find, also, the pattern of putting their money into legitimate businesses. Here we have a man as president of a large steel corporation by virtue of being able to find the ready cash that these people had available. We have heard testimony about other businesses that they have gone into.

"I think the testimony of these two persons shows the general trend that racketeering and persons that may have been engaged in illegal activities has taken in the United States. They have been engaged in rum running and other types of activities, gambling and so forth, and then go into legitimate businesses or get into whatever they can. Of course, gaining respectability as they go along, or trying to."

The reference to "these two persons" meant Dalitz and Tucker.

Senator Kefauver's statements were made in the late afternoon of February 28, 1951. They bloomed on the front pages of the nation's newspapers the next day, and then died. Dalitz and Tucker went back to Las Vegas, where their group then as now controlled the Desert Inn, which it expanded, added onto, shaped and molded into one of the greatest moneymaking machines in Las Vegas. Nevada authorities paid absolutely no attention to the warning given by Senator Kefauver.

From the Desert Inn, elements of the old Cleveland gang have moved into the stock market, where they were participants in stock market manipulations that cost investors about $5,000,000. They have moved into home construction in Las Vegas, bought another casino across the highway from the mother lode, the Desert Inn, and have other branches and interests about which information is unobtainable. They live a good life now, scattered around the country with Kleinman in Florida at Bay Harbor Islands (a community built on two islands in Biscayne Bay); Dalitz in Las Vegas, living in a big house on the golf course that is a part of the Desert Inn; and McGinty and Tucker also moving in and out of Las Vegas as the whim strikes them. As the years have passed, Dalitz has become more and more the motivator, the planner, the overseer. He looks after the Desert Inn, and applies his quick intelligence, his experience-sharpened instincts to the problems that confront the group.

Dalitz is also the tie for one of the most intriguing relationships to be uncovered in the stock market debacle that revealed some of the Desert Inn organization's secret associations. This is the lifelong friendship with Sam Garfield. Sam Garfield lives in Clare, Michigan, a small city in the center of the state, but he travels most of the time. He has extensive oil holdings, he has said, and these require him to move around the United States checking on drilling operations and acquiring new leases.

But Sam Garfield is a lot more than an oilman. Just how much more can be glimpsed through the shadows that hide a great deal of the business activities of such persons as Dalitz and Garfield. For instance, the answer is in doubt to the fundamental question of where he was born. By one account, Sam Garfield was born in Providence, Rhode Island, and spent three years at Brown University, leaving before he took a degree.

It appears more likely that Garfield was born in Russia on December 6, 1899. His family name was Garfinkle, and his parents brought him to the United States as a baby. He acquired American citizenship in 1907 through his parents' naturalization. There is no proof that he ever went to Brown University, and a man who was close to him for a few months said in a dry voice: "I just can't imagine that he ever went to college anywhere."

Garfield grew up in Detroit, Michigan, where he went to Bishop Grade School. Another student was a youngster named Morris Barney Dalitz, whose family had a laundry. The two became friends there, and have been associates all their lives. The full extent of their association disappears behind the shadows.

There has been official speculation that Garfield is a financier for gambling and other underworld activities. The United States government has argued in court that he organized a plan to pay a $100,000 bribe to former Senator George H. Bender, Ohio Republican, to bring about an end to Securities and Exchange Commission stock fraud investigations which led to Garfield's market manipulations. Garfield denied this.

In addition to his friendship with Dalitz, Garfield also has been an intimate associate of Kleinman, while he has an almost father-son relationship with Allard Roen, the son of the late Frank Rosen, who was a Cleveland gambler and associate of Dalitz and Kleinman. (Allard Roen changed his name by dropping the "s.") Both Dalitz and Roen told the author that they have fond feelings for Garfield. Garfield also had a protégé association with another younger man, Irving Pasternak, a Denver construction man and also an oil operator.

But this friendship with Pasternak was on a different basis than the Roen association. Pasternak, according to one story relayed by an official source, began his relationship with Garfield as a chauffeur. Pasternak had been a solicitor for home building repairs, a line that was shot through with fraud and with hoodlum control when it was perfected in the early 1950's. This business faded out when the Federal Housing Administration took steps to withhold the financing that made it so lucrative. It is not clear whether Pasternak was involved in one of these organizations before he became associated with Garfield. At any rate, they eventually became partners in a company called Garnak Drilling which led them into deals with Alexander L. Guterma, the market manipulator, and eventually into convictions for stock fraud. As this is written Pasternak and Garfield no longer are friendly.

One of the most revealing bits of official knowledge about Garfield, and one which indicates most clearly that he has underworld gambling ties, stands out from the details of a raid on a business office in Evansville, Indiana, in 1951. Until then, Garfield had just three arrests on his record, all of minor importance. They were on May 4, 1924, in Detroit, for frequenting a gambling place; on April 12, 1927, by Toronto, Ontario, police for vagrancy; and on October 5, 1930, by Detroit police for investigation. None resulted in conviction.

But in the winter of 1951, at the height of the basketball season, Sheriff Frank McDonald of Vandenberg County, Indiana, raided the offices of the Gar-Dan Oil Company in Evansville. Charges were filed and within a few days Garfield paid a $500 fine on a guilty plea to a charge of keeping a gambling place. In 1963, his explanation to associates from legitimate businesses was that a friend had asked for permission to use a vacant room in the Gar-Dan Oil Company offices. Garfield gave permission, with the understanding that the room was to be used to collect some debts. Garfield said he had no knowledge of the gambling operation. He paid the fine in order to keep down the publicity, he explained.

Sheriff McDonald told a different story. He said that the Garfield offices had been national headquarters for a gambling syndicate specializing in college basketball betting. The sheriff said he had found letterheads from legitimate oil companies, as well as handicapping sheets for college and professional basketball teams and other betting materials. There was a list of prospective circuit court jurors, a piece of intelligence that gamblers would find of interest, but which would have absolutely no recognizable value to an oil company operator. Sheriff McDonald also said that the current phone bill at the time of his raid was $2394.45, something a little outsized for a sedate oil operator's office, but completely in character for a national bookmaking operation.

The final element in Sheriff McDonald's case was this: the other partner in Gar-Dan Oil was Milton Danenberg of Chicago. In Chicago, Danenberg was known widely as a betting commissioner and bookmaker, a fact that fitted well with the sheriff's hypothesis that the Gar-Dan Oil Company offices were headquarters for a national bookmaking ring.

One report on Garfield, from official sources, said that

his circle of friends and business associates includes some of the most prominent individuals in society as well as a number of the notorious racketeers, swindlers and confidence men. Of the latter kind he has had business dealings with Irving Pas-

ternak, Alexander Guterma, Meyer Lansky, Gerardo V.
Catena (Appalachian attendee), Morris Kleinman, Morris
Dalitz, Allard Roen and Edward Levinson. In addition to
high level business activity, Garfield is reported to be a high-
roller type gambler.

A considerable amount of intelligence on Garfield is packed
into those sentences. Pasternak, Guterma, Kleinman, Dalitz, and
Roen have been identified in these pages in their relationship
with Garfield. Meyer Lansky is the "Meyer" of the Bug and
Meyer Mob which had as its other head the notorious Benjamin
(Bugsy) Siegel. Gerardo V. Catena was in attendance at the
Cosa Nostra gathering at Appalachian, New York, when the police raided a meeting that included all the leaders in the Italian
criminal conspiracy. He has been the director in the New Jersey area of the Cosa Nostra activities while Vito Genovese, the
top leader, has been in jail. Association with men such as these
fits poorly in the image of Sam Garfield, oil operator and a leading
citizen of Clare, Michigan. But it fits precisely in the image of
Sam Garfield, friend of Moe Dalitz, bootlegger and gambler.

All this creates a picture of Garfield as one of those businessmen who stand with a foot on each side of the dim, smudged line
that separates the ethical and unethical in American society.
Such men are of inestimable value to such as Moe Dalitz and
Gerry Catena, whose careers have been so much publicized as to
preclude their actually passing across into legitimate society. The
gamblers' and racketeers' money will take them into business circles near the top, but for their social contact with the wealthy
elite, they have to rely on those who come to their gambling traps
for a little excitement. Garfield has been of great value to Moe
Dalitz, and one of the tragedies for the Desert Inn crowd in
the stock market fiasco came from the exposure of Garfield's
associations to the point where some of his former friends in

the legitimate side of life began to steer clear of him. In a subsequent chapter we shall examine the full effects of all this more closely, in particular the effect on the crown prince of the Desert Inn band of racketeers, bootleggers and gamblers — Allard Roen.

Among those half-world figures associated with Garfield, we have discussed all but one. This is Edward Levinson, and he is a figure of as many fascinating facets as is Garfield himself. Like Garfield and Dalitz, Levinson is Jewish, and this deserves consideration as one of the interesting aspects of the sociological phenomenon that is legalized gambling in Nevada. If any single ethnological group dominates in the operating phases of the gambling casinos, it is the Jewish group. Also, for some reason hidden in the accidents of history, many of these now-middle aged or elderly men of Jewish background are descended from families that emigrated from Russia or Poland or elsewhere in eastern Europe. The great Jewish migrations from western Europe produced relatively few of the major figures of American gambling.

Here is a statement of this peculiarity from a high government official who would discuss it only in anonymity.

"When you talk about the underworld you can divide it roughly into two groups. First, there's the Italian mob, what Joe Valachi calls Cosa Nostra and what everybody else for years has called the Mafia. Nobody belongs here but Italians. This bunch does everything to turn a dollar; they rob, steal, cheat, shylock, murder — you name it, the Cosa Nostra does it for money.

"For sure a bunch like this will sooner or later get in the gambling business.

"The gamblers are the second big group in the underworld. There are the bookies, the Nevada crowd, and all the rest of them like the guys who used to run the race wire and make book on the basketball and football. There are all kinds in this like Irish and a few Negroes but the biggest group is Jewish. Beyond that, where the Italians get hold of a good gambling joint, they have somebody run it for them and that somebody is usually Jewish.

"I don't know why this is, but you can see examples of it all along the line. Meyer Lansky is a Jew, and he has very, very close ties with the top hoods in the Cosa Nostra outfit. Bugsy Siegel was a Jew and he was hooked up real close with the Italian mob. Some of the places in Las Vegas today are really controlled by the Mafia and we know this because we see some of their muscle men around. But the front men are almost always Jews."

Levinson is the operating boss at the Fremont Hotel, the only one of the Las Vegas casino hotels located within the city limits. This one is right downtown in the Casino Center where it competes for the rougher, less sophisticated gambling crowd. It is multi-story, built with Teamsters Union pension fund loans, and a money-maker. Levinson promoted the place after half a lifetime in illegal gambling places in Detroit and Miami. As with Garfield and Dalitz, Levinson grew up in Detroit. He was born in 1899, like the other two, but there is no indication that they were close as youngsters.

He was chased out of Miami Beach by the Kefauver Committee, which put a great crimp in illegal gambling operations wherever it held hearings. Levinson moved into Las Vegas in 1952 as a part owner of the Sands Hotel. By 1954 he had a 13 percent interest in the Mob-dominated Flamingo Hotel, the place Bugsy Siegel started. When Levinson left Miami, he announced he was going to Las Vegas to buy into a hotel-casino or else start one. In Florida he appeared to be a man of considerable resources. His company, Gulf Coast Sales, controlled confectionery concessions in some movie theaters.

By 1955, Levinson was ready with his promotion of the Fremont Hotel and withdrew from the Dunes and the Sands, the two Strip casino hotels where he was vice president of the operating corporation. He also had a major interest in the Horseshoe Club, a casino in the downtown area. There are frequent references in official reports to his transfer of minority interests from his holdings to those of others. By late 1963, he still was the largest single stockholder in the Fremont Hotel with about 20 percent, and in the Horseshoe Club with 27 ½ percent.

For at least twenty-five years before coming to Las Vegas, Levinson had been involved in illegal gambling operations. His police arrest record shows that on Christmas Day, 1928, he was arrested in Detroit on a charge of operating a gambling place. The charge was dismissed the following May. In July 1929 Levinson was arrested in Detroit for operating a gambling place, and again the charge was dismissed.

But on August 20, 1941, he was arrested in Detroit for violation of the state gambling laws. This time he was fined $1500. Other gambling charges in Detroit were dismissed in 1942 and 1943. In 1950 he was arrested in Miami, Florida, on a charge of bookmaking and vagrancy, and this case was dismissed. In 1951, he was arrested again in Miami for possession of gambling equipment. This case was dismissed when the arrest was found to be technically improper.

Levinson has an interesting family background. There are three Levinson brothers, Edward, Mike and Louis. Mike Levinson has become associated with Ed in Las Vegas, but in the earlier years he was a part of the illegal Flamingo Club that Louis operated in Newport, Kentucky, across the Ohio River from Cincinnati. This place was closed when the former professional football player, George Ratterman, was elected as a reform sheriff in Newport in 1960.

All three of the Levinsons were prominent in the gambling empire that flourished in Newport and Covington, Kentucky.

In those operations the leader was "Sleepout" Louis Levinson. He got this nickname, he said, from continuing to stay on the move during the Chicago circulation wars in the 1920's, when he would sleep in doorways and soapboxes, never going home to bed. However, around Cincinnati it is said that he is a card player of great endurance, sometimes staying in a poker game for seventy-two consecutive hours, and that his nickname derived from this.

But whatever his family background, Ed Levinson has done pretty well financially for a fellow who started with nothing. In November 1957 an attorney, Bryant R. Burton, who represents various of the Levinson interests, lost his briefcase. It was found at the airport in Las Vegas, and of course carefully examined. Among the things in it was the Edward Levinson bank balance sheet, showing that he had on hand $24,582.33. But there had been several checks written. One was for $350,000 to the First National Bank of Nevada. Two more on that same day (October 18, 1957) had been drawn to the Compañía de Hoteles La Riverside de Cuba for $50,000. Those were the years when the Las Vegas gamblers also were running casinos in Havana under the protection of the man who then ran Cuba, Fulgencio Batista. The Riverside may have been one that Levinson was interested in.

All of these facts about Levinson make him an interesting fellow, a startling example of the sort of man moving about at the top financial level of the underworld. However, more is known about him.

He was a business partner, as this is written, with Bobby Baker, the intimate of some of the most important political personalities of the nation. Baker served them as the secretary to the Democratic majority of the United States Senate. Baker also was the longtime intimate and close political supporter of Lyndon B. Johnson.

What did Baker and Levinson have to do with each other?

Neither man will discuss this relationship, so that where it started is not known. But Levinson was a substantial stockholder in the Serv-U Corporation, a vending machine company that Baker organized, represented, and controlled. This is a startling relationship. Baker appeared to have ready access to venture capital, for he was involved also in a motel, an insurance company, stock speculations and a scattering of other enterprises that all had just one thing in common — the prestige and connections of the secretary of the senate majority was a valuable property for each operation. Through Baker, Levinson had access to many places where otherwise he would have been unwelcome.

Serv-U Corporation, for example, was able to dislodge vending machines in the manufacturing plants of the aerospace industry in Southern California. A damage action was filed over the placing of Baker's machines in a plant in Falls Church, Virginia. He had either to resign or answer questions about his outside activities.

But his relationship as a businesss associate was far more valuable to the gambler, Levinson, than the profits they might share from dividends in Serv-U Corporation. Just how valuable these associations are to Mr. Levinson can be judged by this set of circumstances:

In June 1963, Baker approached Samuel Pryor, a Washington-based vice-president of Pan American World Airways, with the request that a business appointment be made for Baker and a friend to talk with John Gates. Gates is the president of Intercontinental Hotels, Inc., a subsidiary of Pan American for operation of hotels along the airline's routes in some of the underdeveloped nations. Pan American found years ago that if it had good accommodations in some of these places it could sell more tickets, and to have them, it had to run the hotels. Gates was the head of the corporation that controlled the hotels.

Pan American has extensive routes through the Caribbean and into South America where it pioneered many years ago. Some of the hotels that it steers its passengers to are operated by the Pan

American complex of corporations; some are not. In some of them there are various purely local customs and habits and business operations which Pan American subleases for operation by other business firms. One of the most troublesome problems for Gates and Intercontinental Hotels, Inc., derives from the gambling that is encouraged by some of the governments along its routes.

So the casinos are leased out to others for operation.

"We just don't want anything to do with running them," Gates said to the author. "We want someone else to take care of that and keep us out of it. Gambling is a headache for us in those places."

Bobby Baker provided some more headaches for Gates and other Pan American executives. It is an obvious fact that any major American firm doing business in all the fields that Pan American enters will meet a request from such a person as Baker for a business appointment for a friend immediately, pleasantly and with great consideration. Baker was as well connected politically as it is possible for an unelected official to be in Washington, D.C. He had been a close confidant of Lyndon B. Johnson during the years when Johnson established himself as the strongest majority leader in the U.S. Senate in modern times. Baker also played a leading role in the Johnson campaign for the Democratic presidential nomination in 1960. He was one of those who advised Johnson to accept the vice-presidential nomination. Also Baker had been doing favors for senators and protecting their personal secrets for two decades.

After Johnson left the senate majority leader's office and moved into the Vice-president's suite, Baker stayed on as secretary to the majority under the leadership of Senator Mike Mansfield. He was out from under the strong control of the iron-willed and incredibly energetic Johnson. Mansfield is a slower moving and less determined man. It appears, from the disclosures made about Baker, that his branching out into a variety of questionable outside business activities accelerated after the movement of events took him out from under the close control of Lyndon B. Johnson. Baker left his Senate job several months before tragic events put his former sponsor in the White House.

But however this series of actions was allowed to build, it was not at all unusual that by June 1963 Bobby Baker would call an executive of Pan American Airways and in effect assert the private and unofficial right to make a business appointment for a friend.

That friend was Edward Levinson, lifelong gambler, and one of the major targets in Las Vegas of a variety of federal investigations. Yet while the agents of the executive branch of the United States government were watching Levinson's every movement and checking carefully on all his financial transactions, one of the high appointive officials of the legislative branch was making business appointments for him. The flood of money that powers the gambling empire in Las Vegas creates many ironies of this sort.

There was another peculiarity in Levinson's desire for an appointment to see Gates regarding the Pan American hotel gambling casino operating leases. Levinson could not be associated with these places, and still operate in Las Vegas. This was established in 1958 when, under the administration of Governor Charles Russell of Nevada, William Sinnot, the chairman of the Gaming Control Board issued a ruling that no Nevada licensed gamblers could have gambling holdings in any other place. The issue was the flight of Nevada gamblers to Havana to run casinos under licenses issued by the Batista regime.

So why was Levinson there? Why did he go to the trouble of asking Baker to make the appointment for him? Was he representing an interest of some other gambler who had a concealed ownership in the Fremont Hotel casino and was therefore on the record free to consider running one of the Caribbean casinos?

Levinson refuses to talk about these things. When the public became aware of his relationship with Baker and of the meeting
with Gates that Baker arranged, Levinson suddenly became unavailable. Before, he could be reached at the Fremont Hotel,
where frequently he appeared in startling dress.

Levinson is a short man, with a fringe of gray hair and a pair of
the sharpest, most opaque dark, dark brown eyes in Nevada. To
talk with him is to be impressed with many unspoken secrets,
with a quick mind and a cool courage under stress. It is possible
to visualize him angry; but never to see him frightened. Around
the casino he tends to wear white duck trousers and bright green
shirts and perhaps a jockey cap. One who has never been there
could not believe that such dress fits right into the crowd at the
Fremont Hotel.

But when a request was made to him for a picture, what was
produced was Levinson in black tie.

When his involvement with Baker became known, callers at the
Fremont Hotel were told that "Mr. Levinson is unavailable. He
is away." When will he be back? "He is away indefinitely."

But he did come back. He drove into town one day, his car
terribly dusty and mud spattered. He told friends that he had
been to Europe, and that he was in New York when the trouble
"over Baker" came out in the papers. He refused to discuss any
aspects of his arrangement with Baker, however, or to comment
on the contradiction of seeing Gates to discuss gambling casino leases that he could never have unless he was willing to give
up his vastly successful operations in the Fremont Hotel and the
Horseshoe Casino in Las Vegas. He took refuge in constitutional
privilege when he appeared — televised — in the investigation of
Baker.

As the Las Vegas gamblers have become more successful in
branching out into other businesses, their mistakes have been
more rare, so that such an incident as the Levinson-Baker ar-

rangement merits close examination for all the lessons that it shows.

For example, there was just a hint in the episode that Baker and Levinson were playing a game of their own, while at the same time drawing into the operation two other former Las Vegas gamblers who had moved their operations to the Caribbean. The sequence of the meetings with Gates fortifies this suspicion. It was in June of 1963 that Baker asked for an appointment for a friend. In that same month, Baker brought in his friend, who proved to be Levinson, to discuss the status of the casino operations in Santo Domingo and Curaçao, where Pan American controls hotels that have casinos in them. Gates explained to the two men that in Curaçao the airline was the operator of a hotel owned by a group of investors who picked the casino operator subject to Pan American's approval. In Santo Domingo, he said, the airline controlled the choice of the casino operator.

Baker did most of the talking at this meeting, said Gates, and Levinson asked a few questions, but mostly listened. Gates remembered: "Baker told me that this friend of his was interested in the gambling business and had this hotel in Las Vegas and that it was very successful, and that they wondered if there was any opportunity for him in our two hotels in Santo Domingo and Curaçao."

Gates also told Baker and Levinson that he had received an expression of interest in the two casinos from another Nevada gambler, Clifford Jones. They made no comment on this disclosure.

Jones is the former lieutenant governor of Nevada who continued until the fall of 1964 to hold an interest in the corporation that controls the physical properties of the Thunderbird Hotel, but he no longer had interests in the casino at the hotel. He was one of those Nevada gamblers who went to Havana during the Batista regime. He stayed on in the Caribbean to become involved in a string of four small casinos. He lives in Las Vegas, and still frequented the Thunderbird Hotel. But the official lists of holders of interests in the casino did not include his name. His partner in the Caribbean casinos is Jacob Kozloff, a former owner of the Last Frontier, one of the early Las Vegas casino hotels. Jones and Kozloff run three small casinos in Dutch-controlled territories around the Caribbean. They are in Aruba, in the Lesser Antilles; in the Dutch part of St. Martin, one of the Leeward Islands partly controlled by the French; and in Surinam, Dutch Guiana. They also have a casino in a government-owned hotel in Quito, the capital of Ecuador. Jones' group sold the Thunderbird in September 1964.

After the first meeting at which they were alone with Gates, the two dissimilar figures — Levinson and Baker — came back in July 1963, with Jones and took up the discussion anew.

One of the interesting aspects of this second meeting was that Jones thought it was the first, until the author told him differently. He had been explaining that Baker merely had arranged the meeting for Jones, who as a former Democratic lieutenant governor of Nevada was an old political friend of the powerful Baker. When he was told that Baker and Levinson had gone first to Gates alone, and then had later brought him into the deal, Jones was at first silent for a few moments, then went on to talk of other matters.

At this second meeting, somewhat the same ground was gone over again for the benefit of Jones and Kozloff, and Gates let them understand that it was possible that changes might be made by Pan American in the operation of the casinos. The third meeting was held sometime in August 1963, and Baker did not attend this. This time, it was made clear to Gates that Levinson could not appear as a partner in any gambling casino that operated outside Nevada, and that the application that might be filed by Jones and Kozloff would be in their names, not his. Subsequently they did file an application for the Santo Domingo casino. Pan American had not picked an operator there when this was written. Gates' tone as he discussed these incidents was such as to indicate that he wanted nothing to do with the Nevada group. Gates was bitter that the incident had occurred, for he disliked having Pan American involved in public scandals.

The Baker case was a public scandal, and the involvement of Levinson, Jones and Kozloff in it gave it Nevada interest, too. The Rules Committee of the Senate was charged with investigating Baker's activities during his employment by the majority, and a member of the Rules Committee was Senator Howard Cannon, a Democrat representing Nevada. Senator Cannon's home is in Las Vegas, and he has wide friendships among the gamblers who operate the hotels on the Strip.

"I flatter myself that I know every one of them," he has said.

Hardly had the Rules Committee started its study of Baker's deeds before the rumors began to run that Senator Cannon was in effect a friend in court for Baker and was attempting to delay, thwart and spoil the investigation. These reports became current at about the same time that Baker's involvement with Levinson, Jones and Kozloff became known, so that Senator Cannon suddenly found himself widely suspected of protecting Baker because of pressure from Las Vegas gamblers. The senator issued a statement denying this allegation, and supported resolutions within the committee that strengthened the chances of a complete study of Baker's activities.

This series of events involving Baker, Levinson, Jones, Kozloff and the executives from Pan American World Airways has importance beyond the questions of leasing small casinos in the Caribbean. Probably the entire winnings of the string operated by Jones and Kozloff plus the receipts from the two controlled by the Pan American subsidiary would amount to less in a year than the take at just one of the top places in Nevada.

The importance arises from Baker's willingness to be a front man for the gamblers. This is again a symptom of the great power and influence that they can build from their positions as legal gamblers in Nevada. It is highly doubtful that Bobby Baker would have made an appointment for Eddie Levinson, a Miami man who ran illegal gambling places just off Collins Avenue in Miami Beach. But he had no hesitation in moving to help Eddie Levinson, the legal, lawful head man of the Fremont Hotel Casino in Las Vegas.

What makes the difference is being legal. But, as we have seen in studying the careers of some of the gamblers there, they are still the same men they were before. They brought with them to Las Vegas the same set of moral standards, the same set of ethical viewpoints that they collected as young men in the illegal gambling houses of the nation's major cities. One of the remarkable facts that becomes apparent on close observation of the gamblers is the avarice that grips them. Their appetite for money seems to be insatiable.

But there are exceptions to this, as there are exceptions to almost any statement that can be made about the Nevada gamblers.

We have seen how Eddie Levinson continues to scramble even though the record shows him to be the owner of no less than 20 percent of about $10,000,000 worth of gambling houses and hotels. The returns each year from the Fremont Hotel Casino and the Horseshoe Casino must be fabulous. We have had a glimpse and we shall see more of how the old-time bootleggers who run the Desert Inn and Stardust push and shove to make more money, even when they have two of the biggest money-makers in Nevada grinding out the wealth for them. These stories can be repeated again and again with more examples from the hurrying and hustling of the gamblers to fill their bottomless pockets.

Occasionally one comes along that is different, a gambling character out of the ordinary run of things. Such a man is Al

Winter, who was to the Sahara Hotel in Las Vegas what Moe Dalitz was to the Desert Inn. Perhaps the different background Winter has may explain why he operates today on a different plane from his colleagues on the Strip.

Winter grew up in Portland, Oregon, where his father was a circuit judge. Portland of those years was a smaller city in a quiet backwash at the northwest corner. Winter went to law school, passed his bar examinations and then drifted down below his station. He moved back and forth across that line of legality, and somehow at the end of the 1930's became a part of an underworld organization in Portland that controlled the racing wire in Oregon and southwestern Washington. The racing wire was an absolute necessity for operation of a horsebook. Winter and his associates through their control of the wire "drops" controlled the horsebooks in that thinly populated part of the country. They also sat at the top of as smooth a gambling enterprise as ever flourished on the West Coast.

All of this was controlled from a headquarters that included a fine restaurant, a smaller dining room for men and a lunch counter that specialized in putting out the sort of food that gamblers liked. Upstairs, the horsebook and the gambling tables divided the space. There were other horsebooks scattered around Portland, and over the rest of the Winter group's territory.

The organization did well throughout World War II and a few years afterward, for Portland was a center of merchant ship construction for war convoys and the payrolls fed into the illegal enterprises that Winter and his partners ran wide open. There was almost no attempt to conceal these gambling houses and horsebooks. An incident will illustrate just how wide open it was.

It was arranged that two big policemen in full uniform would escort a reporter and a photographer into one of these horsebooks. The premises were upstairs and the doors and windows were open on this Saturday afternoon in late March. Entrance was made with no trouble. No one attended the door. The two uniformed policemen, the reporter and the photographer carrying his camera wandered through the crowded room without anyone becoming excited, or doing more than nod. It was not until the first bulb flashed that the crowd became excited, and it poured down the narrow stairway and into the street, gabbling like a frightened turkey flock.

Winter and his friends ran places such as these until a change in public attitudes brought election of a reform administration. Then they quietly gathered up what was movable and took it to Las Vegas. First they operated a place downtown, but then they built the Sahara, today the largest hotel and the dominant architectural feature of the Strip.

The Winter group also operated the Mint Casino, a downtown Las Vegas place. They ran both places and managed all the property for about ten years. In 1963, they sold the physical property of the Sahara and the Mint to the Del E. Webb Construction Corporation, which now manages both. It has added more hotel space to the Sahara, and is building a downtown hotel to complement the Mint. Winter and his associates retained the casino operations, however. The Webb Corporation will find itself in direct competition with Eddie Levinson and the Fremont Hotel. The Webb Corporation bought the Thunderbird in September 1964, and now rivals Bill Harrah in size.

The Webb concern, incidentally, has been a favorite builder during the years of growth in Las Vegas. Its first big casino job was the first big casino — the Flamingo. Del Webb has told friends hair-raising tales of his experiences with the notoriously unstable Bugsy Siegel.

After the physical plants were sold, there was a realignment of the ownership of the Mint and Sahara casinos, with Winter ending as one of the three persons who own the company that operates the casinos in both places. He no longer lives in Las Vegas, however. Calls for him at the Sahara are answered in surprise, for "Mr. Winter now lives in Portland, Oregon," the caller is told.

There he dabbles in local politics, and has shown no inclination for the frenzied stock market manipulations that entrapped the Desert Inn crowd, nor for the dizzy whirl of top level political friendships that have exposed Eddie Levinson to the public gaze. Winter spends much of his time, as this is written, holding court for longtime friends and retainers at a place called Dunkin's Retreat, a Portland restaurant somewhat like the one he ran so many years ago for the gambling crowd. There is no indication that he is risking his Las Vegas legal standing by getting involved in any gambling operations back in Portland. He seems to be as near retirement as it is possible for a man like Winter to get.

There has been a shift in some of the places in the past few years to new faces and new, unmarked personalities in the top management. The Desert Inn was the first of the Strip places really to make a conscious move in this direction, when Moe Dalitz and Morris Kleinman began to groom Allard Roen as their successor. Roen was the son of their longtime associate, the late Frank Rosen who was also a gambler trained in the illegal joints around Cleveland. He also was a college graduate (Duke University) and was equipped to move in social circles closed to Dalitz and Kleinman. More and more in the late 1950's, Roen became the operating head of the Desert Inn and the Stardust, after the group bought it. He was well situated to do this, for Dalitz liked him very much and had a feeling of continuity with the younger man derived from their shared background in Cleveland. One should always remember that the Las Vegas gamblers rely on their intuition. To them a situation must "feel" right to be right. Dalitz felt right with Roen.

This careful plan for the future was ruined in 1962 when Roen was placed in a position where he had to plead guilty to a stock fraud charge that was the result of the Desert Inn crowd's association with Alexander L. Guterma's stock manipulations. The possibility of Roen continuing even as a part owner of the casino license in the Desert Inn was seriously threatened.

It was necessary to get a new man to be the operating head, since Dalitz was getting older and no one else was around that the various interests could agree upon. After some worrying over the problem, the gamblers turned the place over to John Andrew Donnelley, who had been their lawyer for more than fifteen years.

Donnelley moved into the former board room at the Desert Inn and used it as his office. He could look out on the swimming pool and down toward the golf course, where he also was able to spend a lot of time. Dalitz continued to be around much of the time, and so was Roen, so that Donnelley was not at a loss for advice on past practices, or suggestions for new ways of doing business.

"I love it," he said in an interview with the author. "I've never done any executive work before, and I find it fascinating."

Donnelley had practiced law in San Diego for thirty years when he closed out his office to move to Las Vegas. He was most successful in law. His title is executive vice-president, and he bought a 3 percent interest in the Desert Inn casino paying $10,-500.

Dalitz meantime, through one of those strange and inexplicable sociological developments, has come to have in Las Vegas the reputation of standing as a force for righteousness between the Strip gambling houses and the Mob. Various elements of officialdom look on Dalitz as a known quality, a gambler they can figure is less likely to be a part of some terrible criminal conspiracy. Dalitz is widely respected among observers of the gambling scene. The Desert Inn management group is a sort of aristocracy among the gamblers who control the casinos in Las Vegas.

Morris Kleinman is less often in Las Vegas, preferring to spend his time in Bay Harbor Islands, Florida, where he established a home several years ago.

Wilbur Clark, the small time gambler whose dream is responsible for the idea of the Desert Inn in the first place, had almost nothing to do with running it even before he sold in September 1964. He long since had been intimidated and stared down by the hard-eyed bunch he brought in from Cleveland in 1949.

4

THE GAMBLER AS BUSINESSMAN

THE MEN who dominate the Desert Inn showed near genius as they stepped away from the gambling table and moved into development and finance. In the desert around Las Vegas they put together deals that seem simple, yet are a startling demonstration of the skill of the men who designed them. Tremendous leverage resulted from the investment dollars in the hands of this group through the use of money and credit from the federal government and from the Teamsters Union pension fund.

They manage to make money from different sources work together with the smooth precision of a well-adjusted motor. This is possible, perhaps, because they have the best advice. Another fact that contributes to the success of the Desert Inn group in local finance in Las Vegas is that by now they are local people. The passage of more than a decade has given them status as pioneers on the Strip. There is no apparent indication that the Desert Inn has any concealed ownership that continually syphons off winnings, moving them elsewhere for use in business enterprises of some other kind. This problem interferes with the operation of some of the other places. A run of hard luck sometimes leaves other places with scarcely enough capital to meet the minimum needs of the operation. But gambling tables being the great income producers that they are, these places usually manage to climb back within a few days after the outside ownership has raided the cash drawer. They seldom go broke, although one that did was the Moulin Rouge, a place that was designed and planned to attract the Negro gambling crowd. No one throws Negroes out of the places on the Strip, but they are made to feel unwelcome. It was thought that the Moulin Rouge, built on a back street that parallels the highway on which the big places stand, would meet a need and in the process make a lot of money. But it went bankrupt.

The Desert Inn group never made such mistakes as this. All of its business investments in Las Vegas have turned out to be productive, and it has put together an extensive list of them. The most fascinating thing about this great list of projects is the financing. They get money everywhere, mix it up with a pinch or two of their own assets, and then gather up the profits. The various sources of the money range from the government's housing mortgage guarantee funds, the government's water pollution control programs, to investments made by such persons as Roy M. Cohn, the New York lawyer, and huge loans from the teamsters' pension fund.

One of the first big nongambling investments that the Desert Inn crowd made in Las Vegas was — of all things — a hospital. This Sunrise Hospital is one of the two modern hospitals that serve Las Vegas. The other is the Clark County Hospital. This deal has grown into an investment complex that includes big housing tracts, golf courses, and apartments. More construction is planned.

Corporation records at Carson City show that the Desert Inn crowd's hospital venture started its corporate life on August 12, 1957, as Paradise Hospital, Inc. This company was incorporated with capital stock authorized at $150,000 represented in 1500 shares with par value of $100 each. The corporation papers were signed by Mervyn Adelson, Irwin Molasky and David Zenoff. All three have come up in the world since that day; Lawyer

Zenoff who drew the papers is a district judge and very important man in Las Vegas; Adelson and Molasky have climbed into the ranks of great wealth in Las Vegas, and they live and play with the Desert Inn crowd. For example, they and their wives were so "in" that for the Halloween party at the Desert Inn Country Club in 1963 they had their pictures made with the Allard Roens. The three couples attended in baseball uniforms and wearing clown makeup. The picture was printed as part of the club's promotion.

On September 3, 1959, Adelson and Molasky recorded a deed of sale in the Clark County Courthouse in Las Vegas. It transferred a chunk of desert southwest of the city limits to A & M Enterprises, for a "valuable consideration." There were no federal tax stamps on the document, and this probably means that really no consideration in money changed hands. Perhaps, what happened was this: Adelson and Molasky, who had founded the hospital corporation, had the site picked out and bought in their own names. When they managed to interest Moe Dalitz, they brought him and his crew into the deal, and as a part of this, they agreed to shift ownership of the desert tract to A & M. The tract is surrounded by acres of undeveloped desert land that shows no sign of man's touch.

That same day in September 1959, papers recording the loan of $1,000,000 from the Central States, Southeast and Southwest Conference of Teamsters Pension Fund were filed in the courthouse. They showed that the Sunrise Hospital was to be built with money from the Teamsters, and they also were the first public disclosure that the Desert Inn crowd had a way to get into the Teamsters' millions to help finance their various deals. (We shall explore all the Teamsters' pension fund loans in Nevada in a later chapter.)

The hospital was not built without incident. There was a scandal stirred up by the Las Vegas *Sun*, the militant newspaper operated by Hank Greenspun, who has said he gave up his interest in the Desert Inn rather than be associated with the crew that Wilbur Clark brought in to finish building his dream. A columnist in the *Sun* charged that construction costs had been cut by violating fire safety codes. A considerable storm was kicked up by these and other charges, and in the end the Sunrise Hospital began a damage action against the Las Vegas *Sun* and Greenspun and the columnist. None of the individuals who owned the hospital was named as plaintiff, perhaps on the theory that they could in this way escape the scathing and blistering results of an examination of their pasts, one of the usual deterrents to persons contemplating libel action. The suit was never pushed, although it is still on file. Greenspun has a thick stack of evidence to introduce in substantiation of his charges that various construction shortcuts were taken. He also asserted that the Desert Inn gamblers were able to override the objections of a building inspector.

For their side of this, the Desert Inn group is able to cite the fact that while Greenspun's newspaper was denouncing the hospital as a firetrap, a relative of the publisher was a patient in it. In their logic, this means that the hospital was not so bad as Greenspun's paper said.

But even though these tempests have stilled, the action at the time was of deep concern to the group that owned the hospital. They hired Whitaker and Baxter, a high powered public relations organization in San Francisco, to come to Las Vegas and create the public image a hospital should have. The hospital is highly regarded in Las Vegas, and makes money.

Of course it makes money! That's why Dalitz and company built it. To make money. The Sisters of Charity can run hospitals for the warm feeling that comes to them as they help others; Moe Dalitz runs his to make money and — astoundingly — he is sensitive about it. When we talked in the Desert Inn one autumn day, Dalitz became wary as the questions turned to his investments in collaboration with Molasky and Adelson. I turned toward an area of public interest, which I hoped would give him a feeling of responsibility to answer, and asked if he had used any Hill-Burton Act public funds (federal grants for hospital construction) in building Sunrise Hospital.

"No, we couldn't get those because we're a profit-making hospital," he said.

When I showed surprise that it was a profit-making hospital, he bristled and demanded that I print the list of all the profit-making hospitals in the country. Certainly, there is nothing reprehensible about building a hospital to operate at a profit; the surprising thing is that Dalitz would be touchy as a sore-tailed bear to questions about it.

Other state records showed the extent to which the hospital owners intended to make money, and the various devices they intended to set up to control and spread the profits. There was a Sunrise Hospital Pharmacy, Inc., to gather in the profits from the sale of drugs and other medical needs. There was a Sunrise Hospital Clinical Laboratory, Inc., which would rake in the money from medical tests. The Sunrise Hospital X-Ray Lab, Inc., would have the radiological field to itself. Each one of these was incorporated in September 1958 and each had the same directors, Mervyn Adelson, his father, Nathan Adelson, Irving Molasky, M. B. Dalitz and Eli Boyer.

This proliferation of corporations to handle the medical needs of patients in the Sunrise Hospital was typical of the sort of business arrangements the gamblers make. No device for increasing the take is overlooked. They continually twist and turn and reshape their enterprises in order to get the absolute maximum dollar return out of them.

For example, all of these peripheral corporations disappeared on June 27, 1963, when they were merged with Sunrise Hospital, Inc., and only the hospital corporation survived. Their existence was somehow unprofitable, and so they were put out of business without another thought. The directors of Sunrise Hospital, Inc., after the merger were the Adelsons, Molasky, Dalitz, Boyer, Allard Roen and Dr. Leonard Sloan, a Los Angeles physician associated with the Desert Inn group in the hospital project.

When Dalitz answered a few questions about the Sunrise Hospital construction, he said that the Teamster loan had required "my right arm clear up to the shoulder" as security. He indicated that each of the persons involved in the borrowing had to sign promises to repay the entire loan, should payments be defaulted. Those payments, incidentally, were for $8333.34 a month.

In all these papers filed about Sunrise Hospital, one most interesting fact does not appear. This fact: the hospital is owned and leased by A & M Enterprises, a partnership. That a partnership could borrow that money from the pension fund is strange; but stranger still, the partnership includes a new name — Samuel S. Garfield. Never before, in any of the documents where the Desert Inn's properties are listed, nor on any of the applications, nor on any licenses — in short, nowhere except on the A & M Enterprises partnership papers are Moe Dalitz and Sam Garfield's names found together. This would except the school records in Detroit where they both attended Bishop School as classmates.

Even this is not available in any official source that I could find. I came across the startling juxtaposition of names in a photostatic copy of an accountant's report on "A & M Enterprises, a partnership" while in Las Vegas. The man who gave me the report asked that he not be identified. It was made by Zeman, Tuller, Boyer & Goldberg, Certified Public Accountants, with offices in Los Angeles and Las Vegas. The third named partner is Eli Boyer, the Desert Inn's bookkeeper, a fact noted in the accompanying letter with the audit where it is said that "Eli Boyer, a partner in the undersigned firm of Certified Public Accountants, owns a 3.52 percent interest in A & M Enterprises."

No public explanation has been made of how Boyer came to be a partner. Once Roy M. Cohn, the New York and Washington lawyer who bought Lionel Trains Corporation, was a partner in Sunrise Hospital. No full disclosure of his interest has ever been made, but it has been said that he invested $76,000 in the partnership. When he made this investment and when he liquidated it are not clear. But he was out of it by the time the Desert Inn crowd fell into the well behind Guterma in 1961. Cohn's investment in the hospital came some time after he had left the staff of the Senate Permanent Subcommittee on Investigations, where his boss had been Senator Joseph R. McCarthy. Presumably, his funds were the result of the law practice that he opened in New York on his return to private life from government service. Cohn made money from his practice as soon as he opened the office. Perhaps Boyer took over Cohn's holdings in the partnership; perhaps the accountant was a partner from the start.

At any rate, his accounting firm's report on A & M as of December 31, 1962, showed an investment value of $1,183,033.75 for the hospital building, and land cost of $46,685.83. Hospital equipment had cost new $161,726.88. Advertising signs were up, and new construction in progress (including, strangely, a service station) ran the total fixed assets value to $1,012,875.66. It was the partnership, the audit showed, that held the stock of the peripheral corporations that did business in the hospital — the pharmacy, X-ray laboratory, and clinical laboratory corporations — until these disappeared in the merger.

Another sheet of the audit gave a breakdown on partnership holdings, earnings during the year, withdrawal of funds by the several partners, and standing of partnership accounts at the end of the year. Nathan and Mervyn Adelson together owned 26.37 percent. They had taken out $86,294.27 during the year, and had a red ink balance which meant they owed the partnership $17,-955.13. Molasky — with the same percentage holding — also drew heavily, and his balance of $1,274.37 was barely in the black. All the others had healthy balances. Dr. Leonard Sloan, with 10.94 percent of the partnership, had a balance of $25,420.62 while Moe Dalitz's 16.40 percent interest had a balance of $36,-607.69. Allard Roen and Sam Garfield together owned 16.40 percent and their balance was $38,107.69. Boyer, the accountant, with only 3.52 percent interest, had a balance of $8,179.21. Each of the partners had drawn down heavily that year, for each had a balance below what he had on December 31, 1961, while the partnership had enjoyed a gross income of $353,921.83 that year. The rental income, charged to Sunrise Hospital, was $180,000 which indicates a rental charged by the partnership of $15,000 a month. This gave them a gross monthly return of $6,667 after meeting the mortgage payments.

Many hospitals actually run at a loss.

In addition to the rental income, the partnership in 1962 sold land worth $170,814.95, the audit shows. To whom and what land are questions unanswered in the financial statement prepared by the Boyer firm. There was "other income" of $3,106.88, also undescribed.

Total expenses charged against this were $88,287.76, leaving a net income before depreciation of $265,643.07. After Boyer's accountants had applied what they called the "accelerated method" to depreciation schedules, assigning $102,873.04 to depreciation, the net income was listed as $162,761.03.

The last line of the audit provides what is the probable explanation for the creation of the partnership.

"No provision has been made for federal taxes on income, such taxes being the individual liabilities of the partners."

If the property were owned by the Hospital corporation, they would have been paying at least 52 percent of their net profits to the federal government prior to paying anything to themselves. That would have been about $85,000. But there is more. The hospital corporation charges off the $180,000 a year rental paid to them as a business cost, and to the extent of the depreciation which they can claim this money is sheltered from personal income taxes. So they are able to extract a maximum amount of cash from the operation with a minimum tax liability.

As this necessarily sketchy analysis makes plain, the hospital business in Las Vegas is pretty solid, if you watch the tax angles and play things just right. But for people like Moe Dalitz and Sam Garfield, the Sunrise Hospital is much more than just a moneymaking machine — even though they could never have too many of those. The hospital provides a new status for them in Las Vegas. It enables Dalitz to step up another rung on the ladder of social acceptability.

While the Sunrise Hospital construction has been of great value to Las Vegas and to the men who put it together, these men have been unwilling to rest on their laurels. They have gone forward to other and more grandiose fields, and in each of these there is a glimmer of the shrewd, sharp, penetrating intellect that powered the Cleveland bootlegging coups of the prohibition era and has directed the overall strategy of the Desert Inn group for many years past.

First, consider what has happened with them outside the hospital deal. They established a company called Paradise Homes, Inc. It must hurt each year to see the tax bite that the federal treasury takes out of the corporation's earnings, and to compare this with the painless existence of the partnership that saves so much taxes out of the income of Sunrise Hospital. However, the alternatives of being jointly and individually responsible for legal claims — as partners are — that might grow out of a housing development company are too fearsome to risk. So they created Paradise Homes as a corporation to protect themselves, although they must have done it reluctantly.

The stockholders in Paradise Homes have never been identified publicly, nor even semi-publicly as in the copy of the audit that was given to me as a means of identifying the partners in A & M Enterprises. Irwin Molasky told me in an interview in his office that the stockholders were about the same, and questioning brought out that Dalitz and Roen are in Paradise Homes, while Boyer and Garfield are not.

This was doubly interesting, because while Boyer is not a stockholder in the construction company, he is the company's financial adviser. Molasky said he was unable to discuss the Paradise Homes financing, that Boyer worked out these problems, and Molasky just did not have the answers to my questions.

Examination of records in Washington, D.C., produced some of the answers. Paradise Homes has been the beneficiary of millions of dollars worth of government-guaranteed credit. The first big deal that this group had with the Federal Housing Administration came in 1962 when the gamblers' development company took over an apartment project that had withered and died, even though the F.H.A. was ready to lend millions on it. The place had been started, and the supporting cash to supplement the federal loan could not be raised, so Adelson and Molasky took it over. The apartment house had been called Desert Gardens. They changed the name to Desert Palms. The original mortgage for which the F.H.A. stood ready to make a guarantee was $2,912,000. When Adelson and Molasky moved in, they managed to get the loan guarantee obligation limit raised to $3,000,000. They persuaded the government loan officers to accept inclusion of the wall-to-wall carpet in the construction costs.

This apartment project was finished and today stands right at the edge of the Strip, where the dealers and their families can rent and where Dalitz and his associates can get back some of the money that escapes their slot machines and gambling tables.

But Desert Palms was just a warm-up for one of the most involved and clever meshing of interests and melting together of money from various sources that ever was pulled off in a housing deal in Las Vegas.

Paradise Palms is the name of this great triumph.

Paradise Palms is a very large housing development constructed in the desert near the Sunrise Hospital and a mile or so from the Strip. There are 42 basic designs in the development's homes, all of them repeated again and again. Prices start at $22,900 and run on up to above $42,500. The last the F.H.A. records in Washington showed, 492 of those homes had been sold, and about two hundred of them had federal commitments for mortgage insurance. This would be a credit source of perhaps as much as $5,000,000. It might be even more. Once a housing development gets approval for F.H.A. loans, other lending agencies with other kinds of mortgage packages tend to move into the field. Of course, they would probably stay out if the F.H.A. guarantees were withheld for some reason.

These are nice homes, when allowance has been made for the fact that they are being built in the desert, with no intention of making them stand up to climatic conditions such as those on the eastern seaboard; they are aimed at the sales market that exists in Las Vegas. Roofs tend toward flat, air conditioners are a major item, large glass area is open to the desert scenery, and heating is by electricity. The $22,900 model has these things, according to a brochure: vinyl plastic floor covering in the entry hall, family room and kitchen; wall-to-wall carpeting, aluminum sliding glass doors, indirect lighting, fireplace (wood-burning is specified), all-electric kitchen with built-in oven, range, garbage disposer, electric can opener; three bedrooms, each slightly larger than ten by ten feet; a living-dining area; a family room off the kitchen; two baths, a carport. The $42,500 model features similar gimmicks, except that they are bigger and better and more glossy.

The marketing of these houses was big league, no mistake about it. A whole street of homes was built and furnished, complete even down to the play area with swings and sand piles. It was on a cul-de-sac that ran near the main road leading into the project, and a lot was left vacant right at the road. That lot was used to hold a sales office, which had all the trappings . . . lights . . . signs . . . flags whipping in the wind. Those who came into the sales office were led through and out onto the quiet and lovely street, where models of the various houses stood ready and furnished for examination. The houses were sold almost as soon as they were finished, although the project was scattered over a barren desert tract and some of it looked pretty raw. One explanation of the rapid sales history rests in the availability of Stardust Golf Club. The implications of that availability and the reasons for it will be explained.

The sales pitch on the front of the brochure advertising the development listed these things: FHA-VA and new, low-cost conventional loan terms; Stardust Championship Golf Course; Stardust Golf Club; Paradise Palms Private Park — Tennis, Volleyball and Shuffleboard Courts; Supervised Children's Playground; Little League Baseball Diamond; Barbecue and Picnic Facilities; School Bus Service; Close to Shopping Centers, Churches, Sunrise Hospital and College.

Now to the Stardust Golf Course, a deal that fits into the housing development with all the cunning and charm of a fine Chinese puzzle.

This is a relatively new, eighteen-hole course obviously patterned on the Desert Inn course. This one, too, has building lots set aside along the fairways and along the edge of the course for expensive homes, just as at the Desert Inn. These golf course lots began at $10,000 in price. All of this part of the development was built with a loan of $1,200,000 from the Teamsters pension fund. There was no need to get the union members' money into the action on the housing development, for as soon as the houses were up they would be sold and the less money borrowed, the more there would be available for the division of the spoils among the development's backers.

But to finance building a golf course with their own money — that was something else again. It wouldn't be paid out for a long time, and the gamblers would be violating their guiding principles if they put their own money in it. So they went to the Teamsters and came back with their golf bags full of pension funds. It was on March 6, 1961, that this deal began building up, according to records in the Clark County Courthouse. Paradise Vista Corporation recorded a deed of sale to Star Investment Company for "valuable consideration" and since there were no revenue stamps on the deed, this might have been entirely in love and affection. The officers of Star Investment were M. B. Dalitz, Mervyn Adelson, Irwin Molasky, Allard Roen and Bernard Rothkopf. Rothkopf is a new name in these pages. He is a nephew of Lou Rothkopf, who was one of the Dalitz buddies in the Cleveland days. Bernie Rothkopf is an executive at the Desert Inn casino. The reason for his inclusion in the Star Investment Company is that he owns 2 percent of Karat, Inc., which operates the casino at the Stardust, and the golf club is to be of great importance to the Stardust and its casino.

The mortgage documents made it apparent that this land was to be the site of a golf course. What did these men need with another golf course? They had one at the Desert Inn, a beauty.

They needed it for two reasons, both of them excellent, both of them fraught with opportunity to make more money. First, they could toss in the rights to use the golf course and clubhouse with lots in the Paradise Palms subdivision. This was one of the great allures in the subdivision properties. There are thousands of night workers in the Las Vegas gambling casinos. They love to get up in midmorning, saunter over to the clubhouse to visit with their friends, and then play a round of golf. The conviviality fulfills a need for companionship, for there is no one more lonely than the dealer in a gambling house, the target of all the players who want to beat him. That visit to the golf club in the morning also makes these small-time gamblers feel like the big-time operators, too, for Wilbur Clark and Moe Dalitz do the same thing at the Desert Inn Country Club.

Thus, one can realize readily, the lure of the golf course privileges was a great sales inducement for Paradise Palms, the subdivision.

However, there was another purpose to be served, and this one was perhaps more important in the minds of the gamblers who got the pension fund money to build the course. They were thinking about the Stardust, that monster of a hotel-casino that they were running. It had no golf course. This created a problem, for more and more of the competitors were getting golf courses. So the thing to do was to get one, and they started out to do just that. One can sense Moe Dalitz pushing this. He owned 22 percent of Karat, Inc., as well as the 13 percent of the Desert Inn that he had held for years and years. Dalitz would never forget — no matter what the others might let slip from their minds — that it was the gambling tables that had made them all wealthy. To Dalitz, these side deals with houses and hospitals and the like would be challenging and invigorating and the money would be wonderful — but nothing would replace the casino.

The Stardust Hotel has 1300 rooms in it, making it by far the largest among the Las Vegas places. This space to store the customers may in part account for the great winnings that the casino reports. It has swimming pools — two, as we shall see — and even a convention hall next door for small groups, and the nudes in the "Lido de Paris" show, and everything else including acres of parking space. But it had no golf course.

The thing to do was get one, someone must have reasoned, before it's too late, before the decline sets in and we have to spend great gobs of money to turn it around. So they got one from the Teamsters' pension fund. It serves two purposes — the guests at the Stardust can use it, and the people who bought houses in the Paradise Palms subdivision also can use it. Who knows? Maybe the clubhouse will even make some money.

In the front of a beautifully produced brochure put out by the Stardust, an aerial photograph makes it plain that the place is really the combination of two places — the old Stardust, which has been a money-maker almost from the beginning, and the former Royal Nevada, one of the few Strip places ever to go broke. The former casino and showrooms and restaurant of the Royal Nevada have been turned into a convention center, called the Stardust Auditorium, for the use of groups wanting to meet in easy reach of the gambling tables. This provides an added lure for the Stardust, and also serves the purpose of keeping an aggressive and competing management out of the old Royal Nevada property. The Stardust then books guests into the line of rooms behind the Auditorium and also uses the palm-lined swimming pool there. The Stardust, meantime, continues to fill up its lines of motel-like buildings which feed guests into the casino, dining rooms, and past the slot machines.

The gambler who envisioned this place — the original Stardust — was Tony Cornero, the same who ran the gambling boats at sea off the California shore in the 1930's. His true name, incidentally, was Antonio Cornero Stralla. After a career that included cab driving, bootlegging, hijacking, rum-running, and finally gambling boat operation, he came to Las Vegas when gambling was legalized. He even died hunched over a craps table. Cornero visualized the Stardust — although his first name for it was the "Starlight"; after many incredible adventures with the underworld and with the Securities and Exchange Commission, he built the place . . . almost. He died of a heart attack at the Desert Inn before he got it completed. Cornero had collected about

$6,000,000 to build the place, had it only 70 percent completed, and owed contractors and suppliers about $4,000,000. It would take another $3,000,000 to finish it, and Cornero was dead.

It was at this point that John (Jake the Barber) Factor came on the scene with the money to finish the Stardust. He took over in 1958 and signed a lease with United Hotels Corporation to run the Stardust. This was the same United Hotels that then owned the Desert Inn. When the Desert Inn crowd replaced United Hotels with United Resort Hotels in 1959, that company became the operator of the Stardust's facilities. Later we shall see how it sold the Desert Inn properties in a leaseback arrangement that permitted such great tax savings. So for all practical purposes, the Desert Inn crowd controls the Stardust hotel, as well as the Stardust casino, and operates it as a satellite to the Desert Inn.

But there have been continual undercurrents of talk that the control by the Desert Inn interests merely covers a control of the Stardust by notorious underworld figures. Those reports about hidden interests continually crop up in many of the Las Vegas casinos, and frequently are accompanied by some semblance of evidence. Proving them is another thing. Even when they are well demonstrated, as we shall see in another chapter, they frequently result in court decisions that do little more than slap the wrists of the men whose names are on the license.

Odds and ends of information crop up through the years that show some strange interests on the part of persons who could never get a license to run a gambling place in Nevada. An incident that produced such information occurred the night Frank Costello, the infamous underworld leader, escaped with minor wounds after an attempt was made in New York to assassinate him. The police found a scrap of paper in his pocket with some indications that it was a listing of the business summary of a casino as of April 27, 1957, and that the gross winning was $651,-284.

After extensive searching, authorities showed that this was exactly the winnings of the Tropicana Hotel in Las Vegas for the first 24 days that it was open. The writing on the note was identified as that of an employe of the Tropicana who formerly had worked in Louisiana gambling joints that were controlled by the Costello organization. Such discoveries are interesting, cause trouble, arouse suspicions, but until the recent years of strengthening control of gambling by the state of Nevada, these discoveries never meant anything.

The Desert Inn group's deal with the Stardust Golf Course and the Stardust Country Club turned out so well that as this is written, the organization has moved on into an even more lucrative proposition where they have persuaded the Clark County Board of Commissioners to finance a golf course for them, a golf course that will help sell a new housing development.

This is the Winterwood, Inc., project.

Rumors of this one were floating around in Las Vegas in the summer of 1963. Opposition began to grow. But at its last meeting of the year, the Board of Commissioners voted to go ahead with it. There were indications that agreement had been reached privately before that meeting even started. The deal appears to be unusually lucrative to the group from the gambling casino, and not very good for the county. Under its provisions, the gamblers and their associates will build a golf course and playground to cost no more than $950,000 on about 151 acres of property that is a part of their planned development at the former Winterwood Ranch on the outskirts of Las Vegas. The county commissioners then will enter into a lease initially for three years with options to extend up to 20 years, at which time the county would own the golf course and playgrounds. To give an idea of how it will work out, during the first three years the county will pay $244,800 in lease payments. During the term of the years that the county will be leasing the golf course, it will be making payments at a rate that will liquidate the costs of the golf course construction. Since the gamblers will have paid 6 percent interest on the money they borrowed, and since the county rental-lease payments must cover this cost, the taxpayers will be paying interest at a rate about twice that which Clark County has had to pay on its bonds in the last few years. It has been estimated in Las Vegas that this alone will cost the taxpayers $400,000 more than they need to pay.

Meantime, the gamblers will be building hundreds of houses on the desert land surrounding the course and playground. There will be 170 "golf course lots" alone, and while no price has been publicized for these, remember that the ones on the Stardust course started at $10,000 each. This would mean a minimum for these lots alone of $1,700,000 — all for the Desert Inn group, which retains ownership of the building lots, not for the county which ultimately pays for the golf course. The county already owned 160 acres elsewhere to develop for a new golf course. But this wouldn't have made any money for the Desert Inn.

Initial stories indicated that the Winterwood development would be worth more than $20,000,000 in housing. This time the developers will still have the inducement of a nearby golf course to use in their sales promotion; but they will have avoided the problems of operating the course and of worrying about getting water for it. A golf course takes up to 1,250,000 gallons of water a day. And the water table is falling beneath Las Vegas.

Presumably the Federal Housing Administration has again given its approval to the Desert Inn's promotion activities and plans for construction. Undoubtedly, once again the federal government will be allowed to pay a part of the costs of the sewer construction. Soon, as with the Paradise development, the houses will be sold and someone else will have the problem of collecting mortgage payments on them if some catastrophe befalls Nevada gambling, or Las Vegas should suddenly go out of fashion.

The golf course will be sold — and the Clark County taxpayers will be liable for the payments on it. The Desert Inn group will have its money, much increased by this maneuver, and will be liquid and easily packed again to move on if necessary.

One must admire the sagacity of the gamblers' real estate development operation.

This business is directed from a small, crowded building at 3335 Cinder Lane, Las Vegas. This building is about as far from the Strip and from the beauties of Las Vegas as one can get. It stands at the edge of the desert, across the railroad tracks, and has small industrial plants and a meat-packing house for neighbors. Why on earth out here? No visible explanation appears at the scene. But a look at a map of Las Vegas shows that a super highway is planned that will bypass the city and run near the block of property on which is located the Paradise Homes headquarters. A cloverleaf for entrance and exit to the freeway will be nearby. Someday, the Paradise Homes stockholders will either build a great business property on the site of their present modest headquarters building, or they will unload it for a staggering sum to some other developer. Observers will talk about blind luck and bemoan that the rich get richer; but the truth is that the smart get richer — the careful planners make the big money.

Inside that small office building, the space was crammed with busy people and the bustle of a big business operation. Pictures of Paradise Homes projects lined the waiting room walls, while secretaries moved briskly past and engineers carrying blueprints hurried in and out the door. Mervyn Adelson was away, but Irwin Molasky was in, a short, balding man in his late forties. His actions and attitudes indicated a high level of competence, but none of the flashing sparks that would indicate authorship of some of the inspired maneuvers made by the Paradise Homes management.

He said that he and Adelson moved to Las Vegas from Los

Angeles in 1952. They went into business together in Las Vegas, and soon became acquainted with the Desert Inn group.

"We were socially connected," he said with a quiet pride. In everything Molasky said there was the implication that his fortunes were tied tightly to the moves planned and executed by the Desert Inn organization. Nor did he seem to want it any other way.

This brings us to some observations that need to be made about the boss gamblers who have built the Strip at Las Vegas. Many who have succeeded over the years are men apart from the common run. They have great capabilities, great resources of intelligence and foresight and courage. No one who has studied their lives can help but wonder at the chance that took them out of the slums and turned them into millionaires as gamblers, for most of them came from humble homes in the big cities. They started life with not very much. As Moe Dalitz said to Estes Kefauver: "Well, I didn't inherit any money, Senator." Thus it was with most of them.

This passage expresses no hero worship of these men. But it strives to present them as what they are — talented, capable, their skills sharpened by the abrasive lives they have led.

As young men these gamblers had training in running the illegal gambling places in the alleys of the big cities. They learned things there that no one teaches at Harvard Business School. For example: one has no contract with the district police captain whereby one is obligated to pay him $500 a month and he is obligated to violate his oath to the end that the gambling house gets protection from raids. No legal agreement could produce a situation in which the police in uniform would come to eject a troublemaker, but at the same time would be blind to the crap tables. So the young gamblers' business training included courses in how to conduct business without the benefit of legally binding contracts.

Also, they lived and grew up and learned their trades in a

world where a man's promises might or might not be kept. If the police captain required his $500 on the first of the month for which he was to provide protection and on the second day of that month led a raid on the place in the alley, would he return the payment? Would he pro rata calculate the fee for one day's protection, and give back the rest? Of course not. No one expected that he would. He was a thief, in the minds and language of the men who paid him to be dishonest, and to trust him would have been ridiculous in their view. These gamblers would deal with him, feed his appetites for money and women and liquor; they would build up his ego and his bank account. But they would not trust him or expect him to perform other than in a dishonorable way. This attitude saved them from disappointment; it also saved them from overextending their operations beyond the point where they could pull back in time of betrayal with organization and bankroll still intact. Their experiences taught them also to build reputations for reliability among their own kind. If the pledged word is the only guarantee of performance, then a reputation for honoring the pledged word is valuable beyond diamonds and a reputation for double-dealing is ruinous.

If the gambler had an arrangement that gave him control of some particular operation in some part of the city, or county, or nation, he had it only so long as he could hold it. If another operator came in and by force or by maneuver shoved him out, the prize fell to the new man. There was no contract. How could one go to court to enforce an agreement arrived at in a conspiracy to commit illegal acts? Those were hard lessons learned in the bootlegging and gambling rackets. They were learned well, and when the time came for the gamblers and bootleggers to come in from the outer darkness and assume a place in the legality of the neon-lighted gambling joints in the Las Vegas, they were well prepared. They knew all the tricks that the underworld had invented to protect its investments in the illegal places; they could soon learn the tricks the legitimate world had devised to protect its investments through courts, contracts, and franchises.

This made the gamblers formidable competitors, and this as much as anything else explains why no "square Johns," as they call the people from outside the underworld, have ever been able to take over the big gambling places. Jack Donnelley, the absolutely honorable and reputable attorney who now runs the Desert Inn, would be run out of Las Vegas in a year or so by the competition if it were not for the worldly wise and bitterly experienced Moe Dalitz and the others who came up to the Desert Inn from the other side of the tracks.

The biggest problem for society controlling the gambling wealth derives from exactly these circumstances, and while we will examine that problem at greater length in a subsequent chapter, at this point we should explain why it is that the background of the gamblers produces men of such great attainments once they turn from the racket to the legitimate side of business. The processes of selection were much more violent and compelling in their background. Brains and courage and patience and ability to foresee the course of events were the premium qualities demanded by that society. If there had been some need to be unusually tall to run an illegal gambling place, the managers of the Las Vegas casinos today all would be nine feet tall. The process of selection that produced them was as ruthless as anything known in the jungles. Also, it was unfailing in producing certain characteristics. The problem for Nevada today is that this process of selection paid no attention to those other qualities on which the rest of society is founded. The gamblers produced in the alleys were good gamblers; but they did not always make good citizens.

When they came to Las Vegas, they came in a rush. The Flamingo was the first big hotel casino on the Strip, and after

Gus Greenbaum got it going successfully, the organizations in the various cities of the East began to move their money out to the desert to open more places. The Last Frontier became the New Frontier. (This was in the years when John F. Kennedy was a freshman congressman from that string of towns along the banks of the Charles River, and the name referred to the frontier of settlement, not the J.F.K. rallying cry.) Then the Thunderbird Hotel opened in 1948, with financing that got everybody in trouble and provided a part of one of our next chapters. Wilbur Clark's Desert Inn opened in 1950 while the Sands and the Sahara opened in 1952. The Riviera, the Dunes and the Ill-fated Royal Nevada opened in 1955. The Riviera alone was reported to have cost more than $10,000,000. The Tropicana was opened in 1957 at a cost that no one really can establish. Cost accounting seldom arrives at one of the Las Vegas places until well after it has opened. In the building days, the money comes from wherever it can be had and it may or may not be entered in the books.

After the gamblers arrive, after they have opened a real, legal, wide-open place on the Strip, then they go through a further process akin to those accounted for in evolution by the Darwinian theory of natural selection. The place on the alley demanded and got certain characteristics in the top management. These did not include formal education, or training in the law or business.

This would seem no handicap. The money generated at the gambling tables would pay for the best talent in any field where advice was needed. This answer, however, overlooks the real problem. Who is the best in the field? How does one pick him? These great sums of money also attracted some of the slickest confidence men of the age, and how can the gambler detect him, weed him out, in trying to pick out the most capable lawyer or business adviser? It may sound ridiculous to shed a tear for the poor hoodlum who brought his million dollars to Las Vegas only to be plucked by the operators of a game that was too fast for him. However, these things did happen. Those who could adapt to the new environment survived and thrived and grew. Those who could not disappeared. Recall Bugsy Siegel. In a sense he was the Christopher Columbus for the Mob; he went exploring and found the New World in the desert. But Siegel failed to adapt. It is possible that he became confused between the two ways of doing business and thought that because his name was on so many pieces of paper he really owned the Flamingo Hotel. He was wrong.

The gamblers who came to Las Vegas to run the big casinos and build the hotels must have been confused by the differing advice that came to them from all quarters. Those who could pick out the true prophets had an indispensable skill. But even then they made mistakes. The best of them, Moe Dalitz, allowed Alexander Guterma to walk into his paradise and lead away a trusted old friend (Sam Garfield) and a young man on whom Dalitz had come to rely to provide continuity in the management of the Desert Inn (Allard Roen). True, Dalitz himself was never sucked into Guterma's game — he says — but it would have hurt him less, perhaps, to have been dragged in himself than to see his friends get hurt. In a complicated bit of reasoning that somewhere fell off the track, Dalitz once told me that he blamed himself for Roen's troubles. He said he had introduced Roen to Garfield many years before, and that Garfield then led Roen into the Guterma catastrophe.

"If I never have Sam get him that job in the oil fields so he can go to college, he never would of got mixed up with Guterma and wouldn't be in this trouble now," said Dalitz.

This is foolishness, of course, and Dalitz would recognize it as that if someone tried to tell him such a story to explain a friendship. But it illustrates another side to these men. They can be mawkishly sentimental when they feel like it. Frequently, they use this sentimentality as a gloss to cover things that they do for other reasons. For example, there are two versions of why Garfield and Dalitz are so protective of Roen. Dalitz says that he came to know "the Kid" through association with Roen's father, Frank Rosen, a bookmaker in the Dalitz entourage in Cleveland. He wanted to help young Allard go to Duke University, so he got him a job with Sam Garfield in the oil fields. However, Garfield remembers that he had made a deathbed promise to his old friend, Frank Rosen, that he would look out always for Rosen's son, Allard Roen. Both of these may be true, or neither of them. The significant thing is that both men feel a need to claim a sentimental obligation of friendship to look out for a young man who was extremely valuable to them, and whose interests are entwined with theirs.

There are many different sides to the gamblers' character. This somewhat curious sentimentality is one peculiarity. However, those who have succeeded in Las Vegas are sharp and wise beyond anything that might be expected by someone who had studied them casually. They have learned the lessons of the illegal gambling operations, and learned them well; then they have piled on the lessons of doing business among their bitter competitors on the Strip; beyond that, they have learned to deal with the high-priced entertainers that they must pay fabulous sums to work in their showrooms; and they must master all the intricacies of running an open and legal business.

When they have done all these things, then they can begin to think about moving out into the other business activities of the world, away from the gambling and its related rackets and vices. When they make this move, they tend to carry with them the ways of the gang and the racket — which is what our story is all about.

The outstanding example of this move out into other business activities comes from the story of the Desert Inn crowd, the group of bootleggers and gamblers and their associates who once

ruled Cleveland and Newport, Kentucky. There is a sound reason for this. Dalitz and Kleinman and the rest have managed to
hang on for a terribly long time as the top dogs of the Desert Inn.
This has given them time to make all the adjustments that are
required of a gambler before he can move across the line into the
green pastures of legitimate business. They have had time to plan
and to figure the ways to move, and to pick the deals to go into.
They have had time to live down their mistakes, and to insinuate
themselves into the life of Las Vegas, the home base. They have
had opportunity to live down the reputation built before they
came to Las Vegas, and to forget some of the bad, old times.
Still, however, Dalitz will snap an answer to a question about bootlegging: "If you people wouldn't have drunk it, I wouldn't have
bootlegged it."

Even though his point may be well taken, Dalitz needs to re-
vise this stock answer, for the people he gives it to tend more and
more as the years pass to have been children in the prohibition
years, children who certainly drank none of Dalitz's illegal
hooch.

So these old days grow farther and farther away for Dalitz and
Kleinman and Al Winter of the Sahara and some of the others
who have been around through the big boom on the Strip. Some,
like Winter, go back to where they started and more or less retire.
Others, like Kleinman, go where the weather suits them better
than the desert, and take it easy. Some, like Dalitz, never give up
chasing the dollar. But they now tend to want to get their dollars
in business opportunities away from the gambling joint. They
tend to be formidable business competitors.

5

IF THEY ALL WERE LIKE HARRAH . . .

As THE DECADES have passed, great differences have grown up between gambling on the Las Vegas Strip and gambling in Reno.
Harold's Club, the bustling and noisy, the shirt-sleeved and blue-
jeans-clad place on Virginia Street in Reno, is one type of gambling joint; the Desert Inn, which we have talked about extensively, is another kind. The Harold's Club pattern pushes out a
type of advertising and promotion that attracts the smaller gambler, the visitor with $50 or $100 to spend, or even less. Volume
and more volume is the basis of this sort of gambling operation.
The Desert Inn, the flossy place on the Las Vegas Strip, has floor
shows, a fancy golf course, swimming pools, a hotel, and an atmosphere of opulence designed to attract the high rollers, the
gamblers who are willing to risk losses in a night of $30,000 or
$50,000 or even more. Although some of the places in the Down-
town Casino Center of Las Vegas appear to be weak carbon copies
of the Harold's Club operation, there is nothing like the Desert
Inn in Reno.

It appears from close analysis that the real meeting place of
these two different types of gambling operations is at Lake
Tahoe, high in the Sierra to the west of Carson City. Here is a
casino hotel somewhat similar to the pattern developed on the
Las Vegas Strip, although of course the different climate has required a different sort of physical plant. The man who has

brought about this blending of gambling styles is William Fisk Harrah, who on the record is the most successful gambling operator Nevada has produced. Harrah's style also is widely admired in Nevada for the reason that he has not brought scandal to the gambling business, and because he has supported attempts by the state to control the gamblers.

Harrah was born in South Pasadena, California, September 2, 1911, and grew up in a gambling atmosphere in Venice, a suburb of Los Angeles. His father ran an illegal "circle game," which is a card gambling game somewhat like twenty-one. In those years Venice was a small town where city officials allowed gambling games to operate, but occasionally closed them. Harrah bought out his father, was closed, and decided to go to Reno. He made a few missteps there, but by the beginning of World War II, he was firmly situated, although not the leading figure he is today. His initial entrance into Nevada gambling was as a bingo parlor operator. Without question, he was influenced by the success of the Smith family in Harold's Club, and eventually he established Harrah's Club in downtown Reno on substantially the same pattern. It now rivals the Smith family operation in annual gross winnings. But the Smiths have only Harold's Club while Bill Harrah has moved on.

As this is written, he has gambling operations at Harrah's Tahoe and Harrah's Lake Club on Lake Tahoe; Harrah's Casino Restaurant; Harrah's Bingo and Grand Cafe; and Harrah's Reno, the first place he opened and the one patterned on the Harold's Club operation. Each one of these places is different from the others, but none of them is an entirely new development in Nevada gambling. Harrah's success would seem to come from an ability to pick up an idea from someone else, then shape and improve it through careful management and close attention to business. Many of the gambling operators are nervous neurotics almost totally unable to cope with the details of their businesses.

These men tend to have hired managers who supervise these matters. Harrah is not at all this sort of man. He is cool, quiet, slow in speech and action, cautious, calculating in his business dealings, and for all the world much like the comptroller of a large corporation.

He is the absolute owner of all of his gambling places, and this in itself is a rarity. While Harrah refuses to discuss his earnings, it is possible to estimate that for 1964 they will run upwards of $40,000,000 as a gross winnings figure from his five gambling places. One alone — Harrah's Tahoe — will probably have gross winnings in excess of $20,000,000. Harrah's taxable income will be in the millions, in spite of every maneuver he can execute to keep it down. He does such things as sponsor hydroplane racing on Lake Tahoe, and build up expensive collections of old cars, and invest in expansion of his casino properties. There is indication that Harrah puts his own money back into the gambling operations, a practice not much followed by his colleagues on the Las Vegas Strip, as we shall see in a later chapter.

In his Harrah's Tahoe, he has the only place in northern Nevada that resembles the Las Vegas Strip casino hotels. Harrah puts on expensive shows, has fine food, and plans to build a big hotel fairly soon. I interviewed Harrah in his office on a sunny winter day. His personal press agent, Gene Evans, a former legislator and former Elko, Nevada, newspaperman, took me there. It was Evans who in 1959 helped to write and push through the statute that tightened the state's control of the gamblers. Harrah supported that bill, and this association led to Evans' current employment.

"This is the only gambler that I could work for," Evans told me. "I couldn't work for one of those guys who you have to apologize for all the time. I don't have to apologize for this guy at all."

Harrah is a difficult man to interview. He is quiet and watchful

and slow to answer. He volunteers little. He brightened somewhat in discussion of what he believes to be his most important
business decisions. He thinks that these were to move from bingo
parlor operation into all kinds of gambling, to move into Lake
Tahoe, and to begin to bring people up from San Francisco in
free buses.

Until Harrah bought the Gateway Club in 1955, the places at
the lake had closed at the end of the summer season. By 1957 he
was trying to stay open all winter at Harrah's Tahoe, the reno-
vated and enlarged former Stateline Country Club. The place is
exactly on the state line. A special motel for performers working
in his showroom is across the street in California. It was from
this motel that Frank Sinatra, Jr., was kidnaped in December
1963 and hauled through Nevada and around the mountains to
Los Angeles. Harrah had plans to open a 23-story hotel, at a cost
of $13,000,000. However, the Webb Corporation built before he
could get started and his plans were delayed.

But the atmosphere at a Harrah gambling house will never be
the same as those in Las Vegas. Women deal card games in Harrah's places. There are mirror arrangements in the ceiling that
allow inspectors to watch the casino employees. The Harrah
places are cleaner. Slot machine mechanics, for example, wear
pressed black trousers and white shirts. Waitresses are cleaner.
The bars, the mirrors, the floor, the ashtrays — all are kept clean.
Men are paid to go around with dustrags and clean out the slot
machines, to wipe off the handles, clean out the ashtrays that sit
recessed in each machine, and to gather up debris on the floor.

"We appreciate our customers' business and we want them to
know we do, so we want to treat them the way we would like to
be treated," he said at one point in our talk. "We want the places
to be clean, because that's the way we would like to have places
run if we were the customers."

Harrah has ideas on the customers he wants.

"We want nearly everybody. We don't want the ones who are dirty and noisy."

At another point he said he thought time would bring about the removal of the oldtime hoodlums and racketeers from Nevada gambling, and had this opinion on what should be the state's attitude toward all the gambling operators: "The gambling operator has no rights now to his license and it can be taken away from him anytime he gets out of line. That's the way I think it ought to be. When you start giving them a right to this and that, the end is in sight. You can't control 'em."

Harrah told a story that revealed his short patience with the lack of foresight sometimes shown by Nevadans. He said a group of businessmen had asked him to help get a state law changed so gambling casino stocks could be floated as public issues. He refused, because in his view this would work toward inhibiting the state's control of gambling operators.

"If a gambler had a right, that would be the end of it pretty quick," he said.

Harrah's office in Reno is located in the center of an old warehouse that he has taken over to use as a repair shop and display room for his collection of old cars. The office has no windows and is surrounded by the old cars and mechanics that work on the restoration. There is no commercial angle to the car collection. It must cost Harrah a fortune each year. The cars are not for sale. He does not drive them, except when they are to be shown.

About twenty highly skilled men work in the restoration shops, and the amounts invested in the old cars must be considerable. Harrah had 753 of them on hand the day I visited him, and each of these was completely restored to new condition. Such old cars are judged in competition, the judging being on the basis of restoration to new condition, and on a scale of 100 points. Harrah had a 1928 Pierce-Arrow touring car rated at 100 in such a competition.

One of the restorations, a 1906 Thomas, required 25,000 man hours of labor. This would represent a minimum of $25,000. And Harrah has 753 of these cars! He adds to the number at the rate of about twenty a year. There were 57 Model T Fords, beginning with a 1909 roadster and running through to a 1927 pickup. He also has Franklins and Maxwells, and almost any sort of car ever made in any quantity. His first antique auto was a 1911 model Maxwell, bought in 1948.

There is a little of almost everything in the collection. It abounds in fire engines, and in cars that no one ever heard of except those whose hobby is old cars. Even the names of the body styles ring strangely today — scout, tourists, touring, speedster, phaeton sedan, sunshine saloon, flyer buckboard, cloverleaf roadster. There is a Coey Flyer, a 1907 Compound, a 1912 Corbin, and a 1916 Crane-Simplex built to look like a yacht with a curved line to the sides and a propeller on the rear. Steam cars are represented by the Stanleys, Dobles and Whites. Harrah has thirteen Duesenbergs, and his 1929 dual cowl phaeton must be the most beautiful automobile ever built. Everyone has heard of the Stutz Bearcat, and of course Harrah has those, but who ever knew that Stutz also built fire engines? Harrah has a full line.

He also pours thousands of dollars into hydroplane racing, and his succession of Harrah's Miss Tahoe unlimited hydroplanes have run in the big races for several years. But his conquest here has been unsuccessful. The boats have never been winners.

The people with foresight in Nevada, those who sit and think about the future of the state's gambling business, look on Bill Harrah as a shining example. If more gambling houses were in the hands of men like him, one is told over and over, then the future of Nevada gambling would be completely safe. In short, Bill Harrah is what they wish they had everywhere in Nevada. But he certainly is not what they have, as we have seen, and as yet other cases will illustrate. Harrah's great earnings in the gambling business may have played hell with the price structure in the classic and historic car markets when he shoveled some of his money into his hobby; but even other collectors must approve of him, for they were drawn to the hobby by the same love of perfection that must have been a part of his motivation to enter the field. We do not find Harrah in the stock market, or in great real estate promotions, or borrowing money for questionable purposes from union pension funds, or running with influential political figures who can open doors for him in Washington or New York.

However, Harrah does not run all the gambling places in Nevada. The truth is that no one is ever really certain about who runs a lot of them, for the names on the licenses sometimes are not the names of the men who really control things. The files of the Nevada Supreme Court reveal a shocking story of such a case of concealed ownership, a story that is shocking also because of the eventual result. The gamblers got away with it. The supreme court's decision was written by Justice Charles M. Merrill who later became a member of the federal Ninth Circuit Court of Appeals which sits in San Francisco. Some of his language in the opinion demonstrated a clear grasp of the problems in legalizing gambling. He wrote:

> We note that while gambling, duly licensed, is a lawful enterprise in Nevada, it is unlawful elsewhere in this country; that unlawfully followed elsewhere it tends there to create as well as to attract a criminal element; that it is a pursuit which unlawfully followed is conducive of corruption; that the criminal and corruptive elements engaged in unlawful gambling tend to organize and thus obtain widespread power and control over corruptive criminal enterprises throughout this country; that the existence of organized crime has long been recognized and has become a serious concern of the federal government as well as the governments of the several states.

Throughout this country, then, gambling has necessarily surrounded itself with an aura of crime and corruption. Those in management of this pursuit who have succeeded, have done so not only through a disregard of law, but, in a competitive world, through a superior talent for such disregard and for the corruption of those in public authority.

For gambling to take its place as a lawful enterprise in Nevada it is not enough that this state has named it lawful. We have but offered it the opportunity for lawful existence. The offer is a risky one, not only for the people of this state, but for the entire nation. Organized crime must not be given refuge here through the legitimatizing of one of its principal sources of income. Nevada gambling, if it is to succeed as a lawful enterprise, must be free from the criminal and corruptive taint acquired by gambling beyond our borders. If this is to be accomplished not only must the operation of gambling be carefully controlled, but the character and background of those who would engage in gambling in this state must be carefully scrutinized.

The court's problem was this: in February 1955, the Nevada Tax Commission, which at that time was the state agency that controlled gambling, ordered the suspension of the casino license at the Thunderbird Hotel on the Las Vegas Strip. The gamblers appealed the commission order, and won a temporary injunction that enabled them to continue operation during the appeal.

The tax commission contention was that Marion B. Hicks, who had appeared to be the hotel's promoter, and Clifford A. Jones, the former lieutenant governor, held interests that actually represented other owners. The hidden owners were specifically named as George Sadlo and Jake (or Jack) Lansky, who had operated illegal gambling places together in Florida. The tax commission showed that these interests existed, too.

The Thunderbird Hotel Company was a partnership that ran

the casino in the Thunderbird Hotel, while Bonanza Hotel, Inc., was the corporation that owned the physical facilities of the place. The list of partners in the casino operation, and the list of stockholders in the corporation were substantially the same with Marion B. Hicks holding by far the majority interest in both. Jones held a smaller interest in each, and was secretary of both enterprises.

In 1947, when the hotel was under construction, Hicks borrowed $160,000 from George Sadlo for use in the building job. Jake Lansky put up half the loan, although Hicks said he did not know this at the time. Hicks repaid the $160,000 to Sadlo in 1954, but never in those years did he tell the tax commission that the Sadlo interest existed. This was a direct violation of the rules and regulations set out by the tax commission in its efforts to make certain that some sort of financial control was established over gambling license holders. However, the concealed Sadlo-Lansky interest was in the hotel company, not in the casino.

In a different transaction, in 1948 Hicks borrowed $37,500 from Sadlo for use in the gambling casino as a part of the bankroll for the gambling games. No evidence was produced to show that Lansky participated in this loan. Hicks repaid it in 1952, after using it for four years to help run the casino operation. But neither Hicks nor Jones ever told the tax commission of the financial stake that Sadlo had in the casino.

This was what caused the tax commission to issue its order suspending the casino license until Hicks and Jones should be removed from the partnership. The commission argued that the two men had responsibility to give this information because of a provision in the gambling law that requires the listing of all persons "directly or indirectly interested in the business." The law provides that omission of the name of any person financially participating in the business provides grounds for license revocation or suspension.

The supreme court said in its opinion that it was willing to accept that the $160,000 loan from Sadlo and Lansky to help build the hotel really gave them an interest in the hotel. But the court would not agree with the commission's argument that Hicks' strong control over both the hotel and casino really had the effect of making them an entity. So it refused to extend the concept of Lansky's investment to include the casino. Since there was no evidence that Lansky had participated in the casino bankroll loan, there was no showing that he was involved in any concealment of interest in the casino itself, the court held.

The court then went into a long analysis of what it took to be the aims of the tax commission in bringing the action. The court said it believed that the commission had objected only to the Lansky concealment, and actually was not worried much about Sadlo's interest. Since Lansky was involved only in the hotel construction loan and not in the casino bankroll loan, it would not uphold the suspension order, the court said. The state had not properly emphasized the importance of the loan to the casino, the court said, and held that this led the court to the assumption that the commission really didn't mean it when it asked that the license be suspended because of the casino bankroll loan.

Tortuous reasoning — absolutely. But it became the law of the case. The issues on Jones and Hicks have become moot, anyway, for Jones no longer has an interest in the casino, while Hicks has died. Jones no longer even has an interest in the property, having sold out to the Webb Corporation in September 1964.

Although the tax commission lost the case against the Thunderbird, the full implications of some of the points decided by the court caused reverberations around Nevada. The supreme court said, for example, that in matters that came before the tax commission on licenses, the gambling operators had a right of review of the record, but only of review of the record that was made in the hearing before the commission. In other words, the attorneys for the gamblers were deprived of one of the most time-consuming actions — they could not petition for an entirely new hearing, a trial *de novo*. The courts could review the case only to be certain that the evidence that the commission had heard had been properly applied to the law under which the decision was made.

This was one important point of the two decided.

The other was this: No more temporary restraining orders to block the immediate effect of the commission's orders. The trial court at Las Vegas in the Thunderbird Hotel concealed ownership case had issued a temporary restraining order that continued the casino license in force until the issues were finally decided. This is a common device in law and one of its purposes is to prevent economic loss for a party to litigation who eventually might prevail in further actions on appeal. But it also permits stalling by attorneys representing clients who are certain to lose eventually, but in the meantime can make a pile of money by continuing their business operations. The tax commission had argued that the trial court had no legal right to prevent the effectiveness of the commission's order by such an injunction. The supreme court agreed. This meant that thereafter an order of the Nevada Gaming Commission, successor to the tax commission, would go into effect immediately, even though the person to whom it was directed had the right of court review which might restore him to his former position. He would be closed, however, until he got the favorable decision.

In effect, this gave the Gaming Commission the whip hand over the gamblers in every direction, after this decision put an end to appeals for trials de novo and for temporary injunctions. However, the Thunderbird Hotel crowd won the ball game. Its ownership was tied with members of the Lansky brothers gambling combination, but got away with it anyway.

The other gamblers had no complaint about this, but they were disturbed by the new rules written into the decision. So in the

Nevada legislature's 1957 session the gamblers devised and supported a bill that would have given the right of trial *de novo* to any licensee of the Gaming Commission who was being punished and wanted to appeal. The gamblers wanted the bill passed so that it would give them a delaying action, and also because it would give them a right which the decision in the Thunderbird Hotel case said they did not have. The bill passed the senate, with little opposition, and came over to the house where it went through the judiciary committee. There were two freshmen on that committee — Gene Evans, then the editor of the paper in Elko, but destined to become a press agent for Bill Harrah; and Howard McKissick, Jr., a lawyer from Reno. They began to study this bill, with the wholehearted attention to duty and high motives that freshmen legislators usually have. They found that it conflicted with what they thought the state's attitude should be toward the gamblers. In effect, Evans and McKissick rewrote the senate bill in committee and succeeded in getting it passed by both houses. Governor Charles H. Russell vetoed it, however.

Evans and McKissick agreed to do research in the two years that followed, and to run for re-election. Both won, and they came back to Carson City with an entirely rewritten gambling law which was the toughest one yet. In a sense, then, the lessons learned in the Thunderbird Hotel case were responsible for a general change in the Nevada approach to control of the gamblers that the legalization experiment had attracted. From the time of that decision forward, the gamblers were more and more hemmed in by stronger state statutes, and by a more active and more determined gambling control mechanism in the executive branch of state government.

The question is whether the state will be willing to use the controls that it now has. Gambling is the major business in Nevada, and it becomes important to elected officials there to have the good will of at least some of the gambling operators. This is not to imply a venality, or an unwillingness to perform duties. It is stated simply as a fact of life.

Two cases came up in the early weeks of 1964 that will test the will and integrity of Nevada's gambling control officials. Both of these cases involve elements of the control group at the Desert Inn. Both of them involve extortion cases. In the first, Marshall Caifano, one of the blacklisted racketeers in the famous Black Book, and Charles Del Monico, a lesser underworld figure, were convicted of trying to extort money from Ray Ryan, a wealthy gambler from Palm Springs, California. Ryan, a high roller and habitué of the various places on the Strip, has been a close friend of John Drew, one of the managers and owners of the Stardust Casino, which is also controlled in part by the same group that owns the Desert Inn. When the extortion attempt began, Ryan said that he tried to contact Drew to get advice from him in dealing with Caifano and Monico, and that Drew discussed the problem with him. But when the trial came in Los Angeles of the indictment against Caifano and Monico, Drew refused to testify when the federal government and then the defense subpoenaed him. He said his answers might tend to incriminate him.

Drew could have gotten away with this had the forum been a congressional hearing, but when he took this position in federal court he was in deep water immediately. Harvey Dickerson, the Nevada attorney general, soon demanded that the State Gaming Control Board move against Drew's license. Dickerson's position was simple: If Drew had committed a crime before he got a gambling license, he should never have received the license, and if the crime had been committed since then, the license should be revoked. As this is written, the State Gaming Control Board is investigating the case. If Drew took the Fifth Amendment merely to avoid the embarrassment of testifying against Caifano, a notorious underworld muscle man, he may find that his embarrassment has become much greater with the gambling control officials.

They have the power to deal with him. The question is whether they will use it.

In the other extortion case, the involvement of the gambling license holder is more direct, but the issue is not yet so nearly ready for decision by the Nevada authorities. This case involves Ruby Kolod, one of the old-time bootleggers from Cleveland and Detroit who came into the Desert Inn ownership in order to finance completion of the construction. Kolod, according to the records of the State Gaming Control Board, owns about one-eighth interest in the casino. As this is written, he is under indictment by a federal grand jury in Denver on the charge of attempting to extort money from a disbarred Denver lawyer, Robert Sunshine.

Sunshine was a promoter as well as a lawyer, and was disbarred upon conviction of embezzling money from people who had entrusted it to him for investment purposes. Sunshine has been sentenced to two terms in the Colorado penitentiary which he entered in February, 1964. His career as a high-rolling gambler, a big operator in real estate, and as a top adviser on oil investment opportunities would seem to be finished.

People in his position generally have someone or some situation to blame for their downfall, and in Sunshine's case, the blame is placed on Las Vegas.

"I wish I'd never heard of the place," he said.

Sunshine's story is worth telling, as a prelude to the further examination of the state of Nevada's problems with Ruby Kolod. Sunshine was born in Denver of a poor family, was a Navy fighter pilot in World War II, married, went through law school while working, began practice about 1948, and in short order was making about $50,000 a year as a wonderfully successful trial lawyer. He also began to get clients who needed advice, and one of these was involved in the Royal Nevada, the only Las Vegas Strip casino ever to go broke. This led Sunshine into the inner circle in Las Vegas, and gave him a taste of the wonders of that never-never land the gamblers have built for themselves in the desert.

"I loved it and I wanted to be a part of it," he told me a few days before he went to jail.

He did become a part of it. He was in charge of the Royal Nevada in its death throes. It was just about the end of 1956, as Sunshine recalled the events, and financial pressures were coming from all directions.

"We had Anna Maria Alberghetti scheduled to appear on New Year's Eve," Sunshine recalled. "First, she wouldn't show. There was some problem about the union she belonged to. I got that squared away. Then the culinary workers union had a paper out against the place, and we had bought them off, and about the middle of the evening the constable walked in and served the paper anyway, so that we had to buy it off again. I'd just got that done. Then the state people came in and said we had to close. We talked them out of it, and it was getting on toward midnight and I figured if we got through that night, the place would survive. But about midnight the word went through the help that we were going to close in five minutes. I never saw such stuff. The dealers began giving chips and money to their friends and about that time a moving crew came in and started taking out the equipment. Seems like the people who had the chattel mortgages had foreclosed. That did it. The place closed, and it never reopened."

However, these events failed to dampen Sunshine's enthusiasm for Las Vegas, and he became a regular visitor to the Desert Inn. He came to be a friend of Ruby Kolod, and eventually advised Kolod to invest in an oil deal. As Sunshine tells the story, Kolod took $68,000 in cash out of the cashier's cage at the Desert Inn and gave it to Sunshine to take back to Denver. The money went the way a lot of other money went that came into Sunshine's hands. But Kolod is not the sort of man to relax in the face of such a loss. Moreover, he had been joined in the "investment" by

Willie Israel Alderman, a really hardnosed veteran of the Detroit, Miami, Cleveland and New York jungles. Naturally, they wanted their money back.

The federal government alleges that Kolod and Alderman retained the services of two muscle men to threaten Sunshine. These were identified as Felix Antonio (Milwaukee Phil) Alderisio and Americo DePietto. It is charged that they called on Sunshine in his law offices and told him they were there to kill him. He was allowed to persuade them not to kill him, but only on the basis that he would pay back the money to Kolod and Alderman.

Sunshine maintains that it was this disruption of his financial plans that caused the breakup that led to his conviction as an embezzler. Of course, Sunshine would have to blame someone. He is particularly bitter toward Alderman and Kolod because of the personal relationship that he thought existed between them. The two gamblers once were accustomed to coming to Denver from Las Vegas and staying in Sunshine's expensive home in the Cherry Hills section south of town.

As this is written, in early 1964, no determination has been had in the federal courts of the validity of the indictment against the two Las Vegas figures and the two Chicago underworld figures, nor has there been time for a trial to be held. Consequently, the state authorities in Nevada have no clearcut position to take on the question of lifting Kolod's license since he has not been convicted of a crime. He has only been charged and may be innocent. They can say that they must wait, which is a justifiable position. But what about the evidence that the $68,000 was taken right out of the cashier's cage and placed in cash in Sunshine's hands? What about the indication of a relationship of some sort between such notorious persons as Milwaukee Phil and Pete Pietto and a gambling license holder?

But beyond this, it would appear that in considering the two extortion cases together the Nevada authorities might be struck by one curious fact. There is no connection between them except one — both Ryan, the Palm Springs investor, and Sunshine, the Denver embezzler, were high rollers on the Las Vegas Strip. How many other high rollers have submitted to extortion rather than go through the terribly difficult times that Ryan endured in order to prosecute Caifano and Monico? Ryan had to admit on the witness stand that he had been traveling between Palm Springs and Las Vegas with an airlines stewardess who had been his guest in his hotel in Palm Springs and in the Desert Inn in Las Vegas. There is no way to forecast what problems await Sunshine in the special world of the prison where he must serve his sentence, but the odds are that the underworld can reach inside the prison walls to squeeze him.

So the Nevada authorities should look at these cases, and assess the rumor mill output about others to determine if the gambling tables on the Strip have become a hunting ground for extortionists who survey the crop of high rollers for one who might be willing to come up with a good chunk of money rather than suffer embarrassment. Extortion is not always accompanied by a semi-legitimate excuse, it was demonstrated in the Ryan case.

Testimony there made it clear that Caifano and Monico were trying to take money away from Ryan purely through intimidation. They told him that they had saved him from being kidnaped on several occasions, and that they were going to continue to protect him so he should give them $60,000 a year. Otherwise he would be hurt, he was told. When the final moves in this campaign of terror were worked out in the Desert Inn, Ryan broke away and ran to a phone. Did he call the Clark County sheriff? Or the Las Vegas police? Or the security officers at the Desert Inn?

Not on your life. He called the FBI. And when the agents arrived, they found that Milwaukee Phil Alderisio was talking rapidly to try to persuade Ryan to settle his problems with Caifano and Monico without calling in the law.

What kind of government do they have in Nevada and in Las Vegas? Is it everybody's government, or is it the gamblers' government? Ray Ryan's reaction gives the unconscious opinion of a longtime Las Vegas habitué. There are countless other stories that also give indications. An answer of sorts can be read into a series of events disclosed in the pages of the Las Vegas *Review Journal* in 1963. Jude Wanniski, a reporter for the paper, wrote them and they tell of the strange operation of Clark County Sanitary District No. 1, the sewage disposal district that serves the casino hotels on the Strip.

The management of Wilbur Clark's Desert Inn was the leading group in the establishment of the sewage district. The Desert Inn got its sewage service for $100 a month on a special standby contract based on the argument that since they had their own sewage system they should not pay full charges. But reportedly they are relying now on the sewer without revision of the contract. The other places paid as much as $2000 a month. It is estimated that during the life of the contract, the Desert Inn might save as much as $400,000.

Further, there were stories that the directors and employees of the sanitary district were buying up great chunks of desert land, then voting to have the sewage district build lines to these holdings which had the effect of opening them up to development as subdivisions. Then, other stories told of the world tours and trips to Hawaii paid for out of public funds for directors and employees.

In one transaction, some of the directors bought eighty acres of desert land for $24,000 in 1961. In 1962 the board of directors decided that the sanitary district needed that tract. However, there was concern that there might be some talk if they negotiated the transaction both as buyers (with public money) and sellers. So they went through a condemnation proceeding. The case was heard by a district judge named David Zenoff, who, it will be recalled, signed the incorporation papers of Paradise Hospital, Inc., in his days as a practicing attorney.

The purpose of a condemnation proceeding is the provision of a fair value judgment for property to be acquired by a public body through use of the right of eminent domain. It is contemplated that the owner of the property will attempt to inflate the value, while the public agency will attempt to hold down the price. Yet, in this condemnation proceeding, only one witness was heard and he said that the land suited to the growing of alfalfa was worth $1000 an acre in other parts of Nevada and should be worth 50 percent more in the Las Vegas area. No evidence of the $24,000 purchase price of the property was put on; nor was it brought out that the syndicate also had 320 acres adjoining that it was selling at $300 an acre.

In these conditions, Judge Zenoff set a $100,000 value for the eighty acres of desert land. The judge also was involved as a separate matter in getting about $5000 worth of pipe from the sanitary district for use in a nonprofit youth camp for juvenile delinquents in which he was interested.

After the *Review Journal*'s series of stories, a grand jury investigation was begun of the conduct of the sanitary district directors, and of their use of public funds. The grand jury began to delve into all sorts of things connected with the board, including the matters involving Judge Zenoff.

A motion was offered in district court by others subject to a separate investigation by the grand jury which had the effect of attacking the legality of the grand jury's selection. This motion came before Judge Zenoff, who made no move to disqualify himself. He told me that he had considered his position, however, when I asked him about it.

"That's a good question," he said, with a chuckle, and then turned serious. "Judge Mowbray is the presiding judge and he knew I was hearing this motion and he knew what they were looking into and what it was all about, and no questions ever were raised by anyone about my taking the case. I was afraid it might influence me adversely to bend over backward, but, hell, I can't live my life that way of course."

Judge Zenoff could have avoided any worries at all by simply disqualifying himself to rule on the motions because of his personal involvement in the results stemming from the way the decision would go. However, he did not.

He took the case and ruled that the grand jury was not legally constituted, and this had the effect of stopping the grand jury investigation that was investigating matters with which he had been connected. The state Supreme court overruled him.

Meantime, the federal government has become interested in another aspect of the sewer construction. This came about because through a system of matching grants administered by the U.S. Public Health Service, the Department of Health, Education, and Welfare helped pay for the sewers. The federal contribution appears to have been about $500,000 out of a total expended of about $2,000,000. Among the allegations made in the investigation was one that the sewers had been constructed on a different and less expensive set of standards from those for which the grants were made by federal officials. It also was suggested that some sort of corruption of federal officials had been worked so that this duplicity would not be discovered.

Investigations of these matters were made originally by the Federal Bureau of Investigation in Las Vegas, and the reports were given to the office of the United States Attorney for that area. Prosecution was refused. However, subsequently, when more questions were asked about the matter, the Department of Health, Education, and Welfare referred the matter back to the Department of Justice for possible criminal prosecution and for reassessment of the facts. It is still there as this is written.

There are some lessons to be learned from this examination of the processes of law in the gambler's town. But the odds are that the people who need to learn them will never even study the events. Interest is not high in these questions in Las Vegas. This is a town where the chips issued by the gambling houses are interchangeable with silver dollars or currency. The people who live in Las Vegas are accustomed to the thought that influence and money will permit those who do wrong to avoid being called to account. The reaction to such disclosures is not the righteous indignation that would be felt among the residents of Des Moines or Scranton; in Las Vegas, the reaction is one of envy and fired up ambition to "get mine, too."

This is a town where a street with the thoroughly respectable name San Francisco Avenue is renamed Sahara Avenue merely to suit the needs of the publicity director of the hotel-casino of that name. It is a place where the richest men in town are the gamblers and where the neon from the downtown casinos lights up the block of Fremont Street more brilliantly than Times Square is illuminated.

This is the strangest city in America. It is also the origin of an infectious immorality that rides out of the desert on a golden flood of gambling wealth to spread its peculiar brand of ethics across the nation.

6

BLACK MONEY — THE HIDDEN PROFITS
FEED THE HIDDEN POWER

"BLACK MONEY" is a term used frequently in Las Vegas and elsewhere to designate cash acquired in ways that will not bear examination. In Las Vegas, the term refers to the untaxed profits of the gambling casinos, profits siphoned off through one scheme or another before the casino's profit and loss figures are entered on the books that the tax collectors see. No one can say, even the participants in this highly organized swindle, just how much money disappears every year. One estimate, from a highly qualified official source, was that each of seven places in Las Vegas was taking off $10,000 a day. This comes to about $2,000,000 a month.

"But I couldn't prove it," he said. "I'm not even certain it's true or accurate. I know they take off the top before they enter the day's business in the books. But damned if I know how much. I don't think anyone else does, either."

There are an even dozen of the great casino hotels in Las Vegas, plus a row of casinos on Fremont Street downtown. In all, Clark County, Nevada, had twenty-four places with unrestricted casino licenses when this official estimate was made. The man who made it refused to name the seven places he believed to be taking off such great sums of untaxed profits. Nor would he discuss what he thought about the operations in northern Nevada at Reno and Lake Tahoe, where some of the biggest moneymakers in the state are located.

The most persistent unprovable statement made around Las Vegas is that all the gambling casinos cheat on their income taxes. But the tax collectors themselves insist this is untrue. Not all do, it is said with a wry smile. Just those who think they can get away with it.

The gross winnings of the casinos run to about $250,000,000 a year according to their income tax reports. One knowledgeable observer estimated that this represents, in the state as a whole, no more than 90 to 95 percent of the actual winnings, with some casinos reporting as little as two-thirds of their true income, while others report it all. If this observer is correct, that would mean upwards of $12,500,000 — free and untaxed — that the gambling operators have to play with each year.

This looks to be an unusually small amount to be concerned with, in terms of the national income. However, this money has qualities that make it unique in the American economy. It is concentrated in the hands of an unscrupulous group whose ethical and moral standards have just been exemplified by the very act that gave them control of this untaxed money. There is a continual, predictable flow of it. Moreover, this "black" money is just one of the sources of capital for the Nevada gamblers. They have the money left after they paid taxes on their declared earnings. As we shall see, they also are experts at multiplying the power of their holdings through borrowings.

But the worst of this "black" money is that it can't be spent readily for any legitimate purpose. The men who squirreled it away and hid it from the tax collector are barred from spending it for houses and Cadillacs and yachts. The classic example of the racketeer who did this was Al Capone, who was guilty but unpunished for all his terrible crimes. He went to Alcatraz prison for failure to pay his federal income taxes. Not only do the Las Vegas gamblers have the recollection of Capone's fate in their minds. They have a neighbor and colleague who traveled the same pathway to federal prison in the mid-1930's. This is Morris Kleinman, a major partner in Wilbur Clark's Desert Inn. He served a term for tax fraud in the mid-thirties, and came out to resume his gambling connections. Now he has a seat at the top of the heap.

The black money burns in the pockets of its possessors.

They have two alternatives, beyond the unthinkable one of just keeping it hidden away. The money accumulates too rapidly for that. Either they spend it in some untraceable way; or they go to the trouble of cleaning it up, washing off the moral stains, fixing their money so it has legal status. The latter alternative has the effect of giving this illegitimate money a birth certificate that will pass in polite society.

That portion of the untaxed profits used without any effort to clean it up is a cancerous growth on the American moral fiber. This money has no purpose except an unlawful one. It can be used to pay a bribe, and then it becomes the problem of the bribe taker to give it the color of legitimacy. Or it can go into the narcotics traffic — an agent of Red China operating in Macao cares little whether the American government collected taxes on the stack of greenbacks he accepts in payment for a consignment of heroin. Or it may be used to hire a murderer. The possibilities have limits set only by the limits of need to procure the doing of evil acts.

Some of this money goes by courier every week from a Las Vegas casino to men who live in Florida and New Jersey. The recipients are high in the councils of organized crime in the United States, investigators in Las Vegas believe. One of them has a voice in the Italian criminal organization. The other is a notorious professional gambler and racket organizer. The facts of this transmission are well established by the investigating agencies. But the proof of what they know thus far has been beyond the investigators' reach.

This handling of the black money that goes directly to support the criminal activities of the underworld has little finesse to it. They take the money, hide it and split it up and spend it in the criminal activities that require it. Its social impact is out of all proportion to its size in the economy.

But the process of legitimatizing black money so it may be used in any way its owners wish has as much sophistication as financing the purchase of a New York skyscraper. First, there is the process of getting it. It is most unlikely that the men who are going to clean up the money will be so crude as to just cart it out of the casino. They will use a great many devices, all of them different, and all of them highly effective.

Here is one way.

A high roller loses heavily. The casino extends credit to him readily, for its investigations have shown long ago that he has resources far beyond what he may lose in a week of steady losses. He piles up markers (I O U's) for tens of thousands of dollars. Everyone smiles and assures him that his luck will turn, and he becomes more and more irritable and more and more addicted to plunging in a determined effort to force the dice to act as men do when he forces them in a business deal. But the dice ignore him. They are beyond intimidation. After several days, he suddenly packs up and leaves. The casino manager may even drive him to the airport and all the help will turn toward him in sympathy and kindness. They want this guy back. They love his kind.

Back in his office, the high roller in a week or so will get a telephone call from Las Vegas. After the usual exchanges, the suggestion is made from the casino that those markers could just as well be paid in cash in New York, and the long trip out to Las Vegas avoided unless, of course, "you want to come back and take it away from us at the table. I hate to see you coming when you're hot." (Flattery is a potent weapon on such egos and the gamblers use it with great cunning.)

Well, why not pay it in cash? Besides, this high roller may have a few bundles of currency in a safety deposit box somewhere. If so, he is confronted with the problem of how to spend it and not get caught. All kinds of people, in those walks of life where any access to cash income exists, have an opportunity to salt a little away before the tax man cometh. Lots of them do, particularly those personality types for whom the Las Vegas money traps are a lure and for whom the crap tables are a disease.

So the high roller agrees. He is told that a man will come to him in a few days and will be able to identify himself because he has the markers the high roller left with the casino. Perhaps a slight discount is offered for the cash settlement. The high roller knows full well what is up; as a businessman, he can see a tax dodge being set up when it unfolds before his eyes. But the odds are that no one will discuss this. Both the gambler from Las Vegas and the businessman at his desk in one of Manhattan's towers will act as if this conspiracy did not exist.

Later, when the messenger arrives with the empty briefcase to be filled with cash, the businessman may notice a pronounced accent and a foreign appearance in the cut of clothing, the manners, and the bearing. If so, his intuition serves him well. One of many ingenious devices is about to be played out. This man may have come directly to the office from a session at the United Nations where he represents one of the Latin-American nations. He has a diplomatic passport. This insures him against harm from the police or from federal tax agents or from anyone in any official capacity. The awe in which the underworld holds the people for whom he runs this errand protects him from all but the rankest amateur holdup men. He is safe all around.

When he leaves the businessman, after a few amenities which include his handing over the markers in a sealed envelope, he walks to a pay telephone and places a collect call to an unlisted number in Las Vegas. He announces that he has the money, that it was collected with no trouble, and that the businessman asked no unusual questions. It looked in all respects, he reported, like a solid deal and he would leave the United States on a night plane. Within two days, he said, he would have the money in the bank.

Meantime, the businessman was sitting at his desk, looking at the pieces of paper that had been his markers and wondering if he should go back to Las Vegas again to try to get some of his money back. He probably will go; but he won't get his money back.

The diplomat stopped by his apartment in Manhattan, then went by limousine to Idlewild International Airport and left for home. Everywhere he went first class, and gave gracious tips, and was in every respect what a diplomat would inwardly feel he should be — quietly wealthy, generous, respected, remembered with admiration and envy by all who saw him pass. He had one interesting trait — he never took his hand off the briefcase he carried with him. When the plane flew through the night and most of the others on board slept, he sat staring out the window, clutching the briefcase. If he lost it, he could never come back to the United States because his diplomatic passport would be no protection against the criminal organizations that would hold him responsible. In fact, if he lost the money he could continue to live only by carefully staying within the high-walled home where he was born.

He intended not to lose it.

After hours of flight, the plane landed and he was passed through customs as easily as he had been in New York, for here he was a member of the ruling clique. His name was the same as the name of several of the leaders of finance and government in his country. His face was known to the customs officials, and they passed him without a quibble. None of his luggage was opened, nor was even a glance given to the briefcase. At the inner gate of the customs shed, his brother's chauffeur waited, and together they went out to the sedan where the brother waited in the rear seat. By now it was midmorning and they drove immediately to a small brick building with a sign in Spanish that designated it as a bank.

Inside, they went to a private office, emptied the money from the briefcase and counted it, then made out a deposit slip to a numbered account. The money was deposited to this account, and placed in the bank's vaults. The receipted deposit slip went into the diplomat's pocket. When he returned to New York, he would send it by surface mail, registered, to a man in Las Vegas. When it was received, his sizable fee would be paid to him. But meantime, he was home. There was other business to transact with the officers of his government. He left his brother at the door to the bank and went to the presidential palace.

The Las Vegas gamblers like to deal as high from the deck as possible. Risks are for their customers. They want a sure thing.

This ornate and carefully contrived operation has solved only half the problem. The money is outside the United States safely, and behind a shield that will blunt the inquisitive nose of any tax agent who tries to penetrate the anonymous number on the account. He can never learn how the money went into the account, whether it was cash, or checks, or gold bullion from a shipwreck in the Spanish Main. The small bank will be the end of the line for investigators who may try to trace the money back.

There is hardly anyone among the gambling heirarchy in Las Vegas who wants to truck his money to the tropics so he can go there and spend it. Taking it there was merely a device. The little bank is only a stopping station on a longer journey. It could also have gone to a bank account in Switzerland, or to one in Hong Kong, or to other places where the banking laws permit bankers to be as secretive as their customers want them to be.

The next step is to get the money back into the United States. It would not do for the ambassador to go back, fill up his satchel and fly north with it. No, the whole maneuver to this point has been quiet and still and with no papers signed. Now, suddenly, the entire face of the transaction changes. What happens from here is done in a blizzard of paper. Everyone gets receipts. There are checks and bills and enough pieces of paper to put down one of those trails that children leave in a game.

Of course, these papers are a trail.

This trail is constructed with as great care as the earlier one of the money's journey south was carefully concealed. The intention now is to bring the money out, as a daughter is brought out at her debut. It appears in the hands of someone who borrowed it from a foreign corporation that does business in the diplomat's home town. The lending corporation has no offices or property in the United States. This loan is as bona fide as the papers that record it. There are notes, mortgages, promises to repay, lists of chattels — the whole thing. A bank draft passes from the little bank to one of these big ones in New York. Or Boston. Or San Francisco. The draft goes to the account of the man who successfully negotiated the loan. Now it is his money. He does whatever he wants with it, and the tax collector has no business bothering him about it.

Borrowed it from whom? From "this" company in "that" Latin American nation. The company's name is meaningless. Inquiries as to its incorporators produce a blank wall. One is a lawyer — he might even have the same name as the ambassador — and others are members of his staff. The resident agent: the lawyer. The owners? Sorry, we do not force our corporations to disclose the names of their stockholders.

(In New York City there is a lawyer who is familiar with many aspects of this part of the Las Vegas gamblers' business. He insists that one group there has organized a corporation in Panama which has "bearer" shares. This means, the lawyer will explain, that the person who has physical control of the shares is assumed to be their legal owner. The shares are not registered, no record of their trading is kept by the corporation. But if a share is presented at the company offices, it will be liquidated in cash for its pro rata value in the company as of that moment. The author is not able to vouch for the validity of this story, although it has been set out for him by the lawyer as fact.)

So the borrower has the money. It is perfectly good, clean, untainted money backed by the United States government. He may do whatever he wants with it, insofar as the government tax agents are concerned. Notes eventually will be marked "paid" and a careful paper trail constructed to show that the borrower paid off the loan — whether he did or not.

Up to now, for a group of gamblers following this general scheme to clean up their "black" money, the script would have been much as it is presented here. There would have been minor variances — perhaps an airline stewardess would take the money out of the United States, perhaps it would go to Switzerland, maybe it would come back in settlement of some debt incurred through a foreign operation, with settlement preferred by both parties in American exchange.

But from here on, the opportunities for variance multiply.

Some of the variance will come from the reasons the gamblers have for issuing money from their foreign supply dump. If they wanted it cleaned up so they could use it themselves, they will soon have it. The corporation that borrowed it is probably one of their creatures. If they were settling with someone for a service rendered, a set of papers showing that he has repaid the dummy company in Latin America will be drawn and effectuated after a suitable period of time has elapsed. The possibilities are endless. But the money is back, after a short trip out of the country, and available for use.

They may even want to use it in some respectable business they have opened. This gives them an advantage described once by Henry Peterson, the deputy director of the organized crime division of the Department of Justice. Mr. Peterson was discussing the unfair advantages a racketeer turned businessman has over his competitors. One that stood out in Mr. Peterson's discussion was the availability of large sums of untaxed cash from the gambling tables of casinos affiliated with the business. This means ready lines of credit and full financial support, an asset the competition will not have.

The most startling thought in all this comes as one realizes that this maneuvering has been done to save a small part of the total tax load that the casinos must bear. All the authorities concerned with this problem believe that the casinos all pay taxes on the greater part of their winnings. These little criminal games of international conspiracy are played with the smallest part of their winnings. But . . .

They are certain to take this same set of morals and ethics along with any investments they make of the profits left after taxes have been paid. Or to say it another way, the legitimate profits will be used in just the same sleazy deals as the cleaned up black money.

To use an old-time phrase that has gone out of style, these men who cheat on their gambling profits are crooks. Anything they touch will be soiled by their unethical business attitudes and infected with the virus of their antisocial behavior. These are the men for whom the great wealth generated by the gambling tables has supplied a new force in the American economy.

The state of Nevada does the very best that it can with a small staff of investigators. It must be remembered that a great segment of the voting population is devoted to the continuance of gambling. The agents of the Gaming Control Board, the state's gambling law enforcement agency, prowl through the casinos incognito until a few arrests and open hearings blast away their anonymity. But what can these few do in the long run against such a collection of organized and highly trained law violators?

That is what some of these gamblers in Nevada are. In their formative years they learned to circumvent the law, and developed a cynicism where the rest of us have varying degrees of fear and respect. So they treat the law with contempt.

One should know how the gamblers organize things for themselves in the areas where their operations are illegal in order to understand how they will use their great profits from the legal gambling operations in Nevada. This covert, illegal, conspiratorial gambling operation that exists in every major city is the training ground for the Las Vegas crowd.

The first thing an apprentice gambler learns in an illegal operation is to reject the idealistic view of humanity and of life. He learns to look on people as victims to be plucked, or as confederates in the process of cheating, or as those with authority who must be bought off, or otherwise maneuvered around in order that the gambling may continue. This knowledge, absorbed early in life, creates a cynicism among professional gamblers that seldom leaves them. It creates an unhappiness within their souls and twists and distorts their relationships with the rest of society. Circumstances allow them little opportunity for contact with those elements of society that would give them a different and more balanced view of mankind. The thoroughly decent elements of a community have no contact with the professional gambler. He meets the disturbed ones who want to gamble on his tables, and the dishonest ones who want to share in his profits.

A great many of the procedures and promotional gimmicks of the Nevada casinos originated and were perfected in their basic form by the gamblers in the illegal establishments of the major cities. Now they send out promotional literature in the United States mails; in the old days they called a list of regular gamblers to say "we've moved to a place in the alley off Third Street behind the old theater. It's the green door about half way down on the right. The guy on the door knows you and we'll be open about three-thirty this afternoon." In the old days they put out cards; now they buy four color spreads in magazines.

The customers come, and are regularly fleeced, and they come back when they have more money. The apprentice gambler notes this well and takes it to mean that all of mankind — except for the select few who are clever like him — are idiots who can be manipulated by the clever ones.

Early in the time of his association with the gambling house, he learns the truth about the police department in his city. He learns that so long as a carefully set-out group of understandings is observed, the gambling joint will be unmolested. (If it operates at all in a big city, it operates through some understanding with the police.)

These understandings will vary from city to city and from year to year, for they are dependent on the degree of ascendancy in the public life of the city of those pseudo-respectable elected and appointed officials who are brothers under the skin with the racketeers who run the gambling houses. The understanding may go no farther than the policeman who patrols that beat, and if this is the case the gambling houses' existence is precarious; or it may go to the top of the city's government, and in this case the greatest problem for the gambler is to maintain a balance between what the general public will endure and the terrible costs of buying off an entire city government.

In a sense, this is what has happened in Nevada. The gamblers have achieved an understanding with a majority of the electorate in that sparsely settled state so that they are able to function there, paying taxes as their major payoff, rather than the bribes that they pay in order to continue their gambling operations else-where. They also engage in all sorts of other public-pacifying good works — they give to the churches, they support all the fund drives, they ingratiate themselves with all the leading office holders and molders of public opinion. Meantime, the tentacles of their control reach ever deeper into the life of the state. It has been estimated, for example, that 40 percent of the population of the Las Vegas area is directly dependent on the gambling opera-tions; the total symbiotic relationship of Las Vegas and the gam-blers has not been determined. But the carpenter who drives nails in a new house, the man who washes cars, the clerk in the post office, the policeman who directs traffic on Sahara Avenue at the city limits, the president of the bank — all these are glaringly dependent on the continuation of the Strip gambling palaces. That they would vote to close out the gambling is highly un-likely, for they may believe as individuals that their careers would not survive the transition to the sort of economy that would be supported when the gambling houses closed.

At any rate, the gamblers who run the Nevada casinos learned their lessons well in the years when they watched and ran gambling places in the cities. They came to understand all the mechanics of the games themselves. The means of cheating the house and cheating the customer and getting away with it became a part of their stock of knowledge. They became experts in the psychology of the compulsive gambler, and learned so well how to keep him at the tables until they had all his money.

As they progressed to the level of running a place for them-selves in the alley, they learned the intricacies of dealing with officialdom. At first, it might be the patrolman on the beat. Eventually it was the fat, expensively dressed official of minor capacity who came to them with authority to make arrangements for those of greater power who could not afford the risk of a visit to the place in the alley.

They learned that the percentages for a simple crap game could never bear the heavy burden of expense that their arrangements with authority climbed to. So they had to trim these odds by cheating sometimes and other times by just establishing the more favorable house odds as the basis of the games.

Sometimes the gamblers who later went to Nevada actually had the entire gambling operation of a large city under their control. In one city many years ago the gambling operation consisted of a string of gambling houses and slot machines scattered all over the city in good locations. These gamblers had control to a point where they had established a regular payroll arrangement for police in the various capacities of command. It was weighted to take into consideration the degree of assistance the particular police job could be expected to give to the gambling operation. A patrolman whose district included a tentacle of the gambling operation would get more money than a higher ranking officer who was not directly connected with police protection for the racket. Not all the police took this money; but many did. Those who refused were shifted to positions where they could not hurt the racket. The payroll system was so well organized that it took into account the need to make arrangements with persons outside official status, but in sensitive positions. Newspaper reporters who manned the police station press room were on this list.

In the early 1950's a U.S. Senate committee led by the late Senator Estes Kefauver found a situation like this occurring in city after city, with variables that changed the details slightly in each place. But the major pattern was always the same: The gamblers collected money by the sackful and shared it with persons in official positions who protected them. The Kefauver hearings brought out scandals of American life and rottenness in the underpinnings of American democracy that rivaled those disclosures of the muckrackers who showed the terrible effects of alliances between unethical businessmen and dishonest public officials a half century earlier.

There is an ironic note to all of this.

Things have never been the same for the Mob since the Kefauver hearings. One effect has been for the criminal element to shift where possible into businesses that are legal. One of these is the Nevada gambling casino, for what could be sweeter than to be able to apply the lessons of the underworld gambling apprenticeship to the operation of a completely legal gambling casino? And now, the wealth generated in these operations provides the strength for a move by the very men that Senator Kefauver unseated. They are moving into the nation's legitimate businesses where their lack of ethics and their heavy cash support have constituted a new force in the economy.

As indicative of the kind of public officials the Las Vegas gamblers do business with, consider the late George Bender. He was a congressman from Ohio for fourteen years, and during his tenure he smothered an investigation of the Teamsters Union. In 1954 he ran for the United States Senate, to succeed the then recently deceased Robert A. Taft, and was elected to a two-year term. He was defeated in 1956 when he sought a full six-year term. During his two Senate years, he was a member of the Senate permanent investigating subcommittee, of which Senator John L. McClellan of Arkansas was chairman and a young lawyer from Massachusetts, Robert F. Kennedy, the chief counsel.

In early 1957, after Bender was out of office, Senator McClellan and Robert Kennedy led an investigation of labor racketeering that involved the Teamsters Union. Suddenly, the new president of the Teamsters, James R. Hoffa, announced that he was having an internal and independent study made of the charges of corruption within the union. The man heading this study was former Senator Bender, and eventually he ended up in the witness chair where his fellow Republican, Senator Barry Goldwater of

Arizona, gave him a rough going over. Among many things, they discussed politics and winning elections. Bender told of appointing the "best prostitute" in a certain area as the Republican committeewoman.

"Frankly, unless you get the votes of the washed and the unwashed you can't win elections," Bender told Goldwater. "You don't have to be a prostitute yourself, but sometimes you have to get their votes."

Goldwater said later that he thought Bender's performance had been disgraceful. Robert Kennedy was even more disgusted. In his book, *The Enemy Within,* where he recounted his experiences in the labor investigation, he said of Bender: "To me, it is incomprehensible that such a man should occupy the Senate seat once held by Robert Taft, a man who was a symbol of integrity and intelligence."

Jimmy Hoffa had hired Bender originally at $250 a day, but cut this back to $125 a day when criticism mounted. Bender was paid $58,636.07 in salary and expenses — for doing nothing except lending his title as former United States Senator as a shield of respectability for James R. Hoffa and the Teamsters Union.

The Las Vegas crowd stores up names of people like this, for it constantly needs new influence in new directions. One of the serious needs felt in the late 1950's was to stop a Securities and Exchange Commission investigation of some Wall Street operations that involved some of the group that owns Wilbur Clark's Desert Inn. This represented a disastrous foray into the stock market by the Nevada gamblers. The complex details of this assault on the citadel of capitalism will be set out in a later chapter, but for now it should be understood just what use the gamblers can put their money to, and the sort of people they can hire.

From various records, the allegation comes through that $100,-000 in cash was passed to former Senator Bender so that he would use his influence to stop the S.E.C. investigation. At that time the

Ohio politician was working and living in Washington where he was a special consultant to the Department of the Interior during the Eisenhower administration. He had been a Republican Senator, and administrations generally find a job for party men who have just been defeated. Moreover, a consultancy is a time limit appointment of up to six months in which the authority of the appointee has sharp limitations. Usually he has only advisory functions.

The source of this bribery story was Alexander L. Guterma, the mysterious white Russian immigrant who led the gamblers into the market and who then testified against them when he was himself convicted of stock frauds.

Guterma in his testimony insisted that a member of the Las Vegas group, Sam Garfield, had worked out the proposition and brought it to Guterma. They, and other potential defendants in a federal indictment, would put up the $100,000 in cash and Bender would then persuade the S.E.C. to stop the investigation.

Guterma said he refused to put up his share of the bribe money. But he said the bribe was given to Bender.

"I know damn well it was," Guterma said. "But I had enough trouble without getting snarled up in a bribery case. I just wouldn't have anything to do with it."

Bender died of a heart attack in June 1961, a few days after appearing before a federal grand jury that was investigating stories of attempts to "fix" the S.E.C. charges. There was no indication that any success had been achieved in trying to sidetrack the investigation. Subsequently Guterma was indicted on a variety of stock fraud charges, and after the Democratic administration took office in early 1961, the grand jury investigations turned toward the Las Vegas gamblers' involvement with the result that several of them also were indicted.

So Garfield got nothing for his $100,000, if in fact Guterma's story is true. Garfield denies the entire story.

But George Bender is not the only person said to have been sent by the gamblers to attempt to save them from indictment for stock fraud. In September 1963, Roy Cohn, the young New York lawyer who rocketed to national renown in his association with the late Senator Joseph R. McCarthy, was indicted on a perjury charge. He was acquitted in July 1964. The indictment alleged that Cohn was a part of a conspiracy to thwart justice by preventing the indictment of four men connected with the Desert Inn crowd in Las Vegas. These four men were Garfield and three of his associates, including Allard Roen, the vice-president and manager of the Desert Inn and the Stardust.

Garfield and Roen testified to their relationship with Cohn. They have been convicted on stock fraud charges, and are awaiting sentencing as this is written. The theory of the indictment against Cohn was that he was influential in preventing the indictment of the Desert Inn group when a federal grand jury first studied their Wall Street operations.

Although Cohn was acquitted of the charges, the incident once again shows the trail of conflict, distortion, disruption, litigation and despoliation that follows the movement of the gambling money earned in the Las Vegas casinos.

The Nevada Gaming Commission and the State Gaming Control Board have enough problems in keeping the gamblers in line at home without attempting to check on their out-of-state activities. The Gaming Commission is the policy organization for the state's control of the casinos and slot machines; the Control Board is the law enforcement agency, the policemen of the state's gambling empire.

Occasionally they run into some heavyweight operators. As we have seen, the history of gambling in Nevada is one of gradual imposition of state control on casinos which had been wide open since 1931 when the law permitted casino gambling. This has not been an easy process. There have been steps upward, and slides back many times until the achievement of to-day's comparatively stringent controls.

One of those big steps forward centered around one of the most famous entertainers in America — Frank Sinatra, the talented New Jersey Italian youngster who became a famous singer, then a businessman, a friend of political leaders, the leader of a madcap group of entertainment figures known as "The Clan." In twenty years, through the peculiar force of the publicity machines that characterize our age, he rose from the obscurity of his beginnings in New Jersey to the point where his love affairs and business involvements were of interest to millions of people. From the beginning, when silly little girls squealed at the sound of his voice, Sinatra has shown signs of quick and violent temper. Perhaps as much as anything, this temper ran him out of Nevada gambling.

Sinatra has become the owner of real estate in Palm Springs, the boss of a record company, and until the fall of 1963, he was a major figure in Nevada gambling through ownership of 9 percent of the Sands, a leading place on the Las Vegas Strip, and 50 percent of Cal Neva Lodge at Lake Tahoe. Within less than a month, his gambling interests were eliminated, and he had announced he was selling what was estimated at $3,500,000 worth of casino interests.

What happened?

The answer is far from simple. Only the outer elements of it are known. The true inner relationships that brought about the Sinatra debarment from Nevada gambling probably will never be known to the public.

The surface facts are these:

In 1960 the Gaming Control Board distributed a "black book" among the holders of casino licenses. This was a simple thing to have caused so much trouble to a man of Sinatra's high station. But it did. The volume was bound in black, limp card board such as students use for school themes. It had eleven sheets of letter-sized paper inside. Each page carried the picture and aliases of one man. Also, there was at least one local arrest number in some American city, plus a Federal Bureau of Investigation file number. The men named in the "black book" are these:

John Louis Battaglia, Los Angeles
Marshal Caifano, Chicago
Carl James Civella, Kansas City
Nichola Civella, Kansas City
Trigger Mike Coppola, Miami
Louis Tom Dragna, Los Angeles
Robert L. "Bobby" Garcia, Southern California
Sam Giancana, Chicago
Motel Grezebrenacy, Kansas City
Murray Llewellyn Humphreys, Chicago
Joe Sica, Los Angeles

The black books were carried around to the licensees by agents of the Control Board. The licensees were instructed that the men named were not to be permitted on the premises of a casino, and that the casino license holders were given the responsibility for keeping them out. The idea was that these men were bad medicine for Nevada gambling. For a while, nothing happened.

Then one night everything erupted. Marshal Caifano, who is better known in the underworld as Johnny Marshal, went to Las Vegas and began to circulate along the Strip. He went in one place after another, and soon the Gaming Control Board was aware of his presence. The word was passed to the casinos to keep him out, to eject him, to follow orders. The casinos refused. The state then moved all of its available agents to the Strip and began disrupting the operations of the places where Caifano had been. The agents stopped games, used machines for checking cards and dice, and looking at the roulette wheels. The gamblers began to leave the casinos and go to places away from the presence of the law enforcement officers. Even when the games are legal, cops make the gambling crowd nervous. Caifano continued to move down the Strip.

When he arrived at the Desert Inn, the word had preceded him and he was denied admittance. The casino operators had received the word. The black book was to be treated with respect, not as a joke.

(Caifano, claiming that he was denied his legal rights, sued many of those who dealt with him that night. He lost. A federal judge refused to award him damages but ordered him to pay the costs.)

These events and the vigor with which the position of authority was upheld established the validity of the black book for a year or so. Until it was challenged by Frank Sinatra, the black book was treated reverently by the gamblers. Then on September 11, 1963, the Sinatra challenge of authority became known to the public. This was through a complaint filed over the signature of Edward A. Olsen, the chairman of the State Gaming Control Board. The effect was to force Sinatra to defend himself in a hearing before the Nevada Gaming Commission.

Olsen was a former Associated Press bureau chief in Reno, and came into state government with the election of Grant Sawyer as governor of Nevada in 1958. He radiates intensity of purpose and integrity. Olsen first did public relations work for the gambling control agencies, then became a member of the Control Board, finally its chairman. The early portions of his complaint set up the legal authority under which gambling is operated in Nevada and explained the reason for the issuance of the "black book" as helping to keep nefarious interests out of Nevada gambling. Then the reading begins to get interesting:

The name of said individual, Sam Giancana, under that or other names, was well and unfavorably known to the public press as well as to enforcement agencies so that reports of his activities had appeared in public print for a long time prior to and including July of 1963 and he had been subject of newspaper, magazine, radio, and television reports throughout the United States. Such reports have designated him as one of the twelve overlords in the organization known as "Cosa Nostra," sometimes known as "Mafia," which was and is an organization or society dedicated to supervision and control of criminal activities in the United States of America. These reports continued and resulted in a statement from the Honorable Robert F. Kennedy, Attorney General of the United States, characterizing information received with respect to the organization and activities of Mr. Sam Giancana and "Cosa Nostra," also known as the "Mafia," as "the biggest intelligence breakthrough yet in combating organized crime and racketeering in the United States."

The complaint stated that Cal Neva Lodge on Lake Tahoe's Crystal Bay had received a black book on June 14, 1960, more than three years earlier, and that Sinatra was the chief stockholder in the place. The allegation was made that between July 17 and July 28, 1963, Giancana lived at Chalet No. 50 at Cal Neva Lodge with the knowledge of the employees of the lodge. It was said that he was served food and drinks, was hauled around in cars owned by the lodge, and even drove one of the cars.

True, he was not registered in the lodge or in Chalet No. 50. This was the residence of Miss Phyllis McGuire, the entertainer, who at that time was appearing in the Cal Neva Lodge's Celebrity Room.

"Sam Giancana is known to have been entertained, harbored, and permitted to remain there and to receive services and courtesies from the licensee, its representatives, employees, agents, and directors," said the complaint. It argued that this "is inimical to the public health, safety, morals, good order, and general welfare of the state of Nevada."

Olsen charged that Sinatra "associated with and spoke to said Sam Giancana . . . and did not request Sam Giancana to leave and made no effort to persuade him to depart."

The complaint continued: "Frank Sinatra, principal stockholder, has for a number of years maintained and continued social association with Sam Giancana well knowing his unsavory and notorious reputation, and has openly stated that he intends to continue such association in defiance . . ."

Not only this, it was charged, but "Frank Sinatra originated a telephone conversation with Edward A. Olsen in which Sinatra used vile, intemperate, obscene, and indecent language in a tone which was menacing in the extreme and constituted a threat against the chairman of the State Gaming Control Board." An appointment for Sinatra to talk to Olsen had been made. Instead, Sinatra called, cursed and threatened.

It was said that "Frank Sinatra maligned and vilified . . . by the use of foul and repulsive language which was venomous in the extreme."

There were two other points in the complaint. Paul (Skinny) d'Amato, who had been described by Sinatra as his personal representative at Cal Neva Lodge, was accused of attempting "to force money upon two audit agents of the State Gaming Control Board who were then engaged in their official duties of verifying the gross win at the gaming tables at Cal Neva Lodge."

Olsen said this "was tantamount to an attempt to bribe them and constituted an unsuitable method of operation of the licensee."

Finally, Olsen alleged that Edward H. King, one of Sinatra's lieutenants from the Palm Springs, California, operations, had avoided a subpoena from the control board. King had been at the board offices in Carson City in response to a subpoena, but had refused to testify except after a release from his principals at Cal Neva. He left, and was to be ready to testify the next day. But instead of returning, he went to Palm Springs. Olsen said he thought King was told by Sinatra to leave the state.

At first Sinatra issued statements promising to fight the case, and his many friends in Nevada lined up behind him. It looked to some of the close observers as if the state's control of the gambling joints was to take a backward slip — Sinatra might be able to survive the test. If he did, the black book and the entire philosophy behind it would be down the drain. It turned out differently. On the night before he was required to file an answer to the complaint signed by Olsen, Sinatra issued this statement:

About six months ago, I decided that my investments and interests were too diversified and that it would be in my best interests to devote most, if not all, of my time to the entertainment industry — not only as an entertainer but as an investor and executive. To achieve this, I instructed my attorney to adopt an orderly plan to liquidate my non-entertainment industry investments, and merge my interests in the entertainment industry with one major company so that I can centralize my activities and investments in the entertainment industry.

As a part of that plan I intended to divest myself completely from any involvement with the gaming industry in Nevada.

I was surprised, hurt, and angered when the Nevada Gaming Board asked the Nevada Gaming Commission to revoke my licenses to participate in the gaming industry in Nevada. My immediate reaction was to contest such recommendation, although it was consistent with my future plans.

However, the Nevada Gaming Control Act specifically provides that a gaming license is a "revocable privilege" which the Nevada Gaming officials may grant or revoke at their discretion and that I had no vested rights to retain this privilege of being associated with the Nevada gaming industry.

Since I have decided that I belong in the entertainment industry and not in the gaming industry, no useful purpose would be served by devoting my time and energies convincing the Nevada Gaming officials that I should be a part of their gaming industry. I have recently become associated with a major company in the entertainment industry and in forming that association I have promised not only to devote my talents as an entertainer to certain of our joint investments, but I have agreed to devote my full time and efforts to that company's activities in the entertainment industry.

Accordingly I have instructed my attorney to notify the Nevada gaming officials that I am withdrawing from the gaming industry in Nevada.

For many years I have tried to aid in the growth of the gaming and tourist industries in Nevada — I would like to think that my efforts have been of some help. Since the casinos offer wonderful opportunities for established and new performers to present their talents to the public, I sincerely hope that these major industries in Nevada will continue to grow and prosper.

Such was Sinatra's position. Before he announced it, his attorneys spent two days questioning the members of the Gaming Control Board about just what evidence they had to prove the charges against Sinatra. They had lots of it.

The singer's 9 percent interest in the Sands has been bought up by the corporation for $391,500. It was assumed that his partners in the Cal Neva Lodge would buy up his $3,000,000 interest there. That casino, in the High Sierra, was closed for the season in September 1963 before the Olsen charges were filed.

Who is Sam Giancana, that associations with him would jeopardize Sinatra's gambling interests?

He is one of the nation's most infamous hoodlums. At the time

Giancana came into the Cal Neva Lodge to see his friend, Miss McGuire, he had just finished a successful joust with the Federal Bureau of Investigation in federal court in Chicago. Giancana had a bellyful of being followed by the feds, and with his lawyers' help, he asked the federal court to enjoin them from harassing him.

The federal court agreed, and gave the agents such instructions as that they should allow at least one foursome to be between them and Giancana's foursome on the golf course, that the numbers of them immediately behind him should be held at a minimum, and that they had to allow him a little more room in other ways, too.

In the McClellan Committee labor racketeering hearings, Giancana was a witness who defended "the syndicate" in these terms: "What's wrong with the syndicate? Two or three of us get together on a deal and everybody says it's a bad thing. Businessmen do it all the time and nobody squawks."

Federal agents conversant with the results of investigations in Las Vegas have insisted that Giancana has an interest in some of the gambling places, but they decline to name which ones. Hank Greenspun, the publisher of the Las Vegas *Sun,* said that on New Year's Eve, 1960, Giancana came to Las Vegas where he established himself and his party in the casino of one of the hotels. One of the men whose name was on the license of the casino had a mild argument with Giancana, said Greenspun, and when Giancana issued an order to "shut up and get out," the licensee, the part owner of record of the place, did indeed shut up and get out.

Greenspun also said that Giancana had been able to come and go from various casinos up and down the Strip with no trouble caused for anyone until the situation arose at Cal Neva Lodge. Greenspun, a friend of Sinatra, thought the singer was being picked as an example to emphasize the intention of the State Gaming Control Board to keep the more notorious underworld figures out of Las Vegas where they are drawn naturally through their acquaintances and lifelong business associations with many of the men who have casino licenses.

But Ed Olsen, the former Associated Press correspondent who heads the Gaming Control Board, said this was absolutely untrue. Olsen refused to discuss the Sinatra case in any detail while it was pending and has refused to discuss it at all since Sinatra threw in the towel. Every indication was that for Olsen this was an all-out fight after the abusive telephone call from Sinatra and the attempt to force money onto the two auditors who were checking the casino bookkeeping. The entertainment of Giancana probably would have won Sinatra a stern reprimand, but not much more. Since Governor Grant Sawyer had made a strong point during his first five years in office of his determination to control the casinos, he could not afford to have Olsen resign for lack of backing in dealing with the famous entertainer. Nor has there been indication that Governor Sawyer was in the least perturbed by Olsen's strong stand.

Within a few weeks after he elected to leave Nevada gambling forever, Frank Sinatra was back in Reno, involved in one of the most difficult times of his life. His son, Frank Sinatra, Jr., then nineteen years old, had been kidnaped. Young Sinatra was singing with a reincarnation of the Tommy Dorsey Band, where his father had started so many years before. The band was appearing in the lounge of Harrah's Tahoe, a casino at Lake Tahoe. The young man was kidnaped while he visited with another member of the musical group as they waited in Sinatra's room for their evening showtime. The time was early December 1963, and Sinatra Sr. flew immediately to Reno from Palm Springs. Heavy snows forced him to remain in Reno, and it was there — in his suite at the Mapes Hotel on the banks of the Truckee River — that he took the telephone calls giving him instructions for gathering up and delivering the ransom money. Sinatra Sr. followed the instructions carefully, and kept the F.B.I. informed. When the $240,000 ransom had been paid in Los Angeles, the young singer was released, fifty-three hours after he was abducted, and within a few days he was back at Lake Tahoe, sounding as much as ever like his father twenty years earlier. The three men who took the boy from his room at Harrah's were captured by the F.B.I. soon after the ransom was paid, and most of the money was recovered. They were arrested when one of them lost his nerve and confessed to a relative who persuaded him to surrender.

During those hours when he was so badly frightened for the welfare of his son, Sinatra had some of his close friends and associates with him in his suite in the Mapes Hotel. Among these was Jack Entratter, the manager of the Sands in Las Vegas, the club in which Sinatra had owned 9 percent. When Sinatra left to make the ransom payoff, it was Entratter he left behind, entrusted with the job of lying to the reporters. He told stories that misled them until young Sinatra had been released.

Although Olsen and the issue of close control of the gamblers won the Sinatra fight, there was a question whether they would win the court contest with Marshal Caifano over the night he was "hustled" on the Strip as the first "get tough" demonstration in the history of Nevada's control of gambling.

Caifano lost. But even before that the state won the skirmishes, and in some of the stages has had some strong statements of the state position in some of the decisions. At one step, Judge Walter L. Pope of the Ninth Circuit Court of Appeals, sitting in San Francisco, said this:

"The problem of excluding hoodlums from gambling places in the State of Nevada can well be regarded by the state authorities as a matter almost of life or death. It would be altogether out of place for any court, and particularly a federal court, to say that the State of Nevada could not reasonably anticipate serious and adverse consequences to its peculiar institution if the criminal element is permitted to participate in gambling in its casinos. When this case is tried, if the legislative facts properly to be considered in passing upon the constitutional validity of the orders here complained of, including some of the matters of which I have here assumed to take judicial notice, are developed for the benefit of the court, I think that the court will have no difficulty in finding that the Gaming Board and the Gaming Commission would apprehend the serious possibility of persons of that character carrying into the establishment loaded dice, marked cards, and other means for cheating or otherwise disrupting the orderly conduct of the licensed gambling. The Board's findings that the mere entry of such a person threatened harm could not be questioned by the court . . .

"In view of the situation of peril which always surrounds gambling in Nevada," Judge Pope wrote, "the trial court may well find that plaintiff's entry upon gambling premises would present emergency comparable to that presented by an animal running at large while suspected of being afflicted with the foot and mouth disease."

It has not been recorded what Johnny Marshal — Marshal Caifano — said when he heard that the judge thought he might have foot and mouth disease.

7

THE MYSTERIOUS RUSSIAN

FAILURE has pretty well hidden from most observers the true importance of the Desert Inn crowd's movement into the stock market. The gamblers lost money, were convicted of crimes and slipped back many notches in their search for respectability. Their foray in the stock market has been looked upon generally as a bitter lesson for them. They were seen as yokels among the city slickers. Nobody got hurt except the gamblers, has been the usual summing up.

This is untrue and absolutely misreads the effect of the gamblers' move into Wall Street. The people who got hurt included those who invested perhaps as much as $8,000,000 in worthless stock in a company where the Desert Inn crowd was on the inside. But more importantly, the move into the stock market showed that the gamblers were ready to go big league, ready to leave the noisy casinos where at best the action is slow compared to the New York Stock Exchange whose transactions can amount to a billion dollar rise or fall in the market in one day.

Now that's action!

The steps taken and the results obtained when the gamblers moved to Wall Street make as clear a warning to the American people as any that could be given of the danger inherent in open, casino gambling on the Las Vegas pattern. We have seen that old-time trained law violators are the backbone of the gambling community there, that their voices are the voices that gather respect because of the belief that beyond them threatens the vague outline of the feared Cosa Nostra. It is a peculiar place where Moe Dalitz can be the white knight who fights the dragon.

This desert and mountain gambling town produced the men who marched on Wall Street, clinking their gambling dollars and rattling their chips. But it could not produce a leader; gamblers understand all the percentages and the grind and the vigorish and the rules and ways to cheat at cards, dice and roulette. They were unacquainted with the ways of the stock markets. However, their gambling tables enticed to them just the sort of man they wanted, just the sort of combination genius, con man and gambler that these money-hungry country bumpkins from Las Vegas would follow.

The name he uses is Alexander Leonard Guterma. It may really be his name. No man can say. Compared to the life Guterma says he lived, Moe Dalitz and Sam Garfield from the alleys of Detroit are the pampered children of royalty. Guterma claims to have been born in Irkutsk in Siberia. Once a federal investigator whose hobby is travel included this out-of-the-way place on his vacation trip. Guterma the enigma challenged him, and won. He could neither prove nor disprove that Guterma had been born there. Nor could he find any evidence to bear on the Guterma story that he was a White Russian, born the son of a general in the Czarist army. The truth is that no document exists anywhere that shows anything about Alexander Guterma before he turned up in the 1920's as a teen-ager in Tsingtao, one of the treaty ports of China before World War II. Those places were filled with White Russian refugees and their children, and Guterma was one of these. There is no record of any of his family, nor of his acquaintances of those days. Just one man exists — a slender, energetic, driving, ambitious, talented, unscrupulous sandy-blond kid using the name Alexander Guterma, or when it suited him, Alexander Sandy. His nickname was "Sandy," in those days and now.

Since this was the man who was the spearpoint of the gamblers' move into Wall Street, we should study him well. Bear in mind that the gamblers were childlike only about Wall Street; they are among the most perceptive judges alive of human nature, for they make the weaknesses of other men their sources of profit. They were able to judge Guterma. This is absolutely true and beyond question. They knew him for what he was — a man with the knowledge and lack of scruple that could take them into the stock market and bring them out with great stacks of money seized in the most blatant frauds against unsophisticated buyers of stock. They calculated that his game would be fixed for them to win — their favorite sort of gamble. The people they were willing to let Guterma cheat in their behalf were the same they fed upon in the gambling joints back home in Las Vegas — the inexperienced and stupid. But this time there was a difference. The state of Nevada might protect their right to fleece these little people in a gambling place, so long as they stayed away from outright cheating and let the percentages do their work for them; in the stock market the Securities and Exchange Commission had rules with teeth in them, and if they violated these rules they might go to jail. The gamblers failed to see it then and even today do not understand in their hearts the reason for the different way the rest of society looks at gambling in a casino as against investing in stocks in the hope they will increase in value on a rising market. To the Las Vegas crowd, gambling is gambling, whether in cards or stocks.

The most serious mistake the gamblers made, however, was in the area of character judgment, their area of strength. Perhaps Guterma worked the same psychological tricks on them that they and their predecessors have worked on the rest of the world for centuries. Perhaps he aroused their greed so that its rising tide blocked their vision and helped him to fool them more and more, until the need to deceive was gone in the shattering crash of all they built together. "Don't try to con me," Guterma said to me once. "I'm a salesman and I know your moves before you make 'em."

The place that they misread Guterma's character was not in his motives. He was their sort of man and they knew it at once. They failed to realize that a man with his background would refuse to suffer any indignities to protect them or anybody else. In a word, Guterma would sing. When he was caught he talked and talked and talked, and is still talking as this is written. He even put the Desert Inn crowd in a position where some of its members, too, have become talkers for the law, a situation that must seem to them almost incredible, not to mention distasteful and repugnant.

How did they come together, these men in Las Vegas and this mysterious figure from the Orient?

Guterma first shows in American records in the 1930's when he arrived in Honolulu as a stowaway aboard an American troop transport from Shanghai. In those days the United States Marines still had China stations and Guterma said he had been advised by a marine sergeant that the only way, the best way for him to get to the United States was as a stowaway. He was vague about the sergeant's name. But he was positive he had only acted on the advice in an immigration matter of a man he respected and took to be an American representative. It was too bad he couldn't remember the sergeant's name.

Guterma was permitted to roam around Honolulu for a few weeks, and even worked for a short time. There was some confusion about what had happened to a radio. Then he turned up as a stowaway on a vessel bound back to the Orient. He explained that he thought it best to get back out of United States territory as a means of preserving his right to immigrate legally at a later date. He wanted to avoid deportation. He was around Shanghai and Hong Kong and with his marvelous ability to concentrate, he soon was able to learn a lot about international finance and the existence of various persons who lent money and performed special tasks that sometimes were forbidden by law.

By the beginning of World War II, Guterma was in the Philippine Islands, where he became associated with a group of Filipino international traders and investors. The beginning of the war stopped their trade. Guterma had to come to grips with the problem of living with the Japanese occupation troops. He survived. After the war, there was much talk of his having had trade relationships with the Japanese, but nothing came of this. They told a story of his being the only survivor of an extensive black-market operation. The story was that all the others were lined up and shot by the Japanese before the Americans returned to Manila.

Whatever happened to Guterma in the terrors of the Japanese occupation of Manila, he survived it to re-enter the international trade field with his Filipino backers after the war ended. He was married in Manila to a socially prominent woman, the daughter of an American who manufactured shoes in Manila. In 1950 he came to the United States. His wife was an American citizen; he could immigrate under rules made for such circumstances.

He built up a considerable sum through an esoteric operation typical of Guterma.

When the Communists came into control of China, this created a shortage of ramie, a long fiber much in demand by the Japanese who had come to depend on acquisition of it in quantity from the Chinese. On funds supplied by his Filipino friends, Guterma opened a ramie-growing operation in Italy, and reaped two good harvests. As a participant in these deals, he had a good-sized nest egg when he came to the United States.

He paused a short time in Los Angeles, and in a matter of days discovered Las Vegas and the gambling tables. He was a great fan, for Guterma is a compulsive gambler. He was a high roller in Las Vegas, a plunger, a casino manager's delight. There is indication that he met Hal Roach the film producer during this period. They were to have dealings later.

But the gambling table could not satisfy Guterma. His drives and urges for excitement drove him in other directions. Again with investments from his Filipino friends, he stood ready to go into a new ramie-growing venture. He picked the area to the West of Palm Beach, Florida, in the swampy ground. He leased great blocks of land, and put down his crops. What came up was morning glories.

Whether it is true or not, this is Guterma's story as told by a close associate — the seeds that were given to him as ramie seeds turned out to be morning glory seeds.

This caused extensive losses, and the Japanese began to get their ramie from other sources, as a lull in the Indian-Pakistani dispute over Kashmir enabled trade resumption in ramie in that area. The Filipinos, alarmed at their losses, backed out, leaving Guterma with the Palm Beach Development Company and whatever crop of morning glories he was then planting. It was one thing about Guterma; all his plantings bloomed early. He called this collection of largely worthless leases and swamp and pieces of paper by a new name — Shawano Development Corporation. He had big plans. This newborn Shawano figured in them.

Guterma had been reading and rereading the regulations of the Securities and Exchange Commission. He was hungry to get into the American stock market. Money was to be had there. He wanted it. In his studies he had come to the conclusion that he could avoid the bugaboo that halted the soaring flight of so many worthless stocks, the requirement for registration with the S.E.C. of statements that showed the value of the holdings of the company in which stock was being offered. There was scarcely a stock issued by Guterma that would stand this treatment; the S.E.C. would have refused to accept the registration, for his stocks generally were worth far less than their spuriously maintained value.

Stated at its simplest, what Guterma had found was a regulation that provided for the issuance of stock to be used in a purchase by one company of the stock of another. This is a fairly common device to effect mergers — company A, with 100,000 shares of stock outstanding, wants to buy company B. The owners of B are willing to accept stock in A as their payment. An agreement is negotiated on the sales price of the B company. Enough new stock in A is issued to make the value needed and the old stock in B is retired. B ceases to exist. A has a larger number of shares outstanding, but has greater value because it has absorbed the physical assets of B. If the managers of the two companies have been equally sagacious a balance is achieved. In certain circumstances, the S.E.C. would allow new stock to be issued without registration when it was to be used for such a purchase.

To Guterma's facile mind this opened up an entirely new vista — lined with greenbacks, country homes, yachts, limousines, private planes, apartments and office suites on Manhattan, and friends among the persons that Guterma admired. Around the corner, at the end of this vista, where Guterma couldn't see it then, was a jail cell.

Using the Shawano company as his base, Guterma began to acquire worthless companies by trading stock for them. Soon he was acquiring the companies or an interest in them himself and then having his Shawano corporation issue stock to buy the companies he held. He organized a set of sales practices that got most of his salesmen into trouble, and began gathering money from investors all across the United States. He had boiler rooms where batteries of slick talkers at telephones called people all over the nation, offering them this or that great growth stock, each described as a marvelous investment opportunity. The suckers took it. The stock cost only $1 a share, most of the time, and this was in an era when the stock market had been defying the predictions of conventional wisdom for years on end.

Meantime, Guterma continued to go back and forth to Las Vegas. He continued to make the rounds of the gambling places there, and as Moe Dalitz was to say in the fall of 1963 as he surveyed the havoc Guterma had wrought for him and his organization: "He was a high roller, not here much, but at other places, and we all knew who he was of course."

Guterma was a plunger of the sort that Las Vegas casino managers dream about. He would fly into the desert gambling center and seem to go mad over the crap tables. Even when he was unable to get to Las Vegas, he insisted that his associates play gin rummy with him in his office, or on his boat, or on the train. The farther along his road to disaster that his career took him, the higher became the stakes for which he played. An associate of those years remembered: "In those days Guterma would just get on an airplane and go to Las Vegas. Once he came back with a pair of dice mounted and said he'd made twenty-one straight passes with them. He had a suitcase full of money."

Of course in other times he lost, and certainly on balance over the years that he went there, Las Vegas took more money from Guterma across the gambling table than he took from it. It always works that way for those who keep going back after winning once.

As he moved through Las Vegas, Guterma met many people. He offended lots of them, and charmed others. He is a strange and unusual man, a man of talent and energy and imagination and ambition. He was just the sort of man to fit into the Las Vegas gambling casino crowd, and they accepted him when the time came. They sought to use him. He was willing to be used. His

Filipino friends had sought to use him, through the advantages
his American wife gave to them and to him, and the advantages
of his facility with language and quick absorption of new ways.
He allowed the Filipino friends to use him and it cost them about
$250,000. They put about $350,000 in the ramie venture around
Palm Beach and in the swamplands; after the bubble burst, they
settled for $75,000. This left Guterma with control of Palm
Ramie Company, Gladeview Development Corporation, American Kenaf Development Corporation, and wrote finis to his association with the Philippines where he had gone to make his fortune. He put these things together into Shawano Development
Corporation, and away he went.

Shawano was set up in 1951 in Palm Beach, Florida, as an agri-
cultural company. One of the Guterma associates was an earnest
young man named Robert Leonhardt, who came from New Orleans and who was to ride with Guterma right into the fire. Leonhardt had social connections which became Guterma's and soon
Shawano had on its board John Colgate of the Colgate-Palmolive
Corporation, executives from Foremost Dairies and Charley E.
Johns, a former Florida governor. Guterma always wanted former officeholders on his boards, but he posed as contemptuous of
them. One of his remarks: "I never give a governor more than
$5000 to sit on one of my boards."

Guterma's idea was to expand Shawano rapidly, and issue new
stock to buy companies that could be merged into Shawano, then
sell the stock to the public and make lots of money. Initial capi-
talization of Shawano was $500,000 but soon the stock issued had
par value of $5,000,000 and was being fed into the Guterma
bucket shops and telephone boiler rooms for sale across the continent by the high pressure telephone crews. Some of these salesmen had extensive criminal records and since have acquired more.
Calls were made from lists of persons of substance. Such lists
continually are being built and sold. The callers from the boiler

room told every plausible lie they could think of to get an order placed for the stock. More stock was fed into the over-the-counter market as it was needed, and purchases were made by agents as the artificial values were maintained. Even some of the smart money from pit bosses and other minor executives in Las Vegas was hooked in this deal.

After a while, Guterma set up McGrath Securities. The Securities and Exchange Commission investigators first became aware of it when this firm took over the space formerly occupied by one of the big boiler rooms in the New York Metropolitan area.

At this point it would be well to understand the position of the S.E.C. men in New York at about this time. The stock market had been climbing dizzily for years, and as it climbed, many parasites had hooked themselves onto it, somewhat the way lamprey eels suck onto Chinook salmon as they flutter in the slow water before leaping up the falls. At the top was the slow and cautious administration put together by Sherman Adams for President Dwight D. Eisenhower. The men at the top during Mr. Eisenhower's years were well meaning; but they were slow to move against a businessman who was making money in some way that was criticized by the permanent government employees who had been hired during the long years that the Democrats ran Washington. It was characteristic of the Eisenhower Administration to be slow to move in enforcement of the business-control legislation it had inherited from the Roosevelt and Truman years. No one wanted to protect the looters such as Lowell Birrell and Guterma; the businessmen's administration just failed to understand them for a long time.

This was the situation in which the S.E.C. investigators found themselves in the 1950's. They were unhappy that the market had more and more and more sleazy operators coming aboard, and that they had trouble from the top in getting clearance to move with prosecutions. The United States government is a ponderous

thing when unsure men sit at the peaks of power. The investigators checked endlessly on Guterma and others like him, wrote
volumes of reports, took the complaints from persons who had
lost important sums, and sent all of this up through the shoals of
"in" boxes toward the top where it came to rest in great stacks on
the desks of those unsure men. Nothing happened. Back at the
bottom, the frustrated investigators and low level lawyers began
to take the government worker's classic way of working out
those frustrations. This is the low-level leak. Soon the financial
reporters and observers began to get information about Guterma
and others. It was delivered to them by dedicated public servants
who had no other place to turn. The stories of the incredible
frauds being worked on the edges of Wall Street began to appear
in important newspapers, and that ponderous instrument, the
United States federal government, began to focus its eyes. For
Guterma and his associates, it was like being struck by lightning,
as we shall see. Things were going wonderfully well; profits
were magnificent. Bigger and bigger deals were just around the
corner. It would all go on forever, just as did so many good
things.

Suddenly, the lights went out.

Today, those same investigators who talked so freely and so
anxiously five or ten years ago are as silent as the Sphinx. They
also have her same inscrutable smile. Things went their way.
The men they wanted to see caught were indicted and tried and
punished. The tangled snarl still unravels. They refuse to talk
now for fear something they might say would get the train off
the track.

None of these things had happened at the time when Guterma
was rolling merrily along with Shawano. He bought into many
sorts of firms with it, and one of these was a small hotel in Bay
Harbor Islands, Florida, called the Isle d'Capri. This small community is built on two islands connected by a causeway to Surfside

and Bal Harbour, on the strand north of Miami Beach, and by a bridge to a point north of Miami on the mainland. The Isle d'Capri was a small hotel, and as this is written it has been converted into a health club under the title Harbor Island Spa.

This insignificant little hotel was a pawn in the great games that Guterma played. It has significance in our examination of the investment manipulations of the Las Vegas gamblers beyond anything else in the Shawano portfolios. The Isle d'Capri, worth no more than $50,000, was the pawn shoved forward by Guterma in a business move which almost gave him an unobstructed crack at the Queen of the Strip, Wilbur Clark's Desert Inn, worth perhaps $4,500,000 in those years. But the gamblers pulled back in time — just barely in time — for reasons that even now are unclear. They were frightened off the deal that Guterma was touting, but there are conflicting stories about what frightened them away. The events that brought Guterma and the Desert Inn crowd together were as follows:

We have seen the way the remnants of the Cleveland bootlegging and gambling organization came into Las Vegas in 1949 to help Wilbur Clark complete the financing of the Desert Inn. The organization had changed a little in the years since. Wilbur Clark, the dreamer of the gamblers' Great American dream, had been shoved into right field. Moe Dalitz was older. Morris Kleinman was more accustomed to living in Florida. Allard Roen had become the crown prince, the executive vice president and general manager of all the Desert Inn, subject of course to the whims of Dalitz and Kleinman and some of the others.

The Desert Inn's top command also had buddies on the outside. One of these, and a man of great importance in the events related here, was Samuel S. Garfield. Another was a friend of Garfield's, Irving Pasternak. An associate of Guterma from those years remembered that Pasternak and Guterma had met over the crap tables in Las Vegas.

"Both of them big operators," said this man, who remembered neither of his former colleagues with much pleasure. "They get there shooting craps and begin to talk about what big shots they are. Pretty soon they know a lot about each other. Pretty soon they're acquainted."

A different explanation came from an attorney who represented Pasternak and others during legal troubles that grew out of their association with Guterma. It had become important to him, as it has to others who have studied the things that these men did together, to understand how they met. He had some supporting documentation for his story, although the documentation was susceptible to other interpretations than the one given it by these persons who were trying to put the most innocent possible face on their associations with Guterma. That explanation follows:

In April 26, 1955, a story appeared in the financial pages of the Denver *Post* quoting a Denver promoter, Albert Hayutin of Fidelity Securities Company, as saying he was going to make a public offering of a stock called Garnak Drilling Corporation. This was a successful oil company. It controlled leases, operated producing wells and a pipeline. Garnak was owned jointly by Samuel S. Garfield and Irving Pasternak, and drew its name from syllables in their names.

When the end came for Guterma, everybody wanted his files — the federal officers, his former associates, stockholders, everybody. There must have been a small fortune made just by copying documents for those who wanted full sets. The telegrams he sent were of great interest, and among these Garfield's and Pasternak's lawyers found a copy of a wire sent by Guterma on April 28, 1955, to Albert Hayutin in Denver asking that Guterma be allowed to be the underwriter in the Garnak stock issue. Guterma, you see, had McGrath Securities organized for just that purpose — to underwrite stocks and shove them out and make all the money possible out of every issue.

The answer to this telegram drew Guterma to Denver to meet Pasternak and make a proposal. Guterma suggested that instead of going into the deal the way they had at first planned, Garfield and Pasternak should trade their company for stock in Shawano which had an established market and for which a distribution system existed. It is doubtful if Guterma explained fully to Pasternak just what kept this market up (the Guterma frantic round of buying and selling and manipulating). Guterma was unaware that he probably need not explain: Garfield and Pasternak had been involved in a speculative stock deal before in Canada. They had done well in a sale of stock in something called Sapphire Oil Company, while not many others who invested ever saw their money again.

Garfield was in the Mayo Clinic in Rochester, Minnesota, at the time these developments with Guterma unfolded so rapidly. Pasternak went there to outline them to his old friend, and to get Garfield's acquiesence in riding along with the Guterma plan. In short, Guterma got their company for $6,000,000 worth of Shawano stock which he then proceeded to unload on the public at about $1 a share, making great sums for them, for himself, his other associates, and his stock salesmen. The people who lost were those who bought the stock.

Of course, Garfield and Pasternak were delighted with the money. On their visits to Las Vegas, they discussed Guterma with their friends at the Desert Inn, and certainly Guterma learned from them and from others that the Desert Inn management group was close to Garfield and Pasternak. For minds such as those we are examining here, the next step was obvious. The Desert Inn crowd wanted to use Guterma to make money; Guterma wanted to use the Desert Inn crowd to make money. The problem for each side of this mutual admiration society could be stated simply: How do I keep from being stolen blind while I get what he's got?

Guterma's visits to the Desert Inn became more and more frequent. By this time he was a really large operator, controlling various corporations and becoming a nationally known figure. He even had a company plane which he rode back and forth to Las Vegas. This came with the purchase of the F. L. Jacobs Company on March 2, 1956. Jacobs was an old time automotive parts manufacturing company which had fallen on evil days and came into Guterma's hands. Its importance will be explained later. It may have been his plane, or the temper of the times, or just overpowering greed, but, for whatever reason, the Desert Inn leaders took a fateful step during the late winter and early spring of 1956. They decided to move ahead a few steps on the plan to sell Desert Inn stock to the public. They were not to sell stock in the casino, the golden goose. Certainly not! But the hotel properties represented a lot of tied-up capital, a lot of money that would be irrevocably lost if the state of Nevada ever abandoned its experiment in legalized gambling, or ever did any serious tampering with the law. It would be far better to get the money out, and let others bear the risk. Besides, this fellow Guterma was telling them all that he could get a lot more for their hotel than they could get by selling it themselves.

So a company called United Hotels, Inc., was formed in Delaware on April 5, 1956. When United Hotels was formed, it was created for the purpose of putting Guterma and the Desert Inn crowd into the same business firm. Guterma was to sell the stock created by the transaction. The Desert Inn group was to reap great profits. The public was to be bilked again. This deal was just as fast and slippery from the beginning as any of the other Guterma promotions, and the wise people who built the Desert Inn had to realize this.

Creation of United Hotels, Inc., was the first step. On April 20, 1956, the second step was taken. Shawano Corporation, the Guterma operation, put its Isle d'Capri hotel in Bay Harbor Islands,

Florida, into United Hotels in exchange for 257,000 shares of 10-cent par value common stock of the 5,000,000 shares authorized. The Desert Inn Operating Company in a similar action, got 1,402,-143 shares of preferred at $3 par and 3,285,051¾ shares of common. The division of stock was pro rata based on an appraisal of the assets being put into the new corporation by each of the companies. Thus Guterma's hotel had a value of $25,700 while the Desert Inn's physical plant was valued at $4,534,934.17½. This meant, certainly, that Guterma's little hotel property was gobbled up by the vastly larger holdings represented by the Desert Inn group.

"They just elected the directors and ran things and that was all there was to it," Guterma told me in discussing this deal.

He was satisfied with this arrangement, for it appeared he was about to get all the gravy that would be involved in selling this stock. Just think how a 10-cent par value common stock in the glamorous Desert Inn could be pumped up! The possibilities of promotion of stock in Nevada gambling would be breathtaking. Guterma had the organization already in existence to do this. However, something happened. There are two main stories of what happened, and while they seem to conflict on the surface, both could be true.

Jack Donnelley, the lawyer of impeccable reputation who then was attorney for the Desert Inn, said that he went to the S.E.C. to make inquiries about the plan to sell the stock publicly and found that there were "real problems," to use his phrase. Donnelley would not explain what he meant by the phrase, but whatever it was he discovered in his informal and off-the-record conference with the S.E.C. representatives led him to return to Las Vegas and advise his clients to stay the hell away from Sandy Guterma's stock promotion. However, as we shall see, they were too far in by that point to be able to stay out completely.

The other story to explain the disenchantment of the Desert

Inn group that led them away from selling the stock to the public was this:

The S.E.C. was tipped off to ask questions and when the questions were asked the complicated transaction was placed in jeopardy and the gamblers wanted out before the entire thing fell in around their ears. The scheme reportedly had envisioned one of the group objecting every step of the way to the plan, and then being in a position to sell his stock without registration as soon as he got it. This would be because his stock could not be considered control stock since it had been outvoted along the line. Special rules govern the selling of control stock and the S.E.C. would enforce them, as Guterma and the others were to discover later. But the objector's stock would not be covered by these rules. The theory was that he could sell without registering the stock with the S.E.C.

It was planned that others from time to time would join him and be outvoted, and the theory was that enough of these votes would be taken to have the effect of freeing other blocks of stock for sale without registration. Eventually, it was explained, the gamblers would have sold 80 percent of their stock, but would still be able to control the property with the remaining 20 percent, and besides they would have long leases for their operating companies before they took these actions. They expected to get about $9,000,000, it was said.

It is possible that some elements of this grandiose story are true, and certainly the statements of Jack Donnelley are beyond question. He did go to the S.E.C. and on his advice the plan to "go public" was abandoned. But he might have gone because the S.E.C. asked the gamblers what they were up to with Guterma. Even though they were thwarted here in their plan to save some taxes by getting rid of the heavy investment in the Desert Inn, the gamblers eventually managed to work their will, as we shall see. They were disappointed at the turn the plan took to go public. Moe Dalitz said to the author seven years later: "That was at the time when there was a cartoon with a guy telling his lawyer 'Either I got to go broke or go public.'"

In those times most of the Desert Inn organization was heavily involved with Guterma. He sold great blocks of his Shawano stock to the lower level executives — the gambling pit bosses, the directors, the manager. There was an understanding around the Desert Inn then that some sort of guarantee against loss stood behind the Guterma-backed stocks. The greatest pressure on the Las Vegas crowd to buy came when the stock started to fall at one time and Guterma was without liquid resources to keep it up and climbing. Great blocks of purchases came in. One was for $250,000 worth in one bunch, and this order was placed by Thomas Jefferson McGinty, a longtime member of the Cleveland group and a stockholder in the Desert Inn.

Robert C. Leonhardt, the New Orleans man who was Guterma's partner in McGrath Securities, said he took the order himself. "You don't forget an order like that," said Leonhardt.

One of the wonderments about all this story has been an explanation of why Guterma managed to remain healthy after his stock caved in. There are many reasons. One of the most obvious is that it would have made no money to hurt him. Another is that perhaps if he was still around he could promote something else that would make everybody rich again. This may explain some otherwise inexplicable actions in connection with the United Dye and Chemical Corporation which we shall explore in the next chapter. The question there is this: Why did Guterma allow Garfield, Pasternak and Allard Roen to move in with him without putting in any money?

In addition to costing them all great chunks of money in losses on his worthless Shawano Corporation stock, Guterma also cost the Desert Inn crowd about $500,000 directly through what he did with the 257,000 shares of stock in United Hotels that his

Shawano Corporation got in return for the little hotel, the Isle d'Capri. He distributed the stock to the Shawano shareholders, in spite of anything the Desert Inn crowd could do or say. One morning they woke up with 18,000 shareholders in their hotel and golf course, where there had been thirteen.

Jack Donnelley told the story one October afternoon as we sat in his office in what once had been the boardroom at the Desert Inn. The office had big windows overlooking the pool and inner court that is behind the casino from the stretch of highway that has become known as the Strip. Outside, a bright sun beat down on the pool, and there were scattered sunbathers. Beyond them, the greenery of the golf course could be seen between the low roofs of the expensive homes that line the fairways. Donnelley was the boss of all this, and admitted that he enjoyed it.

"I was responsible for having it formed," he said of United Hotels, Inc. He had two New York lawyers draw up the papers of incorporation and file them at Dover, Delaware, and managed the complicated transfers of stock from the Wilbur Clark Desert Inn Company into United Hotels, Inc., to protect his clients' position. Not long after that, Donnelley had his off-the-record meeting with the S.E.C. and found the "real problems" and advised his clients to steer clear of any public offering of the United Hotels, Inc., stock.

Then came the problem with Guterma. The stock promoter had no reason to love the Desert Inn crowd, and the entire thrust of his relationship with them had been directed toward a mutually profitable business venture. Everybody was to get rich, and Guterma had gone to a lot of trouble. He intended to get something out of it.

"I was a big boy," Guterma said to me years after these events as the two of us sat waiting for the traffic light to change in front of the Americana Hotel in Bal Harbour, Florida. "So were they."

Donnelley was able to understand why Guterma took the action he did. Said Donnelley in explanation: "Guterma was always trying to show progress to his stockholders, so he distributed the part of United Hotels stock that went to Shawano as a stock dividend."

But however charitable might be Donnelley's understanding, his recollection of the events was not pleasant. He said that this action "made a headache for us. It was costly. We had to maintain a registrar and transfer agent and we had to hold stockholders meetings." This was because the Shawano stock was traded in over-the-counter sales, and so was United Hotels stock when it became publicly owned through Guterma's action. Donnelley could see these things coming when the Desert Inn crowd learned what Guterma intended to do, and went to Guterma to plead that he not make the public distribution.

"We were horrified," Donnelley remembered in our interview. "I personally asked him not to do it, but he said it was the best thing for him to do and went ahead with it."

Perhaps there was a bit of petulance in Guterma's action, since the 257,000 shares of United Hotels really made no difference in his financial leapfrogging. He had Garfield and Pasternak with him in Shawano in a big way, and also had Allard Roen, the operating boss of the Desert Inn, involved in his shenanigans. The Desert Inn money was tied to Guterma. But Guterma had made big plans for getting the United Hotels stock listed on the American Stock Exchange. If he could do this, and could push out the famous Desert Inn as a stock issue to be fed to the yammering crowd then storming the doors of the stock market, Guterma would be on his way to one of the great killings in the American history of stock manipulation. At least he thought so. Remember that in those days there actually were thoughtful suggestions that the supply of stocks on the market was insufficient to meet the demand, that the temper of the times required new supplies of stock — ergo, Guterma would be a public benefactor if he could get the Las Vegas gamblers to allow the public to buy stock in their hotel properties. The Desert Inn leadership was the King's Row of the Strip. If Moe Dalitz and Morrie Kleinman permitted Guterma to sell their hotel to the public, the others would line up at Guterma's door and beg him to make them richer, too. In a sense, Guterma was extremely lucky that it was the Desert Inn group that he was dealing with, just as he is lucky that the good sense of Jack Donnelley and the highly suspicious nature of Moe Dalitz kept them from going on with the deal. Had they moved forward with it, following the Guterma Jolly Roger to the hidden gold just over the horizon, they might have lost control of the Desert Inn and been unable to wriggle through the tax loophole that we will examine.

Had these things occurred and had Guterma caused a greater inconvenience for the Desert Inn organization, the animosity its members now express toward him might have held less gentlemanly disdain and more violence. Now Moe Dalitz can say, as he said to the author, "I was afraid of him. He talked too fast. The only reason I gave that bastard any consideration is that Sam Garfield went to grade school with me and brought him to me." What Dalitz's attitude would have been had Guterma caused him to lose control of the Desert Inn can best be described as unspeakable.

There are some other places on the Strip whose ownership would simply have had Guterma murdered if he had done to them what he did to the Desert Inn ownership.

In the United Hotels stock distribution Guterma had to give some of the Shawano holders fractional shares, since there were far more Shawano shares than the 257,000 shares of United Hotels that he had available. Moe Dalitz and Morrie Kleinman found that they had partners in the Desert Inn who had not enough financial stake to turn a dime slot machine once. It is a fascinating effort in mental gymnastics to reconstruct the attitudes of these old-time Cleveland racketeers in such circumstances. They had fought their way up to the top in the gambling business. They were legitimate. The years of jumping ahead of the law were behind them. They had built a castle in the desert. Everything was coming up natural sevens and elevens. Suddenly they had partners who knew nothing, owned almost nothing, but had interests protected by great volumes of lawbooks. One year three of these minority holders attended the stockholders' meeting at the Desert Inn.

It must have been discouraging. But they met the problem.

They bought up the stock, where they could, and held stockholders meetings every year just as the law said they should. They kept careful records of the lists of owners of the 10-cent par value United Hotels stock, and all-in-all spent about $250,000 on such foolishness, all attributable to Guterma's maneuverings. Being out of pocket for the costs was bad enough; but far worse was the realization that all sorts of attractive tax maneuvers were floating around. These loopholes were in danger always of being plugged up — and they could not move to take advantage of them because of the problems presented in getting agreement from all of the minority stockholders. Finally, Donnelley worked out a deal for them. Since United Hotels was a Delaware corporation, they could get rid of it in a simple maneuver. They could create another Delaware corporation that would buy up all the stock at a price set in an independent appraisal. So, under Donnelley's direction, the Desert Inn group created United Resort Hotels, Inc., with papers filed at Dover, Delaware. Then they had an appraisal made of the value of the 10-cent par value shares in United Hotels.

The value then was $1 a share.

This meant that they had to put up $257,000 on deposit to buy up the shares. They did it. It must have hurt. In effect, the little Isle d'Capri hotel that Guterma had thrown into the pot cost them a quarter of a million dollars. There were other irritations, too. They circulated the list of stockholders asking that the United Hotels stock be surrendered for payment. Of course most of the people who held it also held others of the Guterma cats and dogs — Shawano, Jacobs, Scranton Corporation, and so forth. Since many of these were unsophisticated anyway or they never would have bought the Guterma stuff, and because their hearts were full of the hope that springs eternally, they sent these along with the expectation that they were being redeemed, too. At the Desert Inn, the United Hotels stock was paid for but the other Guterma stock was bundled up and returned immediately, along with a curt note that disclaimed all responsibility for it.

When all of the stock had been acquired, United Hotels, Inc., disappeared through merger into United Resort Hotels. This was done on November 27, 1959, and when it was finished, the Cleveland group and Wilbur Clark and his friends again had sole ownership of the Desert Inn. Now they were ready to take advantage of another tax gimmick. What they were doing was to move ownership of their physical plant out of a corporation into a partnership, the same arrangement as in the case of the Sunrise Hospital. The partnership would buy the physical plant and lease it back to the Desert Inn Operating Company.

It should be understood that what was being bought and sold and shifted around in all of these transactions was the physical plant of the Desert Inn — not the casino operating company. The casino operating company is the D.I. Operating Company, and it is this which the state licenses through the State Gaming Commission and the State Gaming Control Board. These fast maneuvers are impossible to work out with the casino operating company stocks, for each owner must go through a close examination by the state authorities, and must pay for a careful investigation of his background carried out by agents of the state. These requirements make it manifestly impossible to wheel and deal with the casino license. Further, this is the main reason why the Las Vegas Strip hotels usually are held under one corporate or partnership structure while the casino licenses are held under another.

Lawrence A. Wien, a New York lawyer who has specialized in such tax-saving ownership switches, was the man who led the Desert Inn crowd through this maneuver. Wien said in the prospectus filed with the S.E.C. in September 1959 that he had put together real estate investment deals that involved the Hotel Plaza, the Graybar Building, the Hotel Taft, the Equitable Building, the Lincoln Building, the Garment Center Capitol Buildings, the Fisk Building, and the Broad-Exchange Building, all in New York. He also had arranged similar deals with the Warwick Hotel in Philadelphia, the Leader Building in Cleveland, the Howard Johnson's Motor Lodge in Springfield, Virginia, the Dyckman Hotel in Minneapolis, and the Roosevelt and Consolidated Buildings in Los Angeles. Since then he also has helped set up a sale of the Empire State Building.

The Desert Inn crowd this time had picked an operator with a proven track record — not another Guterma who talked big and gambled for high stakes. The Las Vegas casino owners want the gambling left to their customers; they dislike involving their casinos in the game. Wien's leadership for the Desert Inn ownership was faultless, too. He sold their property for them for $9,875,000 and they still have it, and are getting good incomes from it.

The purchase price was to be paid this way: $2,875,000 in cash and the $7,000,000 balance in two mortgages. The first mortgage of $2,000,000 was to be liquidated within three years. The remaining mortgage of $5,000,000 was to be paid off in twenty years and really represented payment in 1959 as capital gains what would otherwise have been taxable income to the corporation over this period. The income was to be from a lease of the property to the D.I. Operating Company for twenty years, renewable first for twenty-one years, and again for twenty-two years. Who was the D.I. Operating Company? Why, it was the same people who owned the hotel in the first place. They were selling it to the partnership made up of Wien and his associate Henry W. Klein, and then leasing it back. For the first three years, the D.I. Operating Company would pay a rental of $1,100,-000. Thereafter, the rental would be $1,040,000.

Wien and his law partner were only the recipients of title. The prospectus makes clear that they are selling "participating interests" in their holdings at $25,000 per "interest" for a total of $3,025,000. Who bought those? In part at least the same people who owned the place originally, before all of this transaction came about — Moe Dalitz, Morris Kleinman, Allard Roen, and the others. Just what was it they owned, in addition to a gambling house? The prospectus describes it:

> The Desert Inn offers luxurious guest accommodations and a wide variety of recreational facilities. The Desert Inn property includes the 18-hole golf course which is the site of the annual Tournament of Champions, and is the only golf course owned by a Las Vegas hotel; a Country Club which was erected within the past few years; a 90' by 40' swimming pool, a 3600 square foot casino; the Painted Desert Room, a dinner and supper club accommodating over 400 persons where outstanding stage shows are presented daily; various restauner and supper club accommodating over 400 persons where ment attractions.

There was more. The prospectus described the guest facilities as 329 rooms, which have been expanded since by a high-rise hotel built with one of those Teamster pension fund loans. These are a phenomenon that we will examine in a later chapter. All of this was built in the years since the Cleveland crowd had joined

Wilbur Clark, the small-time gambler with the big-time dream. The prospectus estimated that about $4,000,000 had been put into improvements since 1951. It also made clear that Nevada might close down gambling, but belittled this possibility by pointing out that the state took 29 percent of its general fund revenues from gambling in 1958–59. Also, the following sentences made plain the fact that the Dalitz forces would continue to control the Desert Inn:

> Various corporations controlled by the principal owners of the seller have operated the Desert Inn since its opening in 1950. Such corporations have at all times been duly licensed under the Nevada Gaming Control Act, and a licensee controlled by this group will conduct such operations after Associates acquires title.

In other words, little or nothing was changed except the amount of money the federal government would get in taxes. The prospectus showed through the analysis by accountants that after the first three years, each "participating interest," which had cost $25,000 to begin with, would get an annual income payment of $5000. By binding these to depreciation schedules, even this $5000 payment was only partially subject to federal personal income taxes. In 1966, for example, only 53.9 percent of it would be subject to tax, the remainder being considered to be returned capital. Meantime, the initial gathering up of $3,025,000 from sale of 125 participating interests had provided the money for the $2,875,000 down payment and costs of the transaction. The first three years' rentals have retired the initial $2,000,000 mortgage and have been whittling away on the $5,000,000 mortgage that will be repaid in full in the first twenty years. The holders of the "participating interest" blocks are now reaping $5,000 a year for each block they hold.

All of this is possible, of course, only because the federal government does not collect its 52 percent corporation tax bite on the income of the Desert Inn Associates, a partnership, and because the increased depreciation based on the new high value added further tax shelter. Further, the money the owners get from the sale of the property to their partnership is treated as capital gains, so that again the federal treasury takes a beating. What Wien put together for the Desert Inn gamblers was a far, far better deal for them than the most flowery proposals that Guterma could offer. They not only have eaten their cake; they still have it, and each year the frosting gets sweeter.

There were certain minor disadvantages to the creation of the partnership, and one of these was that the Desert Inn had to give an accounting of its income and expenditures over five years to justify some of the statements made to the S.E.C. in the prospectus. These are fascinating. Insofar as the author is aware, they constitute the most recent complete public disclosures of the full operating experience of any of the Nevada gambling casinos.

The gamblers are secretive by nature, naturally conspiratorial, and it sets badly with them to surrender any information about their operations beyond what they want to give up. They are compelled by law on occasion to give up some bits of data such as the complete disclosure for the years 1954 through 1958 printed here. But they dislike doing it.

By 1961, the collection of former bootleggers and gambling operators at the Desert Inn had survived their entanglement with Alexander L. Guterma, they believed. Business was booming. Income was running high. Their properties at the Desert Inn had been placed in the most favorable possible tax position, and the money was pouring in. Far behind them were the days when Guterma had brought in the proposition that they might sell their stock on the American Stock Exchange, that he could get it

WILBUR CLARK'S DESERT INN, LAS VEGAS, NEVADA, SUMMARY OF OPERATIONS

	1954	1955	1956	1957	1958
GROSS OPERATING REVENUE					
Casino	$5,933,340.25	$6,267,383.20	$7,006,724.95	$7,630,628.90	$8,038,819.65
Rooms department	1,304,443.54	1,321,544.90	1,339,640.10	1,359,281.24	1,592,258.33
Food & beverage	2,495,745.44	2,438,628.35	2,518,634.28	2,752,266.89	3,081,205.53
Other departments	329,607.03	338,753.84	338,513.14	389,971.11	472,627.61
Other income	6,922.69	21,424.50	41,334.89	41,888.52	49,201.02
Store rental	5,841.77	4,011.74	5,060.72	6,315.03	8,151.85
Total revenue	$10,075,900.72	$10,391,746.53	$11,249,908.08	$12,180,351.69	$13,242,263.99
OPERATING COSTS AND EXPENSES					
Departmental costs	$5,097,360.37	$5,732,437.95	$6,045,665.18	$6,652,620.52	$7,245,262.93
Music, entertainment	1,416,851.76	1,675,055.20	1,781,694.53	1,868,035.44	2,059,068.51
Administration	410,386.04	431,932.67	391,667.57	351,463.08	404,756.90
Advertising & promotion	325,751.93	402,341.08	379,466.03	456,612.71	672,457.54
Heat, light, power	109,547.58	111,106.22	118,261.82	112,966.53	133,029.16
Maintenance	549,436.94	900,706.05	652,059.84	718,327.09	944,761.90
Property taxes & insurance	71,978.71	47,424.24	74,023.36	82,608.13	91,759.73
Total expenses	$7,981,313.33	$9,300,103.41	$9,442,838.33	$10,242,633.50	$11,551,096.67
NET OPERATING REVENUE BEFORE RENT, INTEREST, DEPRECIATION, AMORTIZATION AND TAXES ON NET INCOME	$2,094,587.39	$1,091,643.12	$1,807,069.75	$1,937,718.19	$1,691,167.32

This table is based on the prospectus filed with the Securities and Exchange Commission at the time of offering participations in partnership interests in Desert Inn Associates. The date of the prospectus was September 9, 1959. The audit was made by Zeman, Tuller, Boyer & Goldberg, certified public accountants. Eli Boyer, of that firm, is a longtime business associate of various of the figures in the Desert Inn group.

listed, if only they would go along with him. In those times Guterma had claimed a close friendship with Edward T. McCormick, the president of the American Stock Exchange. Robert C. Leonhardt, who had been Guterma's partner in McGrath Securities, remembered in a talk we had that Guterma told him that McCormick had agreed tentatively to the proposition that the United Hotels stock would be listed on the American Stock Exchange. Leonhardt, looking out of his apartment window into the play of the sunlight on the trees in Central Park, remembered that Guterma related that McCormick had said he would have the stock listed and would designate the Gerard Re firm as the specialists in it. Leonhardt turned away from the window and said: "Guterma said he told McCormick 'My God, don't do that. They'll steal 'em blind.' "

The Re firm was among the fixtures in Wall Street which came tumbling down in the intensive investigation that the Securities and Exchange Commission staff eventually was allowed to make. Its leaders were convicted of stock and securities law violations. They were friendly with Guterma. McCormick also fell on evil days. He had been a member of the S.E.C., and left it to become the president of the American Stock Exchange. Among the Wall Street operators with whom he became friendly was Alexander L. Guterma. At that time Guterma owned a yacht, had great resources for entertainment, and made lavish use of these in his relationships with McCormick. In one instance, they went together on the Guterma yacht from Florida to Havana. This was in 1955, during the period when the Batista regime was enticing American visitors and dollars into the island by promoting gambling in the big hotels in Havana. In those days, the Nevada gamblers were heavily involved in Havana casinos, although later they were forced to withdraw by an order of the Nevada Gaming Control Board that told them they could have casino interests only in Nevada.

On this trip, the Guterma-McCormick party ended the night at the Havana Riviera where McCormick, who had been drinking during the evening, began to fight the dice. His losses mounted, and Guterma was in a quandary. He felt he needed to maintain his friendship with McCormick and also that he must protect him here since the place was controlled by Meyer Lansky, the major underworld figure who would insist that McCormick's losses be paid off. The upshot of it was that Guterma paid off $5000 in losses directly and took some stock from McCormick for another $3500 which made up the $8500 that McCormick lost that night. McCormick's debts were settled, but he was a ruined man from that moment. Guterma, of course, let it be known that he had made the settlement in McCormick's behalf, and eventually — in December, 1961 — the American Exchange president was asked about it in an investigation. Guterma was in jail by that time, and the admission by McCormick brought about his resignation as president of the American Exchange. It was widely known that Guterma had been attempting to have his Shawano stock listed on the American Exchange. The criticism was vicious against McCormick for, first, his close association with Guterma, and, second, for having allowed the promoter to pay off his gambling debts.

However, Shawano was never listed on the American Exchange.

By the time that these disclosures came about, Guterma was all through, his bailing-wire and fast-promise financial empire had stopped teetering and had fallen to bury him. His former Desert Inn associates had left him and hoped they would never hear from him again. They had even tried a little to contribute to his burial a bit deeper. Their deal with the tax loophole and the partnership arrangement was building up, and they were almost ready to clear up the last of the United Hotels stock.

Things were beautiful, almost never better.

All the Desert Inn crowd was happy, carefree and gay. The money was rolling in. They had acquired control of the Stardust Casino across the street and it was turning out to be one of the biggest money makers on the Strip, particularly since they began to feature a show made up of almost naked women. The Guterma dealings were all long ago and far away, although there was an undercurrent of criticism toward Allard Roen from some of the employees of the Desert Inn and Stardust who had lost heavily in their investments in Shawano stock. They felt that Roen, as an insider, should have told them it was worthless so they could sell out before the crash.

Hardly anyone gave a thought to the profits made by the Roen-Garfield-Pasternak group in a firm called United Dye and Chemical Corporation. Then Guterma began to talk and that was all they thought about. It turned out to be the most expensive money ever brought into the Desert Inn.

8

CATASTROPHE AT UNITED DYE

IT WAS in 1955 — if we believe the stories of the only two witnesses — that Alexander Guterma stumbled across the carcass of a company that had been looted by Lowell Birrell, a New York lawyer who became a member eventually of the colony of American stock manipulators who went to live in Brazil. Guterma places the time in 1955, as does Virgil D. Dardi. The company was the United Dye and Chemical Corporation, a firm registered on the New York Stock Exchange. Dardi was allowed to stand guard over the bones left by Birrell, who in 1957 fled from the United States when his financial operations were exposed in the Swan-Finch scandal. (Birrell returned in 1964 to surrender for trial.) Dardi had been in United Dye and Chemical for about two years, since October 1953, at the time that Guterma came into Dardi's office. The story told by both Dardi and Guterma is that they had never met before, that they had no business ties, that the meeting which meant so much to so many came about just because Guterma needed office space. A rental agent working for Dardi brought Guterma to see a vacant office suite, and the stock market manipulators began their conversation because the desk used by Dardi was exactly like one that had been made especially for Guterma.

Or so the two men have said. There is a vigorously argued opinion among investigators who have studied the United Dye case. They hold that some other and more devious connection was established previously between the two men. After all, empires teetered, empires fell, great scandals erupted — all traceable to many things, but traceable most to the chance meeting of Guterma and Dardi on that winter day in late 1955. Credence boggles at the idea of a rental agent being the catalyst of these catastrophes.

Guterma was looking for office space after his bust-up with Robert C. Leonhardt, the New Orleans neophyte who followed Guterma into Wall Street. Together they had owned McGrath Securities, a company which Guterma expected would help him expand his slice of the profits accruing from the stock he was floating on the rising tides of public demand. He planned to use McGrath Securities to market the stock in the Las Vegas casino hotels which he hoped would come his way in his United Hotels, Inc., manipulation. However, this hope was unrealized, and the relationships between Leonhardt and Guterma deteriorated to the point where Leonhardt wanted Guterma out of McGrath Securities. Guterma left. There is irony in this. The company had been named from the maiden name of his wife, a fact that Mrs. Guterma is said to have resented.

On the day that he went looking at new office space, Guterma was not at loose ends. He had lots of irons in various fires. But he always had an eye out for a good deal. He fell into conversation with Dardi, rented the office, and within a few months had bought up the remains of United Dye and Chemical Corporation — the remains that had been stripped first by Birrell, the master manipulator, and then picked over by Dardi, who followed Birrell. Guterma has claimed since that he had no knowledge of what he was getting. He has asserted that Dardi deceived him. Birrell was in Brazil by the time United Dye blew sky-high. But whatever happened — and it goes down hard to think that a man of Guterma's background and fast footwork around the stock market could be deceived by such a simple maneuver — he ended by buying up 38,500 control shares in United Dye from Dardi, paying $10 a share.

Those control shares sent lots of people to jail.

After a few maneuvers, he distributed them this way: he kept 18,000; Irving Pasternak, the partner of Sam Garfield and the friend of the Desert Inn crowd, took 12,000 shares; Dardi got 6500 shares; Robert Leonhardt got 1000, as did Robert J. Eveleigh, a man whose association with Guterma went back to the years when both worked for the Bunge Corporation, a British firm in the jute trade in the Philippines before World War II. Eveleigh was Guterma's oldest associate. He literally had followed the dynamic financier to the ends of the earth. Eventually, he followed Guterma into jail. Guterma told me one night that he had invited Pasternak to participate in the control share ownership of United Dye.

We have discussed Guterma at length in these pages, and our examination of him will continue throughout this chapter. The atmosphere of an interview we had, the disclosures of Guterma's attitudes that came out of it, the pressures under which he now lives — all of these matters make it worthwhile to tell the story of the interview in detail.

Since his fall from his throne in late 1959, Guterma has shunned reporters. He was careful with them before, and there are few records of interviews in the files in the morgues of New York papers. Even pictures of him were hard to get by the time he was arrested. But he agreed to the interview in the fall of 1963 as a favor to a friend who had helped him during his troubled times. He agreed to it reluctantly and with the intention of saying very little. Here was the way it developed:

He was to make himself available at 4:30 on an afternoon in late September. He would be at his home in Miami Shores, north of Miami on the mainland. When the 4:30 call was made, he was not there. Nor was he there at 5. At 5:15 he was home, and began to try to move away from the interview commitment. He had to go to New York. We would go together. Could we talk before the plane left? He had to take his wife to dinner. But we had about an hour. He gave directions for reaching his home. It was a low, fairly new home on a point of land where the Biscayne drainage canal empties into Biscayne Bay. The view across the bay is magnificent; the house probably is in the $60,000 class — a sum of money which is below what Guterma used to win or lose on the Las Vegas crap tables in one night. (The property is in his wife's name.) The driveway curves around a palm tree in the small front yard and Guterma was inside waiting for the doorbell to ring. He came out into the heavy, humid weather between the tropical rainstorms that were sweeping Miami at intervals that day. He is a tall, loose-jointed man with a peculiar resemblance to the Danny Kaye who is never seen on camera but is seen in repose. There is the same sharp, quick intelligence springing from the eyes. But this resemblance disappears immediately when Guterma takes off his hat, for he is bald. Guterma allowed himself to be looked at by looking away. After permitting this brief examination, he turned his attention fully to the problems of the interview.

It was obvious he regretted the invitation and had decided that he would say as little as possible. He would limit his remarks to whatever he may have said before in court. He started by denouncing the New York *Times*, which had sent me to see him, and Harrison E. Salisbury, the director of National Correspondence for the *Times*. Salisbury was my boss. He also was the author of a penetrating study of Guterma made at the time the stock manipulator had been riding high in the 1950's. Salisbury nailed Guterma long before anybody else did. Guterma resented it.

Interview subjects such as Guterma tend to have established

patterns for ending the conversation, but they all can be met by fairly simple means. One of the simplest is to conduct the interview in a car from which there is no easy escape. During the first part of our interview, we drove up U.S. 1, turned across the causeway and through Bay Harbor Islands to Bal Harbour and north on Highway A1A which parallels the seashore.

Did he feel any animosity to Pasternak, Garfield and Roen?

"I'd protect myself better next time. I was a big boy and I knew what I was getting into with them."

A question described Pasternak as a professional gambler.

"He's not a professional gambler," Guterma snorted. "He's a sucker for gamblers. He can't win. Doesn't know the first thing about it. They take him every time."

Guterma refused to criticize his former business associates, and the feeling developed that he had achieved an understanding with them. They had left him alone in the woods with the snipe sack (as we shall see) and he had protected himself as best he could. He had done what he had to do; but anything further to antagonize them would be unwise. He repeated again the explanation of his meeting with Dardi that led to the takeover of United Dye and Chemical: "I was taken there by a rental agent."

It became apparent from this response to one question that Guterma is sensitive about the numbers of people who have been convicted of crimes through his willingness to be a witness against them. He refused to answer a question of how many had been indicted through his testimony. There was a certain melancholy in his discussing whether he would ever come back as a stock market operator. He insisted that "all I want is to be left alone." But he brightened at the suggestion that at age forty-six a man with his experience and skill might be able to rise from the ashes of his defeat. There was another remarkable action as this portion of our interview ended. We had agreed to ride to New York together on the night jet. The hint was dropped that he might

try to go on a different plane to avoid resuming the talk. With
the air of a man who has become accustomed to being required to
provide corroboration for every statement, he pulled his airline
ticket from his coat pocket and showed it.

Five years before he would have spit in my eye.

This question of the value to prosecuting authorities of
Guterma, the voluble, has never been discussed in public by any
of the officials who have made use of him. At one point, it was
said in court that Guterma had been most cooperative with the
federal government and that he had helped some of the companies he mismanaged to regain about $3,000,000. But no pin-
pointing of these helpful actions was given by the federal prosecutor who was explaining to the court why a suspended sentence
was being recommended for Guterma in stock frauds that
amounted to upward of $10,000,000. It was just a sort of "by the
way, your honor, he has helped us very much" speech of the kind
prosecutors make everyday for law violators who have become
prosecution witnesses.

The list of persons that Guterma dragged down with him is
impressive, even just those that are known and appear in these
pages. The Desert Inn crowd, Roy M. Cohn (who was badly
damaged although he was acquitted), and Dardi and the stock
manipulators from on Wall Street lead the list. But there were
others. There was George A. Heaney, the president of the
Security National Bank of Long Island, who was utterly destroyed
by his association with the Guterma brigands. Heaney was permitted to gratify all his appetites, so long as he made loans
secured by the worthless stocks in the Guterma portfolio. Of
course, the end came. When it did, the charge was that Heaney
had made $2,525,000 in improperly secured loans to Guterma and
others among the high-flying stock manipulators. There must
have been others, many others, who fell when Guterma began
to talk; but this was a subject that Guterma refused to discuss —

the list of prime trophies that he delivered up to the prosecutors.

At the Miami airport several hours after our talk in the car, Guterma was surprised that seats had already been arranged that put him next to me, barring the possibility of avoiding further talk. He returned to his complaints as soon as the plane left the ground. But, after about half an hour, he slipped and committed himself to answer questions about any aspect of the Handridge Oil deal. For his plans of limiting the interview, this was disaster, but he answered questions about Handridge Oil until there were no more asked. Handridge Oil was the business acquisition that ruined the Desert Inn group. We will examine it in its proper sequence in the story of their stock market assault and defeat. Guterma broke off the talk at the point where he was being pushed to explain why he had allowed these Las Vegas gamblers to move into his United Dye and Chemical Corporation operation. He said he had invited Pasternak to buy the 12,000 shares of control stock. But on repeated questions about Garfield and Allard Roen, he refused to answer and finally said he wanted to sleep. He sprawled his long legs in the aisle of the plane where stewardesses and other passengers stumbled over them for thirty minutes while he appeared to sleep soundly.

When he awoke, we resumed the talk, but he had nothing else to say. We separated at about 2 A.M. at the baggage rack at Idlewild.

Except in the early phases of our talks, Guterma showed no accent, and even then it was very slight — just a hint. This has been a trait that has contributed much to the air of mystery that surrounds him. His only business associate over the years spanning his life in Asia and the United States has been Robert Eveleigh who worked with him in the Philippines and came with him to the United States. Friends he made here have suggested that his grasp of American English, and his acquaintance with the minutiae of American life indicate a knowledge beyond what he could have from the brief time he has lived here. He knew two years after he hit New York where the good delicatessens were, the background and batting average of various baseball players, and he spoke with an accent that fitted these suspicions, but did not fit the story he told of his life.

There is another explanation of these things. Guterma is an extremely clever man, who is quite capable of learning a somewhat esoteric fact and steering the conversation to a point where he could drop that fact. Also, he has a facility for languages, and his New York accent is perhaps only the expert linguist's innate ability to catch and reproduce the sounds of a new language.

Guterma also is expert in the uses of the air of mystery he always wears. He uses it to create an aura of romanticism — as in the story of his father having been a czarist general. Or to create new myths about himself, as in his statement to me that he never sold stock to people who couldn't afford it. When he first came to the United States and was living in Los Angeles, there were suspicions that he represented some foreign power, perhaps the Soviet Union. By the late 1950's, when he had acquired Mutual Broadcasting System, these rumors were very strong, and were in part responsible for the careful analysis of Guterma made by Harrison E. Salisbury for the New York *Times*. Salisbury concluded that Guterma was just a free lance stock manipulator, and a highly successful one. (It is laughable now to discover that once photographers around the U.S. marshal's office in Manhattan mistook Guterma in a jail transfer van for Colonel Rudolph Abel, the Russian spy.) But by the time Salisbury was studying him, Guterma's success was leaking out of the gasbag that he had pumped up.

By 1958, Shawano was in bad shape. The F. L. Jacobs Corporation was in such bad condition that it was destined to provide the reason that the government of the United States would lock up

Guterma as a menace to society and in the hope of reforming him. Guterma took over this company in March, 1956, at the time he was also wheeling and dealing with the Desert Inn crowd toward the dream of getting to market stock in all the gambling joints on the Strip. The Jacobs Corporation made parts for the automotive industry and had been family controlled, but had gradually gone down hill. In the first year that he owned it, Guterma spent little time worrying with it, but he went through quite a few maneuvers internally. He was in such little evidence around the Jacobs firm that his critics among the S.E.C. investigators assumed that he was running it on good business lines, staying away from the stock kiting and other dilly-dallying that characterized Shawano and the others.

However, the stock in Jacobs continued to climb on the market, and associates said that Guterma had promised to run it up to $15 a share. He bought it at about $4. When the end came for Guterma in early 1959, the stock of Jacobs was at about $9.

In early 1958 the pace for Guterma began to get faster and more frantic. He had borrowed all the money he could from usual sources, and his transactions now were at the point where small sums in the hundreds of thousands of dollars were of no use to him. Now he had to have it in the millions. Through the Jacobs company, he had acquired an old established company called the Scranton Lace Corporation, and immediately had it issue 40,000 shares to buy the assets of the electronics division he had established in Jacobs. Then in June 1958, when Guterma had less than a year left of free wheeling, he acquired control through Scranton — the "lace" had been dropped — of the Hal Roach Studios. In September 1958, this combination announced the purchase of Mutual Broadcasting System. There seems to have been some idea to create a great entertainment industry empire. Whatever it was, Guterma today refuses to discuss it. And whatever it was, it disappeared in the wreckage of the Guterma debacle that came about in 1959. He was indicted by a federal grand jury on a charge of violating the securities laws in connection with the mismanagement of the Jacobs company. This indictment came down at the turn of the year, and it was tried in 1959. Guterma was convicted, and lost his appeal of the conviction. He was sentenced in February 1961 to four years and eleven months in jail for looting the Jacobs company. At the time he was sentenced, a prosecutor advised the judge that Guterma had made no less than $919,000 from the Jacobs company stock manipulations.

Subsequently, and for reasons that shall become clear as we examine what happened with Guterma, he pleaded guilty to a whole string of indictments and was given an overall sentence of five years. Sentence was suspended, an apparent kindness of the government which will become understandable later.

When his world caved in, Guterma used all his skill and all his courage to try to save himself. One of his first actions was to file a $10,000,000 suit against a company called U.F.I.T.E.C. and the owner of that company, Abdulla K. Zilkha of Paris. There exists a positive charm in considering that Zilkha and Guterma did business together. Zilkha is an international moneylender, one of those men with great resources in ready cash of any nation, and a willingness to lend it at great interest rates. Guterma needed money when the music began to speed up for his death dance on Wall Street. He went to Zilkha to get it. When I asked him about Zilkha, he was reluctant to answer, but said eventually that an American banker had introduced them in the Netherlands. Guterma borrowed $1,000,000 from Zilkha and put up the control stock of the Jacobs company for security. He pledged his Jacobs stock as collateral, and as an indication of how closely people like Zilkha play the cards to their chest, the moneylender had a provision in the loan that if the New York Stock Exchange delisted the stock, he could sell it immediately to secure his position.

But as Guterma's empire crumbled and the S.E.C. came closer

and closer behind him, like the wolves after the sleigh in the old Russian prints, the stock exchange suddenly stopped trading in Jacobs stock. The smashup was just ahead, and Zilkha moved rapidly and smoothly. He sold out Guterma's Jacobs stock in a private transaction. This was what Guterma sued him about — on the argument that Zilkha by selling the stock had put Guterma in the position of violating an S.E.C. regulation by selling control stock without going through all the process of announcement and revelation. Of course, the suit was one of those political suits that important men file at moments of crisis in the hope of spreading the glare of publicity for a few days and helping their chances of escaping the drop of the big flat rock. However, the rock fell on Guterma while Zilkha calmly followed his normal pursuits. The damage action was never pushed. For one thing, Guterma was too busy defending himself in criminal court.

By the time he arrived in the federal prison in Atlanta to do his sentence, he was persuaded of the futility of suffering all these indignities alone. The department of justice in January 1961 had come under the control of Robert F. Kennedy, a vigorous young man with a great hunger to have malefactors caught, tried and locked up. There were a number of malefactors at liberty, but attached to strings leading to Guterma who in effect could be the puppeteer from his jail cell. Among these was the Desert Inn crowd — Irving Pasternak, Samuel S. Garfield and Allard Roen. They had been hip-deep in the swirling waters of Guterma's United Dye and Chemical Corporation dealings. This possibly is the case which got more S.E.C. attention than any involving Guterma and certainly is the one with the greatest effect on the affairs of the Desert Inn.

So now, having studied Guterma, having followed the tortuous trail of his attempt to get in position to float stock in the Nevada gambling casinos, having seen how his financial empire came down with such a shattering crash, let us see how all these elements fit together with the United Dye and Chemical Corporation shenanigans to engulf the great gray wolves from the Desert Inn.

Remember the story that Guterma bought up the control stock in this company after a chance meeting with Virgil D. Dardi who was guarding the bones left in the masterful looting by Lowell Birrell. Remember that he paid little attention to the Jacobs company in early 1956 right after he acquired it. Remember that Guterma had cost the Desert Inn crowd and its friends a considerable amount of money in investments in Shawano Corporation stock that was worthless and also in expenses connected with the ill-fated United Hotels, Inc., scheme. Remember that Guterma could be persuaded to talk only about the United Dye and Chemical Corporation deals and about the Handridge Oil deal that was a part of United Dye.

The fact is that the Handridge Oil deal was the thing that ruined Allard Roen, Irving Pasternak and Sam Garfield.

It had all the overtones of a night at the crap tables for the Las Vegas crowd. A sure thing was being constructed. They moved in with Guterma as soon as he took over United Dye. He was concentrating on this company to the extent that he seemed to have no interest in any other. A big killing was in the wind. Soon after Guterma moved into United Dye, his former partners in Shawano came forward with a new proposition, the Handridge Oil deal. How soon?

"Immediately," he said. "Garfield and Pasternak brought it to me."

This deal followed the pattern of so many of the earlier Guterma transactions. The idea was to generate a great block of stock through purchase of another company, then to sell this stock at a price that was inflated by all the tricks that Guterma and his crew could pull out of their hats.

This time the deal was to be a little different. In the other deals, sometimes Guterma had been satisfied to get control of the stock so he could get the sales commission money. In those instances he had not owned the companies that he brought together to create the blocks of stock that were necessary to fuel his operations. His procedure this time gives further insight into his character — and also the characters of the Las Vegas gamblers who picked Guterma to be their leader in the assault on the stock market.

Handridge Oil Company was controlled by the Murchison interests — that collection of investments held together by the wheeling-dealing sons of old Clint Murchison, himself one of the pioneers in the use of almost tax free oil money to control other businesses. Pasternak and Garfield located this Murchison operation. They found that it could be acquired for about $3,000,000, and on a small down payment.

"I put up the only money that went into the deal," said Guterma. Remember this. According to Guterma, neither Pasternak nor Garfield nor Allard Roen invested "even $10" to finance the Handridge Oil deal. Guterma put up $800,000 for the down payment. A mortgage of $2,200,000 was accepted by the Murchisons. The earnings of the companies paid off the mortgage, said Guterma. However, there is indication elsewhere that Guterma may have paid it off with the money he took out of the treasury of the Bon Ami Corporation. He had arranged for Bon Ami to be purchased by United Dye and Chemical in May 1956, at the same time the Handridge deal was in the making. Bon Ami was reamed out in an extremely complicated transaction.

Whatever the facts on the payout of the mortgage, Guterma insists that he alone put any money into buying Handridge Oil Company. This small and virtually unknown company was vitally important to Guterma's schemes and the schemes of the Desert Inn group. By now, through what had happened in the sale of the Garnak Drilling company to Shawano, the Desert Inn crowd understood how Guterma could generate stock that would be sold at good prices and make everybody associated with him rich.

The deal in Handridge Oil Company was a typical Guterma operation. Handridge had 575,000 shares of stock. The Murchison interests owned it all. When Guterma and his gambling buddies bought the oil company, they got that much stock. Guterma already owned and completely controlled United Dye, which had a total of about 153,000 shares of stock in it. So the next move was for Guterma, acting as United Dye and Chemical, to propose to Guterma, acting as Handridge Oil Company, that Handridge be merged into United Dye through an exchange of stock. Obviously, Guterma could not appear publicly to be doing this. The interests conflicted. He used his buddies from Las Vegas as the fronts. The deal was worked out. United Dye suddenly issued 575,000 new shares of stock and absorbed the properties of Handridge Oil. The owners of Handridge Oil got the 575,000 new shares of United Dye stock.

A crucial question arises at this point. If Guterma had financed the entire deal, why did he not get the entire bulk of stock — or at least the lion's share? He did not. He got only 80,000 shares and the other 495,000 shares went to his gambling casino friends. Why? He refused to give anything more than monosyllabic and unsatisfying answers. When he was pressed, he just closed his eyes and went to sleep. He would not say. Just before he went to sleep, it was suggested to Guterma that his generosity was to settle for the drubbing his friends had taken in the United Hotels and Shawano deals. At first he said he was "just stupid, I guess." When he was told that of course he was not stupid and he knew it, and an answer insisted upon, he began to yell. Heads began to turn in the cabin of the plane. When the yelling came right back at him, Guterma shut up. It was suggested that he was giving his associates a chance to recoup so he could get them off his back. He said "that's an interesting story." Then he took his nap.

Another explanation is offered by a man close to the Desert

Inn group. He pointed out that Guterma had been forced to use these men as his stand-ins to negotiate in behalf of Handridge Oil, since as the chief owner of United Dye Guterma had to work from that side of the table. Perhaps this is the explanation. It is true that United Dye put out a brochure explaining the Handridge merger that contained outright lies about Guterma's hands-off part in the transactions. The brochure was in fulfillment of an S.E.C. requirement to explain to stockholders.

Whatever the reason, Guterma says he financed the deal, yet he gave the better part of it to the people from the gambling crowd. As an indication of what those profits amounted to, the government prosecutor told a judge who was ready to pass sentence that Irving Pasternak had made $2,100,000 in the deal. Pasternak's lawyer argued with this. He said the profits were only $1,494,-789. But before these sad and pointless arguments could be held in a Foley Square courtroom a few blocks from the New York Stock Exchange, many things had to happen. The stock from Handridge Oil had to be transformed into United Dye stock; it had to be sold in violation of securities laws; the crime had to be discovered; indictments had to be voted and trial juries had to be persuaded. This was a long, rocky road and to study it, to chart it, is to marvel that the processes of justice ever can be brought to bear on those persons who have great wealth. But they are brought to bear. The law is served. The wealth melts away in the great heat generated in the pressures of an all out investigation such as those that have characterized the United Dye case since Guterma decided it was time for him to talk.

What caused Guterma to become a government witness? Who can say? A very personable federal agent may have persuaded him. It may have been an understandable wish to get out of jail sooner and to be absolved of further punishment for transgressions of the securities and exchange act beyond those in the Jacobs company case. These reasons all must have figured in it.

However, any realistic appraisal of the possible reasons must put at the top of the list the voting of criminal indictment No. 159-275 by a grand jury in the United States District Court for the Southern District of New York. To be blunt about it, this indictment served notice on Guterma that his old buddies from Las Vegas had shoved a shiv in his back, and were galloping over the hill toward the sunset, headed back to their desert sanctuary. He was left there among the wolves of Wall Street, the little empty snipe sack in his hands. It is possible to draw a very pathetic picture of Sandy Guterma at this point. Except that he doesn't deserve it.

This indictment was the forerunner of the 1963 indictment that charged perjury against Roy Cohn, the one-time boy wonder of the Senate Caucus Room. In fact, this indictment was the forerunner of more and more and more trouble for more and more people. Guterma's fall was like a big rock dropped in a small fishpond, for the waves continued to pound against the shore and to churn up more mud from the bottom.

The people who were indicted were Guterma, Virgil Dardi, Lowell M. Birrell (who long since had taken off on an extended trip to Brazil), Robert C. Leonhardt (the young man from New Orleans who had been involved with Guterma from 1952 onwards in McGrath Securities), and three minor parties in the United Dye operations, Louis Levin, Pierre A. Duval, and Harry W. Bank. Read it again. Nowhere appear as defendants the names of Samuel Garfield, Irving Pasternak, Allard Roen and A. K. Swann (their lawyer who was tied up in it all with them). It was astounding. Guterma must have been ready to tear out his remaining fringe of hair. He was facing trial in the Jacobs case, was in the most serious trouble of his life, and there his associates who had made sacks of money from his Handridge–United Dye promotion and manipulation obviously had moved out to sink him.

The physical appearance of this indictment itself made the

matter more striking. The practice is to list the names of defendants throughout in capital letters, and those other names are in lower case. Thus the indictment talked of a conspiracy between "ALEXANDER GUTERMA, VIRGIL D. DARDI, LOWELL M. BIRRELL, ROBERT C. LEONHARDT, LOUIS LEVIN, PIERRE A. DUVAL, HARRY W. BANK, the defendants," and "Samuel Garfield, Irving Pasternak, A. K. Swann, Allard Roen," and a long list of others. The effect must have been quite startling on Guterma's disposition. Obviously, he would have decided, his former buddies were now federal witnesses against him, contributing their little knives to the general attack on his position.

Guterma's unhappiness was matched by that of the investigators who had worked so hard to bring him and his friends to justice. They were dumfounded when the indictment was handed up. They also became suspicious when it became known that the Securities and Exchange Commission lawyers had not been asked to write the indictment. This was generally the practice, since the S.E.C. men were more familiar with the pitfalls of the highly technical jargon that was required.

At any rate, the whole sorry story of Handridge Oil and United Dye was set out in the indictment. Birrell's looting, Dardi's bonepicking, Guterma's rejuvenation with an injection of blue-sky stock all came through in the indictment, showing that the truth was known by somebody, but that the truth was not being served. Even as his world was being turned upside down, Guterma had resources in friendships and supporters. These men since have not rested in their campaigns to see that their version of the truth is brought out about United Dye and about the strange indictment that was voted that day in 1959 by the federal grand jury.

Immediately, when this indictment was brought in, all manner of hell was raised throughout the legal and financial circles around Wall Street and in Washington. In 1960, another indictment charging securities law violations in the United Dye matters was voted in the Southern District of New York. This time the list of persons indicted was, to follow the capital letter style, SAMUEL S. GARFIELD, IRVING PASTERNAK, ALLEN K. SWANN, ALLARD ROEN, VIRGIL D. DARDI AND ALEXANDER L. GUTERMA.

At last, Guterma and his buddies were in the soup together. But this was a far different document from the one voted earlier. It began with forty-one counts of using the mails to sell securities that had not been registered with the S.E.C. Each count was based on a letter written in connection with the stock. The forty-second count alleged a conspiracy to violate the securities act.

This 1960 indictment is a very simple, and relatively short, and clean-cut looking document. But it apparently will never be tried, for in 1961, after Robert M. Morgenthau became United States attorney in Foley Square, yet another indictment was voted out in the United Dye case. This time, the names left off were Guterma and his associates such as Robert Leonhardt and Robert Eveleigh.

Guterma then was in jail. Leonhardt had been convicted in connection with the Jacobs case and had been barred from selling securities as a condition of probation. Eveleigh also was more or less square with the law. In short, insofar as stock promotions were concerned, these men had had it. Moreover, they were willing witnesses and Guterma had told the grand jurors all they wanted to hear. If they were indicted, their evidence would be less easy to bring into court against the defendants who up to then had gone unpunished. It was a great long list of defendants, but the six names at the top are the most interesting. They were SAMUEL S. GARFIELD, IRVING PASTERNAK, ALLEN K. SWANN, ALLARD ROEN, VIRGIL D. DARDI, HERMAN W. BRANN. The first four of these we have identified in detail.

Dardi is the fellow who had the desk like Guterma's and who had an office to lease. His background was checkered. He was born in California and had a connection by marriage with important financial figures there. In about 1952 he became the head man of Blair Holding Corporation where he lasted two years. There he was forced out after being accused of dealing with the late Serge Rubinstein, who was without a doubt the greatest phony securities dealer that the country knew during the mid-century period. Rubinstein was killed in his plush New York apartment during the time that Guterma was a rising star. There have been frequent comparisons of Rubinstein and Guterma, since both came from Russian-Chinese backgrounds and both had a flair for breaking the securities laws. Guterma has always resented such comparisons. Undoubtedly, Rubinstein would have resented them, too, had he not been murdered.

Dardi was closely associated with Lowell Birrell, who left him in command of United Dye to protect Birrell's withdrawal with all the United Dye money. He also had been associated with Stewart B. Hopps, a San Franciscan who was mixed up in the great Inland Empire Insurance scandals, and the Maryland savings and loan scandals. Dardi was one of those men who served on many boards of directors, and in three instances he served with William Zeckendorf, the real estate operator whose frenzied financing has sometimes had the smell about it of Abdulla K. Zilkha or the Hong Kong moneylenders or those in Panama. Whoever put these boards of directors together also had some of the Guterma philosophy, for other well-known names appear on them as a cachet to indicate respectability.

Herman William Brann, the sixth indictee in whom we are interested, has had a career that might well have been plotted by E. Phillips Oppenheim. Brann was a graduate of the University of Pennsylvania where he took a masters degree in engineering. He was decorated for his work as a spy in Europe and around the Mediterranean in World War II. After the war he was in the United States briefly, then in 1946 went overseas to stay. Brann ended up in Tangier, where he started one of the multitudes of banks that opened in that free port in those years when Tangier was the site of all kinds of strange dealing and smuggling and criminal activity. Europe was rebuilding after the damage of World War II, and the legal shortcuts were being taken in such places as Tangier. Herman William Brann was an expediter in these shortcuts.

His bank was called the American and Foreign Bank of Tangier. That was a good title, for it created in the unsophisticated mind the feeling that somehow this was an American bank, protected by American rules and laws, and perhaps even with a little policy in the Federal Deposit Insurance Corporation. Such thoughts were silly. Brann showed his depositors just how silly.

As North Africa moved toward independence, the free-wheeling free port system disappeared, and this meant that the bank had to be closed. It could not possibly conform to the laws of Morocco. So a notice was sent out to the depositors, who had about $4,000,000 in the bank. (It was a favorite among oil company employees and service personnel in North Africa.) The notice said the bank was going to move to Panama and that the depositors would soon get notices of the new address and other particulars.

That was the last they heard.

The American and Foreign Bank of Tangier went down without a ripple. There were many searches and much hue and cry, but the money was gone.

Brann also had some problems that grew out of the movement of some stolen securities from Miami to Switzerland. They were shares in the Pan American bank of Miami, worth $400,000 and they belonged to a former Cuban official. Brann was arrested in Switzerland, then released so he could come to the United States and be rearrested. This was in 1961. Brann had been away fifteen years. He returned to Europe and brought his family over. When he got off the boat that time, later in 1961, he was served with the warrant in the United Dye and Chemical Corporation stock fraud case.

At first glance it seems curious: what could Brann have been doing in this Wall Street operation? He was living in Europe all that time. So how could he have violated the American securities law? The answer reveals more about how Guterma worked, as he and the Las Vegas gamblers tried to multiply their loot from the stock market.

"Why, he was buying stock for me to hold up the price," said Guterma. "Except I don't think he ever bought any. He just took my $130,000 and that's all I ever heard. No stock. No money."

Guterma had thoughtfully arranged to have United Dye and Chemical stock supported not only in New York and on the over-the-counter market in the United States, but also to have frequent price supporting purchases made by agents overseas. This was Brann's assignment. It cost Guterma $130,000, and there is no indication that his buddies from the Desert Inn kicked in a few bob to help defray the costs. They just took the profits he made for them and left him in the lurch when the end came.

The instruments the Las Vegas crowd used in these transactions were Guterma and such of his henchmen as he called on. The rest of the indictment on which Roen, Swann, Garfield and Pasternak were named as defendants listed a string of boiler-room operators and stock pushers that had worked for years in the Guterma entourage. They were all convicted or pleaded guilty as did the six at the top of the list.

Like so many things connected with Las Vegas, this trial was superlative in various ways. It was the longest ever held in a federal court. It started in March 1962 and ended on February 4, 1963. By the time it was finished the jurors were old-time friends,

celebrating birthdays, anniversaries and other events. There
were more than 100 witnesses, 1447 exhibits, 26,700 pages of
testimony. The jury fees alone cost $50,000. While most of the
publicized figures pleaded guilty in the first month or so, four —
including Dardi — were still around to be found guilty by the
jury at the trial's end.

One of the first witnesses was Alexander Leonard Guterma,
brought over from a room in the Public Health Service hospital
at Staten Island. He was off and on the witness stand for four
months and there was never any question but that he was a
cooperative, willing and anxious government witness. He wanted
to convict his old buddies from Las Vegas. His former partner
in McGrath Securities, Robert Leonhardt, also testified along the
guidelines laid down by Guterma's testimony. There were
others. The Desert Inn group had fought hard at the beginning
and had resisted making any sort of deal. But the end was in
sight.

The early days of the trial were taken up with arguments on
motions, procedures, and the usual time-consuming courtroom
ritual dances of a large group of lawyers representing the many
defendants named in such conspiracy cases. It was not until
March 9, 1962, that Guterma took the witness stand and in the
first day began to destroy the complacency — if they had any
left — of the group of men he'd met first over the gambling tables
at Las Vegas. He described in detail the plan to generate 575,000
new shares of stock in United Dye through the Handridge Oil
Company absorption maneuver. Garfield, Pasternak, Roen and
Swann must have been frozen in their seats as Guterma sat there
and calmly began to talk them right into jail cells. One of the
first things Guterma talked about was the time Garfield wanted
to bribe former Senator George Bender to stop the 1956 investigation by S.E.C. staff members. Then he built it on up from
there.

On the afternoon of March 12, 1962, after four days of listening to Guterma's memory perform for the prosecution, Garfield and Roen left the court and outside found a cold, wet, windy storm had struck Manhattan Island. They couldn't get a cab, and settled for the subway for their uptown hotel. Sam Garfield had been tough as a kid, but by then, at age sixty-two, he was old and tired and sick and worried for his future. Aboard the subway he collapsed at Allard Roen's feet, and began to hemorrhage from an ulcer perforation. This delayed the trial temporarily, but it also gave Garfield and Roen a little trading stock with the prosecution. If the government insisted on continuing the trial, what would it do about Garfield who plainly was to be hospitalized for weeks? Would it consider a deal of any sort? It would consider a deal.

The deal was simple. The government didn't really give much away. Garfield and Roen and Pasternak and Swann would be permitted to plead guilty to one count in the indictments and the other counts would be dropped. They would not be sentenced until the government had made whatever use of them it wanted. They would tell the government whatever they knew about any matters it wanted to ask them about. The trial of the others would proceed.

Pasternak wouldn't buy it. He wanted to continue to fight, and did so. By July, he too, was convinced that he would be found guilty, so he pleaded guilty to the United Dye conspiracy charge, and also to another indictment growing out of his and the others' involvement with Guterma in Shawano Development Corporation. Pasternak, while he pleaded guilty, was reluctant to go whole hog for the government as the others were committed to do. So in June 1963 he was sentenced to two and one half years in jail and to a fine of $50,000. As this is written, he may have had a change of heart and his tongue may have been loosened, for he has not had to serve the sentence or pay the fine.

But while Pasternak was stubborn, Roen and Swann readily followed Garfield's lead. On March 19, 1962, they pleaded guilty and Judge William Herlands deferred sentencing indefinitely. A special session of court was convened in Garfield's hospital room to take his plea of guilty.

The trial dragged on through the summer, the fall, and into the winter before it reached its end. The end found that everyone who had not pleaded guilty was convicted. There were just four who had not pleaded guilty earlier. Virgil Dardi, 57, was sentenced to seven years in jail and a $40,000 fine. Charles Rosenthal, 58, got four years and a $25,000 fine. Robert B. Garvis got five years and a $15,000 fine. Charles M. Berman, 53, got six years and a $35,000 fine. Appeals were filed. Rosenthal, Garvis and Berman all were associated with the stock-peddling operations. A sort of epitaph to Dardi's career on Wall Street was spoken by Gerald Walpin, the prosecutor who had directed the government case and who asked Judge Herlands for heavy sentences. Said Walpin of Dardi: "He served his apprenticeship with Serge Rubinstein, got his master's degree with Lowell Birrell and his Ph.D. with Alexander Guterma."

Walpin could have added that Dardi is the type to which the Las Vegas gamblers gravitated when they came to Wall Street.

Now, the end of that long trial did not finish the government's interest in the events surrounding Guterma's involvement with the Las Vegas gamblers, or the involvement of all of them in the nation's stock markets. A burning interest arose from the strange things that happened at the time that Guterma and his crew were indicted for the United Dye frauds, but the gamblers and their buddies were not.

A grand jury was convened in early 1963 to study those events, and a parade of witnesses passed before it. It became obvious to those associated with Guterma, Roen, Garfield, and the others from the heady days when United Dye was making them all rich that the grand jury was checking into some allegations that a "fix" had been arranged to prevent the indictment of the Desert Inn group, while doing nothing to stop the indictment of Guterma and his associates.

A special crank was available to turn the screws on all of the Desert Inn bunch. We have seen how Allard Roen was a protégé of Sam Garfield and Moe Dalitz. He was a boy they had watched grow up and work his way through Duke University. He had been associated with the Desert Inn from the days when he came to Las Vegas from Florida to help Moe Dalitz and Morris Kleinman keep track of the construction after they put up the money to finish building Wilbur Clark's dream.

As Dalitz and Kleinman became older, they turned more and more to Roen as their heir apparent in the management of the Desert Inn and the rapidly expanding series of other investments the Desert Inn group had made. Roen's future was assured. Moreover, it was a future that helped make a brighter outlook for those older men.

This future was conditioned, however, on Roen being able to continue as the front man at the Desert Inn. There seemed to be slight likelihood that it would ever be in doubt, for it had seemed that all he needed was the approval of Dalitz and the others — an approval he certainly had. But the Guterma involvement, which had made so much money for them all at one time, suddenly changed this rosy picture of the future for Allard Roen. Almost overnight, his future became dark and cloudy. When he and Garfield and Swann pleaded guilty, this was a step that could mean the end for Allard Roen.

Conviction of a felony would mean that he would be forced out as a holder of an interest in the license for the Desert Inn casino. The state Gaming Commission in Nevada certainly would be forced to require his removal from that license, and if he had no part of the license, the commission also would resist allowing him to remain as an officer of the corporation either there or at the Stardust casino. Such a turn of events would be ironic for many reasons, but none more so than this: while a felony conviction would be forcing Roen out of the Desert Inn, a partner in it from the beginning has been Morris Kleinman, a man who served three years in 1934-37 for federal income tax fraud. Kleinman, of course, is one of those "grandfathers" discussed by Clifford Jones and Senator Tobey. He was licensed before the state became strict.

It is with this in mind that the Desert Inn has imported its long-time attorney, J. A. Donnelley, from San Diego to succeed Roen as the executive vice-president. Donnelley has moved into Roen's job and Roen now moves quietly around the place where he formerly was the crown prince.

However, he has a hope. That hope is based on the legal advice of his attorneys that if he can escape a jail sentence for the United Dye stock frauds, he will not be judged a felon and thus might be able to keep his casino license. So his future may rest in the hands of Judge Herlands. Whatever Judge Herlands does will be based in great part on the advice given to him by the staff of District Attorney Morgenthau.

That advice will be shaped a great deal by the degree of co-operation given to the federal authorities by Roen. Not only Roen's actions will bear on that question, however, but also the actions of Garfield and Dalitz and the others will govern the words that are spoken by some prosecutor on the morning that Roen stands before Judge Herlands for sentencing.

In short, if Roen and Dalitz and Garfield and Swann and others involved and controlled by the Desert Inn organization are willing to tell the prosecutors what happened in 1959 with the first indictment voted by a grand jury charging fraud in the United Dye case, then the odds are high that Roen will get a suspended sentence and a fine. That will permit him to have a fighting chance to stay in the Desert Inn, and restore to him at least some of the future he thought was so secure.

Roen and Garfield testified for the government — as circumstances dictated they must — in the two trials of the indictment against Roy M. Cohn. The first trial ended in a hung jury which was dismissed during deliberations when a juror's relative died. The second trial ended in an acquittal.

Many strange events were related by the government's witnesses during these two presentations of evidence. The actual charge was that Cohn and Murray Gottesman, another New York lawyer, had perjured themselves and attempted to obstruct justice in 1962 and 1963 in connection with a grand jury investigation attempting to learn why Roen, Garfield and two others were not made defendants in the first United Dye indictment in 1959. The evidence, however, was thought by the prosecution to show that Cohn exceeded his functions as a lawyer by participating in an attempt to thwart justice in 1959 by blocking indictments of the Las Vegas group.

Drawing conclusions from the evidence put on in these trials is tricky business, for violent charges were made against Cohn, while at the same time the jury found that the charges as set out in the indictment against Cohn were not proved. On the one hand the Las Vegas gamblers testified in open court to things that Cohn was said to have done; but on the other hand the jury said that he was not guilty of the main charges of perjury and obstruction of justice in 1962 and 1963.

In any event, Cohn was cleared, but the testimony against him is still relevant in examining the Nevada system of legalized gambling and the attitudes which it generates.

Both Garfield and Roen were willing witnesses for the government. Their testimony was that $50,000 had been taken from the cashier's cage at the Desert Inn and used to pay for stopping the indictment of the members of the Desert Inn group who had been involved in the United Dye and Chemical Company operations. Garfield testified that he gave $16,666 to Cohn in the lobby of the Desert Inn. Roen testified that acting on Garfield's instructions which Roen said he understood originated with Cohn, Roen paid out $33,333 more. Roen said he gave this to a man he identified from a photograph at the trial as being an assistant U.S. attorney. This man testified also; he denied the Roen story and evidence was presented that he was elsewhere. All of this money came out of the cashier's cage at the Desert Inn casino, and an I O U from Garfield was left in its place.

This is truly a shocking state of affairs, however one assesses it. Roen, then the chief operating officer of the Desert Inn casino, testified he took large sums of cash from the cashier's cage, part of which he says was paid to a federal official. This is what Roen said under oath in a criminal trial that he did. Either he did or he committed perjury. And in either case this is as fine an example of the seepage of back alley morality into the legal trappings of Nevada gambling as exists anywhere.

The picture of Garfield being able to tap the till merely by phoning Roen also should be enlightening to the uninitiated. Garfield has no ownership of record in the Desert Inn casino. His right to dip into its cash reserves derives from his lifelong friendship with Moe Dalitz and his longtime sponsorship of Allard Roen. What now portends is the action to be taken by the Nevada gambling control authorities.

The testimony given by Roen and Garfield is an open scandal against the state licensed gaming casinos. Roen is convicted of a crime, a crime involving the cheating of investors in the stock market. What happens now? Will action be initiated against the Desert Inn, some action to punish and set an example? Will Roen be forced out of the ownership of the casino?

These and many other questions arise.

In a certain sense, the hand of Alexander Guterma also drew

Roy Cohn into the quicksand, along with his clients the Desert Inn crowd, although Cohn managed to tug himself free while the others could not. Cohn had been a business partner with the Las Vegas gamblers in some nongambling deals. But he had nothing to do with Guterma, insofar as records now available show. Cohn had his own stock market deals in Lionel Trains Corporation, and provided his own service in grand ideas and quick-minded grasp of the possibilities. He had no need of Guterma and Guterma had none of him.

The connecting link between them was the Las Vegas crowd and the great sums of money generated every year across the gambling tables, money that has to be invested somewhere, that has to go out because it comes in so rapidly.

This is money that has great weight in the American economy, weight far beyond its size, because of the way its owners are able to multiply its strength and effect through resort to all sorts of far-ranging enterprises. In the case of the ill-fated attempt to put the physical properties of the Desert Inn into the stock market we have seen one way their minds work. Yet, when this failed, they were able to demonstrate the elasticity of their purpose by shifting gears into a "participating partnership interest" arrangement whereby they sold the company and still owned it and still controlled the hotel properties, also managing to arrange great savings every year in federal income taxes.

When finally the gambling crowd became fully committed to the pursuit of the stock market dollar in Guterma's entourage, we see another side of its collective personality. Here the gamblers showed a greedy desire for the lion's share of the pile of stocks generated in the Handridge Oil deal. Since at the time United Dye was selling at about $38 a share, those 575,000 shares of United Dye created in direct violation of the securities laws had a market value of about $20,000,000. This is what the gamblers intended to sell them for — or more. Yet they knew, as did Guterma and everyone else on the inside of that deal, that the stock was worth perhaps $5,000,000 in actual assets of United Dye, and perhaps was worth not even that much.

What happened to the people who bought United Dye and Chemical stock from those manipulators? They lost everything they invested, is the practical answer, although it is true that the company's few remaining assets eventually were absorbed by another firm and some stock equity salvaged. But it was so little as to be meaningless.

Meantime, while Guterma was going to jail for his part in it, while the investors were being wiped out, while the tangle of companies destroyed the employment of an uncalculated number of simple people who traded the hours of their lives for small salaries, while the S.E.C. investigators and lawyers labored to bring the malefactors to justice — while all others involved underwent great stress, the Las Vegas gamblers reverted to the lessons of the back alley gambling joints. They tried to put in a fix, both Roen and Garfield said under oath.

The consternation of Guterma and the S.E.C. crowd when the first United Dye indictment failed to name the gamblers must have been more than matched by the glee of Sam Garfield and Company.

However, their time was coming to worry in the dark hours of the night. The immense pressures that built up when Guterma began to talk about all his business deals, the shocks in the halls of justice that followed the presidential election in 1960, the new impetus to prosecutions by federal authorities that came with the swearing in of Robert F. Kennedy as attorney general — all of these things turned the tables so that those once sad were happy and those once happy were sad.

Perhaps that second act curtain in this drama was the scene in Sam Garfield's hospital room where he pleaded guilty to a serious charge for the first time in his life. There should have been thunder rolling offstage, for the entire order of things was to change. The world had turned. The hateful light of publicity was to shine on Garfield, who had shunned it, and on the business dealings of the Desert Inn group, which wanted to avoid it. Allard Roen was in serious trouble, while the stock fraud gains of Irving Pasternak long since had gone into phony deals created for him in a Cuban gambling joint by Alexander Guterma and into squaring up his troubles with the law.

In a situation full of tight circles where men must sometimes feel that they chase their own tails, so often do they meet themselves coming and going — in such a situation, the indictment and acquittal of Roy Cohn in the administration of Attorney General Robert F. Kennedy is yet another tight circle.

In the years when Senator Joseph R. McCarthy was riding high on his witches' broom, his flight patterns directed by the radar inside Roy Cohn's head, a young attorney just a few years out of the University of Virginia law school joined the staff of the committee headed by Senator McCarthy. This was Robert F. Kennedy. He and Cohn became bitter enemies. While Kennedy has many unique distinctions, this is not one of them. Roy Cohn has many bitter enemies — as well as close friends. When he was indicted, Cohn hoped to capitalize on this enmity with the attorney general. He filed motions, arguing that he was the victim of persecution for this old conflict with Robert Kennedy. The court dismissed the motions. But who can read the minds of jurors?

The interest to our narrative here arises not from any question of whether or not Roy Cohn was able to maneuver a "fix" for the Desert Inn gamblers. The jury said he did not and we must agree. Our interest stems from the demonstration that wherever the gamblers from the Desert Inn took their money, the way of the racket including willingness to make payoffs went with it.

In the United States we have built a system wherein we hope that men will not be able to buy themselves out of trouble when they have done things against the general welfare. We know that they do; but we strive always toward the end that the system may be improved so that others cannot. In earlier chapters we have examined some of the deals that the Nevada gamblers have worked in their home fields. Some of these are revealing and startling. None, however, is as illustrative of the national problem that their great wealth creates as is the story of their march on Wall Street with Sandy Guterma.

⑨

THE TEAMSTERS'
PENSION FUND LOANS

MUCH needs to be understood about the psychology of the boss gamblers if we are to follow and comprehend their actions. This is particularly true in understanding the huge loans from the Teamsters Union pension fnuds. One of the men responsible for enforcing the Nevada gambling laws showed a lack of this comprehension when discussing the Teamster loans. A light broke on his face, which had been clouded during our earlier talk about the practice of skimming.

"You see," he said. "If they were hiding all that money you think they are, why would they need to borrow from Hoffa?"

Why indeed? This is just the way that "outside" people, unaware of the ways of the gamblers, would think of it. The reasoning: the borrowings indicate a need of money and if money is needed, then the gambling business cannot be very profitable and certainly no resources of hidden wealth from concealed income could possibly exist. The interest costs on the loans would prevent a reasonable businessman from borrowing when he has money at hand to do the job. People on the outside might think that way, but it is lamentable that a public official charged with regulating the gamblers should be so naïve about their intentions and psychology. This line of reasoning is entirely correct, if you're running an ordinary hotel in an ordinary city, financed with money raised in the financial district and profitable at the ordinary profit levels for hotels. But in considering the maneuvers of the Nevada gamblers, such reasoning leads to false assumptions.

Let us examine this in terms of gamblers' psychology.

First, the gambling business, particularly in Las Vegas on the Strip, has the capital investment demands of any growing business. The casino hotels need more hotel rooms, then they need larger casinos, and then they need to expand their supper club showrooms, and then they need more hotel rooms and so on until a balance is reached somewhere. It has not been reached yet. The crowds visiting the Strip get bigger every year and the competition for their attention becomes tougher all the time.

Second, all of these operations produce money as if they picked it off the palm trees. As we have seen earlier, these places literally crank out money in bales of currency and small electric cartloads of coins. There is no shortage of money around the successful gambling casinos. (Certainly no one is going to lend much to an unsuccessful gambling place, for the possibilities of being wiped out through inept management are as great in a gambling house as in any business one can name.)

Third, the ownership lists in the casino operations are short. The most successful places in the state are owned by one man, William Harrah of Reno. The Las Vegas Strip casinos usually run to about a maximum of twenty owners, and some have a very few. So there is plenty of income for the individual owners. No need exists to borrow improvement money just so a dividend pattern can be maintained.

Fourth, the places are run by professional gamblers, and this is the point where all the conventional wisdom goes out the window. These men are not at all interested in business risks for their own money. They want to get that money out of the operation as quickly as they can. They are unsure of the future, they are worried about their money, they always want it right where they can pick it up in a satchel and move on with it. If there is

$1,000,000 available to take out of the operation, they want to take it out immediately. Money in the hand is better than money on the gambling table or tied up in buildings.

This is the chief reason why the treasury of the Teamsters' pension fund has become so immensely important in Nevada. What life insurance company is going to lend money to expand a gambling joint when the loan must be for a term of years and the gambling house would become an abandoned ruin if the state law should change? What bank has the resources to risk in such loans? Individuals with that kind of money to commit would want to buy into the ownership, and the gamblers could never agree to that. This was the only way Wilbur Clark could finish the Desert Inn— and his financiers took over the place.

Then, the gamblers feel the compulsive need to get the money out and let somebody else take the risk that the Nevada noble experiment will founder before the mortgage is paid out. This appears to be universal among those in Las Vegas. The feeling may also stem from the checkered history of some of the places — the top banana today is tomorrow's has been, afraid to go to court to try to regain his position because too many things come out in court, and besides there is lots of unmarked graveyard space still left in the desert for people who thought court was the place to assert the rights better asserted with naked power.

So the top command of a successful place today faces those three fears that limit using the profits in expansion — the place may be taken away from them by another mob with greater strength; the state of Nevada may decide to try to get along without gambling; and the cutthroat competition among the casinos may force them to the wall within a few months. If any of these things occur, the money is gone. But if the money is scooped out, and shoved into the pocket or in some other safer investment, then the gambler can rest his head more easily. How much better it is to let the truck drivers take the risk!

The total of loans in Nevada from the Teamsters is astounding.

As of the time this is written, they amount to more than $20,000,-000, and all from the treasury of the pension fund of the Central and the Southeast and Southwest Conferences of the union. This is the area in which James R. Hoffa, the international union president, has his greatest strength. The Hoffa control throughout the Midwest is ironclad. But none of the teamster pension funds for the Western Conferences has gone into loans such as these. Hoffa's dictatorial powers have not yet shredded down the layers of resistance against doling out the Western Teamsters' pension funds to gambling joints.

The relation between Hoffa and the Western Conference is something that future historians of the labor movement will unsnarl. Today, it is far too entangled to enable us to do more than follow the main threads. In the days when Dave Beck was the pushing young union politician in Seattle, he created the Western Conference as a power seat for himself in crowding Dan Tobin, Beck's predecessor as international president. James R. Hoffa years later did the same thing to Beck with the Central Conference. As Hoffa took over the union presidency, he found the greatest blocks of resistance in the Western Conference. This explains in great part why the money to support that great and unique Western enterprise — Nevada's legalized gambling joints — came in loans from the Midwest Teamsters' pension funds, not from the West. The simple reason: Hoffa dominates the Central Conference fund; he does not dominate the Western Conference fund.

In these matters of the pension fund loans to the gambling casinos, we again have another series of those tight circles in the lives of men. When Beck lost the Teamsters' presidency to Hoffa, it was in part because of the disclosures of his financial chicanery with union funds. The man who brought out those disclosures was Robert F. Kennedy, the chief counsel of the United States Senate Select Committee on Improper Activities in the Labor or Management Fields. This came to be known as the McClellan Committee, named for its chairman, Senator John L. McClellan of Arkansas.

Thus Beck and Hoffa and Kennedy had bitter relationships in those days. Beck long since has disappeared into McNeil's Island Federal Penitentiary in Puget Sound, serving a sentence for income tax fraud. When he finishes that, he must come to terms with the state of Washington, to whom he is obligated for one to fifteen years in the penitentiary at Walla Walla. This sentence was imposed by a state court in Seattle where Beck was convicted of selling union-owned Cadillacs bought for his use, and then putting the money in his own bank account. Robert Kennedy had prepared the coffin of Beck's union career in those spring days of 1957 when Beck was unable to explain his stewardship of union money and took refuge in the Fifth Amendment when questions about it were asked before the McClellan Committee. But the nail was driven into the lid on the coffin in that trial in Seattle in December 1957 when Beck was convicted of a felony and was sentenced to a jail term. That was a wonderfully well-managed trial, from the prosecution viewpoint. Beck had been a power in Seattle, a moving force of so many things that had happened there, both good and bad. He had helped organize many aspects of Seattle life into union membership. As a regent at the University of Washington, for example, he helped persuade the legislature to appropriate the money to build the university's great medical school. It was no small matter to be able to convict him, and then to make the conviction stick.

Two men represented the state in that trial. The prosecution seemed to be focused through Lawrence Regal, a talented trial lawyer who completely destroyed Beck in a scathing cross-examination that skillfully exploited Beck's personality traits. But some of the most difficult problems were met and solved by a quiet, almost shy Negro attorney who worked with Regal and prepared all the briefs and handled all the arguments on law that were tossed into the proceedings by the excellent defense counsel for Beck. The trial court and the courts of appeal found his performance to be immaculate, for Beck's conviction was upheld in successive appeals.

That lawyer's name is Charles Z. Smith. His job as this is written is in the United States Department of Justice where his boss is Robert Kennedy. Smith's assignment is to examine the administration of the funds in another Teamster treasury — the pension funds of the Central States Southeast and Southwest Conferences. Smith's target again is a high Teamsters Union official, but this time his name is Hoffa, not Beck.

Smith is one of a group of attorneys and investigators in the Department of Justice which examines the way James R. Hoffa runs the Teamsters Union. Smith's job is to discover whether the pension funds have been managed properly, and to this end he has conducted several grand jury sessions in Chicago where the pension fund's headquarters are located at 29 E. Madison Street. As this is written, a jury in Chicago has convicted Hoffa and others on a number of charges in a complex case involving allegations of fraudulently obtaining more than $20,000,000 in fourteen loans for themselves and others. (Hoffa and the others have moved for a new trial and will no doubt appeal if the motion is denied.) The indictment accused them of diverting more than $1,000,000 of this to their personal benefit. The pension fund stood at about $200,000,000 at the time the indictment was returned. This means that about $40,000,000 or about 20 percent of the entire fund was involved in loans either to the Nevada gamblers for their casinos and related enterprises, or to a group of borrowers elsewhere in questionable circumstances colored by the suspicion of fraud.

Seven other men were indicted with Hoffa, and none of the matters involved had to do with the loans to the Nevada casinos.

However, one of the men indicted figures heavily in one of

the Nevada loans. This is Benjamin Dranow, fifty-five, a former Minneapolis department store executive who went to jail for mail, wire and bankruptcy fraud and tax evasion. He also was convicted for jumping bail, in circumstances that will make a part of our story. This indictment returned in Chicago accused Dranow of seeking out persons who needed loans and representing himself as able to get pension fund loans because of his association with Jimmy Hoffa. It was said in the indictment that Hoffa used "fraud, deceit, misrepresentation and overreaching" and abused his position of trust to get the loans approved.

Then, according to the indictment, the defendants would demand and get fees, stock options or stock interests in payment for arranging the loans. Fourteen loans were mentioned in the indictment — for shopping centers, hotels (such as the International Airport Hotel in Miami) and other commercial buildings in Florida, Louisiana, Alabama, Missouri, New Jersey and California. But as this is written, no indictments have been returned in connection with any of the Nevada loans. But Smith and the other Department of Justice lawyers in his section have dug into all the aspects of the Nevada loans.

The pension fund was set up in March 1955 to collect contributions from employers for retirement, disability and death benefits for more than 177,000 Teamsters Union members in about twenty states. The money being loaned to the gambling casinos in Nevada and in the controversial loans in the South and Midwest is meant to guarantee the integrity of these death, illness and retirement provisions in union contracts which require employer contributions.

To the extent that these funds may be available to Hoffa's cronies, it should be remembered that Hoffa has had some very strange cronies indeed. A series of his associations and relationships was explored for weeks in the hearings of the McClellan Committee and since then in books, in trials and in investigators' memoranda over the past several years. Which of these cronies first interested him in the Las Vegas gambling houses is unclear; who interested him in Reno is startingly clear — Benjamin Dranow, who is a co-defendant with Hoffa in the Chicago indictment for pension fund abuses.

There appears to be little question that Benjamin Dranow's connections with the Teamsters Union president had a bearing on the issuance of a $2,750,000 loan to the Riverside Hotel in Reno at a time when it seemed to be on its last legs, ready for closure. Dranow came to the Riverside in July 1962 at a time when he was getting ready to drop from sight. He had been convicted in Minneapolis of wire and mail fraud, of bankruptcy fraud and of violating the income tax laws. He was freed on $25,000 bond during appeal proceedings. He also was facing arraignment on a new indictment over the attempt to sell at discount a $100,000 U.S. Treasury bill that had been stolen. He sold the bill for $80,000 which was taken away in cash. So in the summer of 1962, Benjamin Dranow disappeared and a man named Ben Davis checked into the Riverside Hotel, a place then under the control of William Miller, who was a longtime friend of Benjamin Dranow.

Dranow behaved for all the world like a man with the key to the Teamsters' pension fund treasury. He was able to get loans of more than $1,000,000 to support the Thomas department store in Minneapolis, in spite of its shaky financial condition. He also was involved on the edges of Hoffa's disastrous Sun Valley, Florida, land sale promotion schemes and even made $17,000 out of a Hoffa-backed deal to sell jackets to teamsters in the Midwest. This was the man who showed up at the failing Riverside Hotel in July 1962 as Ben Davis.

William Miller, who had been running the place, had once worked as an entertainer in Florida, and had finally drifted into the business of booking entertainers. Once he was the entertainment director of the Sahara Hotel in Las Vegas. He acquired the management interest in the Riverside, after it had been almost ruined by an amateur management that effectively spoiled the hotel's longtime reputation as the "class" gambling hotel in Northern Nevada.

Miller was in sad straits when his old friend Dranow, alias Ben Davis, showed up in Reno. "Davis" immediately began to maneuver, and to give orders and to act as if he were a part owner of the place. He somehow played a part in persuading Raymond Spector, a wealthy New Yorker, to put $800,000 into raising the standards of the sinking Riverside. Spector, once chairman of the board of the Hazel Bishop cosmetics firm, should have known better. But he did not; he put up his money as a loan and then found that Miller was unable to repay it.

Along in this period, in the fall of 1962, Spector loaned $35,-000 to "Davis," too. This has never been repaid. "Davis" — Dranow, Jimmy Hoffa's friend, also gave advice to Spector and Miller on filling out a loan application form for the Teamsters' Union pension fund. This loan was filed and approved in short order, and instead of having to wait for the payout until the fund had accumulated enough uncommitted money, the loan was paid out to the Riverside in about three months. Usually, those close to the loan fund activities have said, it takes about three years for a large loan to be paid out to the borrower.

Spector has denied that the $35,000 he loaned to Dranow-Davis was in any sense a finder's fee for helping get the pension fund loan. But he has not received the money back from Dranow as of the end of 1963. Soon after the pension fund loan was paid into the hotel accounts, Dranow-Davis disappeared. He must have felt that the time for surrender to serve his sentences was getting near, and he intended to avoid this eventuality if it were possible. It was not. He took off from Reno. People who worked around the hotel have said since that they took him to be Spector, who they knew had big money in the place, or at least to be

Spector's overseer. None of them knew him for what he was —
a convicted fraud law violator on the lam.

Dranow eventually was found in Miami, living in the maid's
quarters of an expensive home, and trying to conceal his identity behind hair dyes and the walls of the house. As this is written, he is a prisoner in the federal correctional institution at
Sandstone, Minn. Spector withdrew from the Riverside, but
he had to put the hotel corporation into bankruptcy to get out.
He has said that he lost $80,000 in the venture.

Closure on the Riverside came in December 1962, a few days before Christmas, when suddenly the hotel management told the
350 employees that it was all over — the most famous gambling
hotel in northern Nevada was bankrupt. What about the $2,750,-
000 mortgage held by the union pension fund? Was it secure?
That was a big question and as this is written, it still is a serious
question. The place closed in late 1962, and reopened in the
summer of 1963, under new ownership. The new owners are
professional men from the cities in the Central Valley of California. They must make payments of $20,000 a month on the pen-
sion fund loan, in addition to whatever other commitments they
may have. Whether their management can make the Riverside go
or not is a question to be answered in a year or so. In the
months after they reopened, business at the casino was very, very
slow. Meantime, the Teamsters' pension fund has made a loan
that could be lost.

This was the only loan made by the pension fund in northern
Nevada and it appears to have been made on an entirely different
basis from those that were made in so much greater number in
the Las Vegas area. There has never been a public disclosure of
what prompted the Hoffa-led fund board to grant the Las Vegas
loans. There has been indication that E. Parry Thomas, the president of the Bank of Las Vegas, enjoys the trust of the pension
fund board, and that his bank has an interest in many of the
loans. These loans usually pass through his bank.

There are aspects of Hoffa's background that might bear on this Las Vegas loan series, too. In the years when he was moving around beneath Dave Beck's throne, organizing his own support toward the day when he would challenge Beck, Hoffa had very close relationships with a hoodlum who also had close relationships with one of the top figures in the Cosa Nostra. This man is John Dioguardia, or Johnny Dio, as he was called for so many years around New York. Hoffa used him when Hoffa wanted to take control of the New York City Teamsters organization. A series of charters for local unions was issued from Hoffa to Dio and men associated with Dio. When the test of strength came, Dio's crowd voted to support the Hoffa candidate, and the opposition was voted out of office. This solidified Hoffa's control in New York, and for this he has been grateful to Dio. The hoodlum used his local union charters to start up locals that were used for labor racketeering. Dio eventually ended up in Atlanta federal penitentiary for extortion in labor matters. Two other important underworld figures were there. One was Joseph Valachi, a Cosa Nostra "soldier" who was doing a long sentence for narcotics law violation. The other was Vito Genovese, one of the most important men in the Italian criminal conspiracy, also doing time for narcotics violations.

Valachi has told in detail how he discovered that Genovese wanted him killed, and how he himself killed an innocent prisoner in the mistaken belief that this man had the Valachi murder assignment from Genovese. One important detail of Valachi's story may not be remembered — he told of Johnny Dio trying to entice him into the prison showers in order to kill him there. This Cosa Nostra hoodlum was the man Hoffa used to help get control of the Teamsters in New York. In the Atlanta penitentiary, he was serving Vito Genovese.

Federal investigators in Las Vegas suspect that Genovese has a part ownership of one of the major casino hotels there. They insist that Genovese's share of the profits is carried away to his

representative in New Jersey by special courier. Is there a connection between the loans in Las Vegas and the former association of Dio and Hoffa and the more recent association in jail of
Dio and Genovese? Probably not, although various investigators
have raised these questions.

A much more solid connection with Hoffa exists among the
Nevada gamblers than this farfetched one with the Italian criminal group. Morris Barney Dalitz, the moving force for so many
years at the Desert Inn, and Jimmy Hoffa were doing business
together as far back as 1949. This was one of the many discoveries that Robert F. Kennedy made as chief counsel of the Mc-
Clellan Committee. Kennedy found that in 1949 a determined
business agent for the laundry workers in Detroit was trying to
force the laundry owners' association to agree to a five-day week.
The owners thought the cost would be more than they wanted to
pay. Remember that Jimmy Hoffa lived in Detroit, was president of the Teamsters there, and rose from the obscurity of a
warehouse loading dock in Detroit to his present position of
power. He was a powerful labor leader in Detroit in 1949.

The negotiations of the laundry workers and laundry owners' association bogged down completely on the five-day week
issue. A strike date was set. The union negotiators appeared
ready for a strike. So the management group called up Moe
Dalitz, whose proud boast has been that no matter how far from
home he has roamed in the gambling and bootlegging rackets, he
has always owned a piece of a laundry, his family's traditional
business. The laundry owners asked help from Dalitz, a bootlegger and gambler but also one of them. Within a short time
the owners were talking with Hoffa's advisers. The price of
peace, they were told, would be $25,000. The laundry owners
were shocked. Dalitz was not a part of these discussions. He
would not have been in the least astounded. Dalitz is a realist, and
these men could provide what the laundry owners had to have.
Eventually, the management negotiators, who failed in trying

to achieve some agreement with the union that represented their employees, managed to negotiate the bribe down to $17,500 to have the rug jerked out from under their employees. Moe Dalitz had shown them the way.

At the crucial time, late in the last session before the strike was to begin, Jimmy Hoffa came to the negotiations and ordered the union representatives to sign on the employers' terms or he would take over the negotiations himself. They signed. The employees' position was undercut through an arrangement reached behind their backs. This was possible only because Moe Dalitz had shown the way.

So perhaps Moe Dalitz and the Desert Inn crowd showed the way for the Las Vegas gamblers into the union pension fund treasury. For there may have been a lot of different open doors. Hoffa had many acquaintances and business associates over the years, and the pressure for new money from such sources as the pension funds is a continual fact of life in the business world — whether in Las Vegas or on Wall Street.

At any rate, the first of the Las Vegas loans was made to a business operation with which Dalitz was closely connected, although it had no direct connection to any of the gambling casinos. This was the Sunrise Hospital, a private, profit-making institution described in chapter 4. This little project got $1,000,000 from the Teamsters.

In Chapter 4 we also told how the Desert Inn group was the beneficiary of a $6,000,000 loan to Stardust, Inc., and Karat, Inc. This loan was just a straight provision of funds for building up the plant and expanding the facilities of the Stardust. The place is run on a lease arrangement by our old friend, United Resort Hotels, Inc. Moe Dalitz is also president of Karat, Inc., which runs the casino in the Stardust — the money machine. In 1961, remember, this casino ranked third behind Harrah's Tahoe and Harold's Club as the most profitable in the state.

When I talked to Moe Dalitz in the fall of 1963, in the executive suite at the Desert Inn, I asked him to explain the Teamsters Union loans his organizations had received. He made a great show of being sorry almost that he had become involved with them, for he said the security demanded was too great and the guarantees of repayment too strong. He also said that none of the Teamster money was involved in the Desert Inn, only in the Stardust. But J. A. Donnelley, the lawyer who now runs both places as executive vice-president, corrected Dalitz. A high rise hotel addition to the Desert Inn is being paid for through this $6,000,000 loan made in December 1962, with the Stardust properties and rentals as security.

Of the nine pension fund loans in Nevada, the Desert Inn crowd had its hand in four of them one way or another. The Star Investment Company got $1,200,000 in March, 1961, to build a golf course; this story was told in Chapter 4. However, the fourth of the Desert Inn loans from the Teamsters has Allard Roen out in front.

This was a loan of $850,000 in April 1962 to the Three-O-One Corporation of Las Vegas. This outfit owns and operates an office building at 301 Fremont Street in Las Vegas. This is right in the center of the downtown district. The structure, four stories high, is called the Nevada Building, and contains offices and shops. The other officer with Roen is William Israel Alderman, an old-time racketeer with the colorful nickname of Izzy Lump-Lump, and in other quarters, the more foreboding nickname of Icepick Willie.

We have traced Roen from his beginnings through his rise to prominence at the Desert Inn and his present status in suspension while he awaits sentencing when the government has finished with him in its prosecutions of Roy M. Cohn and whomever else it may want to use him against. But Alderman is new to these pages. The police across the Midwest and East have tied Alderman for years to the top figures in the underworld. He has been arrested for robbery, larceny, carrying concealed weapons, assault, disorderly conduct, and suspicion of murder. He has not been convicted. His "Icepick Willie" nickname pretends that he formerly did murder with an icepick. His arrests have been in Las Vegas, New York, Minneapolis and Chicago. His associates over the years have included Bugsy Siegel, of the Flamingo Hotel, and Tony Cornero, who ran the gambling ship *Rex* off the Los Angeles shore and dreamed of the Stardust hotel and casino. Alderman had business with Gus Greenbaum, who ran the Flamingo after Siegel was killed. Later Alderman moved to the Riviera. Greenbaum was murdered in his home in Phoenix and his wife was killed at the same time. At one time Alderman owned a part of the Flamingo Hotel, as well as the El Cortez Hotel and the Riviera Hotel. All of these associations and investments stamp him as closely connected with the New York criminal organizations that came to Las Vegas with Bugsy Siegel and stayed to grow and prosper.

What is Allard Roen, the cleancut young man from Cleveland, Duke University and the Desert Inn, doing with such a man?

Making money, that's what! Roen got tied up with Alderman in April 1961, before Roen was indicted in the United Dye and Chemical Corporation stock fraud case. They got the $850,000 from the Teamsters and set themselves up in business. Moe Dalitz and Morris Kleinman of the Desert Inn are the other directors of the Three-O-One Corporation. In the mortgage documents filed in Las Vegas, the Roen-Alderman combine shows that it was getting about $12,500 a month rental on the Nevada Building, with the prospects of getting more later on. This would pay off the loan handily. To show how little effect the court actions of the federal government have had on the attitudes of the Teamsters' pension fund trustees, it was three days after Roen was indicted in the United Dye case that the loan was granted to him and Alderman and the others. Further, the Teamsters would never worry at all that Alderman once was gathered up in a big federal investigation of national gambling syndicates — or that he took Fifth Amendment protection when questioned. Among some elements of the Teamsters' power structure, such actions would be worn like badges of honor.

Divining the ultimate explanation of the association of Izzy Lump-Lump Alderman and the satin-smooth, educated, polished and cautious Allard Roen is impossible at this stage in the proceedings. Perhaps later someone's foot will slip and it will become clear. Not now.

There were a couple of other curious loans made in Las Vegas outside the gambling field. One of these went to Hank Greenspun, the publisher of the Las Vegas *Sun*, and it was for $475,000. Greenspun borrowed the money to build a golf course from which he hoped to realize some tremendous profits in real estate developments in the desert. Like so many other loans that ultimately were paid out of the Teamsters' pension funds, this one started at the Bank of Las Vegas. Greenspun has said that the loan was entirely worked out with the bank, and that after it was granted to him, the Teamsters Union bought up the mortgage. He also said his loan was paid off within a few years after he took it out. It was used to pay for construction of the Paradise Valley Country Club. This is located in a suburban area of Las Vegas and is near the Las Vegas Strip.

In his early years in Las Vegas, Greenspun was a close associate of Wilbur Clark. At one time, Greenspun owned 1 percent of the Desert Inn, a portion designated for him by Clark who was very grateful for the help that he had received from Greenspun. But later Greenspun sold his stock. He told me that when the Desert Inn opened in April 1950 he was doing publicity for the place.

"We brought in all kinds of reporters and photographers," he said, "and the guys from Cleveland finally told me who we were doing business with — who our partners were — Moe Dalitz and

Morris Kleinman and that bunch. I quit the job because I couldn't stand to be around them."

This would make it appear that no connection with Moe Dalitz helped Greenspun get his loan from the Teamsters' pension fund.

Las Vegas is one of the best taxicab towns for its size of any in the nation. This is because of the great influx of well-to-do persons who fly into the desert for a fling at the gambling tables, and then want to visit all the places in one night. This means a lot of cab riding, for the Strip itself is about four miles long, while more mileage is involved in getting to the Downtown Casino Center where the Fremont Hotel and other casino operations are located. For the cabdrivers, the frame of mind of the visitors is good — a "let's live it up" attitude means good tips and no arguments about the bill.

The system of flying great herds of customers in from the Pacific Coast cities to the Las Vegas Hacienda miles out in the desert also is a boon to the cabbies. If they get tired of the hustle at the Hacienda, these visitors may hunger for the quieter and more sedate places nearer to town. A cab is their only chance of getting there.

Cab business is good in Las Vegas.

The cabbies are organized, too. They belong to the Teamsters Union, and this brings up another ironic note, for one of the major companies — the Checker Cab fleet — is owned by a former Teamsters Union official who bought it with a loan from the pension fund. This man is Homer L. Woxberg and he borrowed $225,000 in early 1962 to buy up the Ardmore Leasing Company in a carefully concealed business deal which kept Woxberg's name off all the documents involved in the transaction. This loan from the pension fund is another of those that has all the earmarks of being based on a personal relationship between the borrower and Hoffa.

For about ten years Woxberg was secretary in Los Angeles to the local union to which the long route drivers belong. These are the men who handle the big produce trucks that roll up the Central Valley of California for more than a thousand miles to Portland and Seattle. They herd the big diesel rigs pulling two big trailers across the deserts and mountains of the West. They are the elite of the Teamsters there and their annual earnings are very high. These were the men that Dutch Woxberg served as a local union secretary. But in those days he also served Jimmy Hoffa's interest. Remember that in the days before Robert F. Kennedy and John L. McClellan toppled Dave Beck from the presidency of the union, Jimmy Hoffa was tunneling and burrowing, trying to soften the foundations of the throne so he could shove the aging Beck off and move himself on.

One of the foundation stones of the Beck control was the Western Conference of Teamsters, and of course Los Angeles is within that area of control. Dutch Woxberg was Jimmy Hoffa's man in Los Angeles in those days, a figure around which the growing Hoffa strength in the area was able to gather. The time came, however, for Woxberg to move on. The hour arrived when he was convicted of embezzling union funds. Others became Hoffa's spokesmen in Los Angeles, but the faithful Woxberg was not forgotten. Hoffa bought him a cab company in Las Vegas.

The documents in that purchase and loan effectively concealed the identity of the man for whom the money was provided and for whom the cab company was purchased. But it became so apparent after a year or so that Woxberg was really the operator of the Checker Cabs in Las Vegas that the fiction was destroyed and the union officials admitted that the loan had been made for Woxberg's benefit.

What could anybody do about it?

Thus another big bundle of Teamsters' pension money came into Las Vegas. For a cab company purchase in a desert town, the loan was large. However, compared to some of the others made there, it was tiny.

There are indications of startling laxity in collateral requirements in some of the loans, too, although a federal investigator who has studied them carefully gave his opinion that the Las Vegas loans generally were well secured. Even in the light of this judgment, the weakness of the $4,600,000 in two loans to the Fremont Hotel is glaring as it shows in the files of records in the Clark County Courthouse in Las Vegas.

The Fremont Hotel, remember, is the one controlled by the sharp-eyed Edward Levinson who was the business partner of Bobby Gene Baker, the wonder boy of the United State Senate's staff. Levinson promoted the construction of the hotel after leaving Florida in the wake of the Kefauver gambling exposures in Miami and Miami Beach. It is the only one of the casino hotels operated in downtown Las Vegas, and by the look of it has been highly successful. But when it came time to add a fourteen-story addition, the use of the gambling casino profits for the job was never even seriously considered. Levinson, as president, and Bryant R. Burton who said that he managed properties for Joseph W. (Doc) Stracher of Beverly Hills, as secretary, of the Fremont Hotel, Inc., signed the documents which got them a total of more than $6,500,000 in loans, $4,600,000 from the Teamsters, the remainder from a San Francisco syndicate headed by Louis R. Lurie, the San Francisco financier. The first mortgage on the property was held by the San Francisco group. What secures the interest of the Teamsters Union members in their $4,600,000 doled out of their trust funds is a traditionally shaky second mortgage in a highly speculative enterprise with questionable backers.

The final loan that we will examine from the pension fund to the Las Vegas gamblers was a $5,000,000 package paid over to Western Realty, the owner of the Dunes Hotel, in April 1962. The

Dunes is said to have been closely associated with gambling and other underworld activities operated in New England. But today it is controlled by James Gottlieb and M. A. Riddle, according to statements made by local observers of the Las Vegas casino operations. However, Gottlieb does not appear on the ownership lists available from the state licensing officials at Carson City. These show that Riddle has 37.28 percent of the casino operation. Gottlieb owned various trucking and related companies in the Midwest while Riddle was in an oil operation, although he also was said to have been interested in some gambling operations near Chicago.

The operating company for the Dunes Hotel, as contrasted to the casino, is M & R Investment Company, which also holds some of Gottlieb's transportation interests. The best guess about why the Teamsters poured money into the Dunes Hotel is that Hoffa and Gottlieb knew each other because of Gottlieb's transport holdings.

Not everyone who wanted a loan from the Teamsters' pension fund got it, as gossip around Las Vegas and Reno makes abundantly clear. Further, these stories indicate the close control that James R. Hoffa exercises over the lending operations of the pension fund board of trustees. When Frank Sinatra was promoting money to establish himself and his partners in the Cal Neva Lodge at Crystal Bay on the north side of Lake Tahoe, he went to the Teamsters Union to try to get the money.

The gossip around Nevada tells what happened this way:

Sinatra, certainly an excellent loan risk from all accounts, had given the pension fund board a fully documented disclosure of all his financial dealings and standing, and of the possibilities of earnings of the Cal Neva Lodge and casino. The story is that Sinatra had word that Hoffa disliked him for some reason, and would look for an excuse to reject the request. So no effort was spared in turning out a financial statement and set of disclosures that might almost have met the standards of the Securities and Exchange Commission for listing a new stock for public offering.

But this didn't faze Hoffa. He just said that it didn't look to him as if the Sinatra interests were being quite square with the trustees. Hoffa thought they must be hiding something. Hoffa thought the loan should be refused. It was refused.

The reason for this peculiarity in Hoffa's outlook on Sinatra puzzled the Las Vegas crowd for a time, and then someone remembered that Sinatra has had varying degrees of friendship with the family of the wife of one of his good friends, Peter Lawford. Lawford was one of the members of the Sinatra Clan, which also included such as Dean Martin and Sammy Davis, Jr. Mrs. Patricia Lawford, his wife, is one of the daughters of Joseph P. Kennedy, the former ambassador to the Court of St. James's. One of her brothers was the late president, John F. Kennedy. Another is the attorney general, Robert F. Kennedy.

If there is any man on this earth that Jimmy Hoffa hates, that man is Robert F. Kennedy. An indication of that hatred came soon after that November day in 1963 when John F. Kennedy was assassinated in Dallas, Texas.

"That makes him just another lawyer," gloated Hoffa of Robert F. Kennedy.

Hoffa's hatred of the entire Kennedy family also led him to an open breach with Harold Gibbons, his most trusted adviser during the years when he was moving up from Detroit to take control of the Teamsters Union. Gibbons had wanted to issue a statement deploring the murder of President Kennedy. Hoffa exploded in rage at the suggestion and instead issued his statement of comment on his view of Robert Kennedy's new status.

At any rate, the Las Vegas gossip about the refusal given to the Sinatra loan application explains that Hoffa turned it down because Sinatra had been close to Lawford, a relative by marriage of the Kennedys, and also had put together entertainment spectacles in connection with some of the campaign needs of the politically oriented Kennedy family.

Any friend of the Kennedys will get none of the Hoffa-controlled millions, seems to be the rule.

Lending money to the gamblers is not a new trait in Hoffa, not something that he just picked up when he found himself surrounded by the stacks of money pouring into the pension funds. The McClellan Committee showed that he had many transactions with underworld figures. It seemed that when they needed money and couldn't get it from the banks, Hoffa was the next stop. Teamster treasuries under Hoffa's control have provided $12,000 to a numbers racketeer named Ahmed Abass, a man with seventeen arrests. Another numbers racketeer, John Bitonti, with twenty-three arrests, got $40,000 out of the Teamsters' treasury. Then there was the time the Teamsters bought a large estate outside Chicago to use it as a school. At least, that was the explanation that Hoffa gave to the McClellan Committee; but the property has never been used as a school.

This transaction showed a couple of interesting traits among the people who control the Teamsters' money, traits that may also crop up in the huge loans made from the pension funds to the Las Vegas and Reno gamblers.

First, the money — $150,000 — went to help a hoodlum in trouble; second, the business controls on the transaction were so sloppy as to be almost beyond belief. The hoodlum they wanted to help was Paul (The Waiter) Ricca, whose true name is Paul De Lucia. Ricca once was a bodyguard to Al Capone. In 1955, Ricca needed money in a hurry to pay up his tax bills with the Bureau of Internal Revenue. He had to have money that he could account for, and this barred him from any access to hidden stores of cash that the racket crowd might have on hand. He had to have money from somebody who could produce legitimate, taxed, capital in a hurry and then be ready to explain where it came from. Certainly, the internal revenue bureau would slaver at the thought of racking up Ricca and anyone who would step forward to help him. The money involved had better be able to stand the most strict inspection.

Hoffa and the Teamsters turned out to be Ricca's benefactors. They bought his showplace home for $150,000, which was his asking price and far above the appraised value. There was a terrible sense of urgency surrounding the deal, too, it seems. The union got title to only half the place. The swimming pool and the tennis court were both only partly on the land the union acquired.

Of course, this was just a technicality which Ricca and Hoffa and the lawyers straightened out after they got some expert advice. The advice came from Jerome S. Alderman, who was the chief assistant to Robert Kennedy in the McClellan Committee investigation, and now has succeeded his former boss as the occupant of Room 101 of the Senate Office Building.

(This is a historic office, incidentally, for its former occupants include William P. Rogers, who was attorney general in one of the Eisenhower administrations, Roy M. Cohn, who served Senator Joseph R. McCarthy from that room; and, of course, Robert Kennedy.)

After Alderman had drawn out the explanation of how the Ricca property transaction had been fouled up and suggested how it could be straightened out, James R. Hoffa, the supreme egoist, announced benignly: "We want to thank Mr. Alderman for giving us the information so that we could properly clear the title."

There are many lessons to be gleaned from the examination of the Teamster's pension fund loans to the Las Vegas gamblers. One of the chief ones seems to be that once the gamblers find a source of new money to bring into their financial manipulations, they work it to death. As we have seen in the examination of some of the non-gambling business operations they get into, the Desert Inn group had ample resources to swing all the expansion plans they could think of for the casino and hotel. But they wanted to use their money in other deals. The risks in loans guaranteed by the gambling house were too great for their tastes; much better, they thought, to let the truck drivers run the risks there.

Another lesson appears to be that this business is done on a personal — not a business — basis. For each of the loans that was disclosed in the hearings, there seems to be some personal involvement of the borrower with James R. Hoffa. Even in the most notorious refusal, there was a personal reason on Hoffa's part to turn down Frank Sinatra.

Further, there is an immense air of mystery that shrouds the dispersal of the great earnings of the casinos. The millions generated in the gambling pits and by the banks of slot machines just fade away. Nothing is left, they would have us believe, for expansion needs of the casinos. This is ridiculous.

As we have seen elsewhere, one Las Vegas Strip casino hotel over a five-year period showed net earnings of more than $10,000,000. This was the profits on which taxes were paid — the open, declared profits. Yet, at the same time this place was borrowing from the Teamsters Union pension funds to pay for expansion. The answer is simple. The Teamsters had the money and Hoffa was willing to let go of it. The gamblers had the money and they wanted to keep theirs, not tie it up in their gambling joints.

Given access to the great sums that the Teamsters' pension funds will continue to produce from an hourly levy on the work of the members, the gamblers could do many things, and a lot of them would be anti-social by almost any standards that we could use to judge. What will be the future relationship between the Las Vegas crowd and the truck drivers' retirement money?

Much will depend on what happens to Hoffa in the various criminal actions that now face him in federal courts across the Midwest. If Hoffa survives, it appears likely that his friendships that prompted the first loans will hold so that other loans will be made in the future. In short, more and more the truck drivers are likely to be the owners of mortgages on the Las Vegas gambling joints.

"Isn't that a hell of a place to invest pension funds?" asked one high government official a few months after the total involvement of Hoffa and the gamblers became known.

His question was rhetorical, but he was right. It is.

10

MORE CONTROLS THAT DIDN'T WORK: FROM HOT SPRINGS TO THE ISLE OF MAN

SOMEPLACE in these pages we should describe the grandest illegal gambling operation that functions anywhere in the United States — that of the hallowed resort town of Hot Springs, Arkansas. All the things that happen in Nevada happen in Hot Springs, except that in Hot Springs gambling is absolutely illegal, punishable not as a misdemeanor but as a felony with a term of up to three years in state prison. Serving mixed drinks is illegal in Arkansas, but in Hot Springs this is ignored. (This describes how it was — and how it may come to be again. Gambling and cocktail bars have gone from Hot Springs — at least for a time.)

Walk into the Vapors, a trim, neat, clean place a block or so from Bathhouse Row in Hot Springs. On the right, just as in the Desert Inn, is the casino, and on Saturday nights they sometimes turn away people because there is no room inside to stand, much less room to get at the tables. Even on a slow night the players stand in line behind blackjack players waiting to get at the table. The play is magnificently good, the crowd well behaved, and heavily inclined to throw away its money.

There are three such places in Hot Springs, and they run absolutely wide open and with the full knowledge and assistance of the law enforcement officials. The chief of police, whose next-door neighbor is Owney Madden, the one-time lord of the beer business in Manhattan in the 1920's, told me that it was all political. What he meant was that the people who ran the gambling did so on political grounds. He meant that they had backed the right side in the last election and so were permitted to violate the laws. If the other side had won, a different set of law violators would have been protected. The gambling and bootlegging would go on; in any case the only question decided by the elections was which of the contesting sets of operators would be allowed to make hundreds of thousands of dollars a year by running illegal places.

The federal government — at least as it was constituted when these words were written — would like to close down the Hot Springs gambling, unless the state of Arkansas were to make it legal. The Department of Justice has made extensive and expensive investigations of the gambling there, and holds that this illegal gambling constitutes a violation of federal law in that it makes use of interstate commerce to carry on an activity that is illegal within the state where it is operated. However, the Department of Justice has been unable to get a grand jury to indict the Hot Springs operators. This has been a point of irritation between various local public officials and those from Washington. For example, Senator John L. McClellan was told off by Nevada officials last year when he complained about what some of the Nevada gamblers had been doing. He was told that at least the Nevada gamblers were legal at home; his own gamblers from Arkansas were illegal and why didn't he do something about them, he was asked.

Senator McClellan had no answer, for he has resisted attempts to destroy the arrangements arrived at in his constituency long before he ever went to Washington. Hot Springs has been a gambling center since Civil War days, and only three times for brief periods have the games been stopped. The last time was in the late 1940's when Sidney McMath was elected prosecutor on a reform ticket. He closed it all down, and ran for governor the next election. He won, but his colleagues of the reform ticket lost in Hot Springs and the gamblers returned to open up again. (A fourth closure came after I reported in the New York *Times* in March 1964 on the Hot Springs gambling operation.)

The operation there is for all the world like Las Vegas. I saw Mickey Rooney playing to 450 people in the showroom of the Vapors. The food was delicious. The entertainment was fine. The place was neat and clean and well run. Off-duty policemen stood around to discourage any rough ideas.

It it almost impossible to discover even an approximation of the total profits of the three main gambling places and their smaller allied places. But it must run upwards from the $3,000,-000 which someone advanced to me as a minimum figure.

However, it seemed to me when I visited there in 1964 that the Arkansas authorities had done something that the Nevada people had not been able to do — the gambling was controlled by home-town boys and there was no indication whatsoever that any of it fed tribute to the national criminal organization. There are several reasons for this: first, the local boys have the "fix" with the law; they don't need help from the Mob in getting this. Second, the operation is self-contained. This takes more explaining.

Usually, the Mob gets its teeth into a lucrative business operation by furnishing something that the business needs. Maybe women. Maybe narcotics. Maybe money. Maybe muscle. Maybe a wire service to give sports and racing results. The Mob furnishes this, gradually moves its agents into positions of influence (remember Bugsy Siegel who went to Las Vegas to peddle the race wire) and eventually takes total command of the whole thing.

The Mob uses the race wire service to great advantage. Perhaps once it had its fangs sunk into Hot Springs' operation, too, for Owney Madden used to be the big race wire operator. But the wire folded and Madden now lives in semi-retirement. The local boys in Hot Springs run things. The two main operators, Dane Harris and Jack Pakis, both were born in Hot Springs. They know the local officials and are able to talk with them in terms of lifetimes spent together in this little mountain resort community. In many ways, this aspect of the Hot Springs operation is like Reno; although the method of operating the places themselves is much like Las Vegas, the Las Vegas pattern of Mob interest is not duplicated. What would happen if Arkansas legalized gambling in Hot Springs? The same men would continue to run it, and they would be reinforced in their positions by the legality they would then enjoy. As things are now, they could be forced out at the whim of their political sponsors any time they wished. Governor Orval Faubus looks on the Hot Springs gambling as a local problem, the time-honored out for any official who wants to sit and not act. But he opposes legalization of the gambling. (A law was proposed that would permit gambling only in Garland County, where Hot Springs is located. The voters turned it down and as this was written the casinos were dark but the flame of hope burned brightly among gamblers.)

The argument is that Arkansas could not control the gamblers if they were legal. In some ways the history of legalized gambling in Nevada fuels this argument, but on balance the Nevada experience shows that controls can be effective.

A different situation exists in some of the places abroad to which the Nevada philosophies have spread. Remember Clifford A. Jones, the lieutenant governor and gambler who came to grief before the Kefauver Committee? Now he is a big operator in the Caribbean. His partner is Jake Kozloff, who once ran places in Las Vegas. The unwary officialdom of out-of-the-way places, after a look at the glorious dollar-making operations in Las Vegas, tend to want these things transplanted back home. The latest to join the throng is the government of the British West

Indies. It has granted a gambling concession at Freeport on Grand Bahama Island, to the Lucayan Beach Hotel, and immediately all the familiar patterns that have been worked in Las Vegas for the past thirty years became visible on Grand Bahama.

Handouts from public relations firms announced that the Timmins Mining Company of Montreal was building a hotel, which the Molly Corporation of Toronto would operate. The casino would be operated by the Grand Bahama Port Authority, Ltd., through a subsidiary, the Grand Bahama Amusement Company The rest of the story spoke of the glories of climate, of the varius ways of reaching the place, and of the wonderful things to do and places to stay once this Mecca was achieved.

It didn't say that a former stock promoter from Toronto named Louis Chesler was the money behind this deal. Chesler also has another interesting business. He is the head of a film company called Seven Arts Productions. In 1963 this company provided months of titillation for the tabloid readers by taking Richard Burton (who brought Elizabeth Taylor) and Ava Gardner (who brought nobody) and Sue Lyons (who brought her intended) and a film production company to a village on the west coast of Mexico. Tex McCrary, the one-time public relations wonder boy in Manhattan, is associated with Chesler in these matters. McCrary is a director of the Seven Arts corporation, among other things.

There were all sorts of conditions attached to the deal Chesler made with the British in the West Indies. The croupiers were to be British, Irish or European — no Americans or Canadians. The casinos on the island must be operated as a part of deluxe hotels with no less than 200 bedrooms. The profits must be retained for further development of Grand Bahama Island. All of these things are meaningless to a really clever bunch. Who cares where the dealers come from? They deal right or we break their hands! So we have a 200-room hotel — great! More room to store the players so the tables will always be full. The profits? What profits? We took in a lot of money but we spent it all on this and that.

The man whose feelings were most hurt by all this was Huntington Hartford, the American millionaire. He had pioneered, he felt, in a big tourist attraction on an island near Nassau. (It had been called Hog Island, but Hartford renamed it Paradise Island.) He had put $25,000,000 in the place, and felt that this presentation of a gambling casino permit to his competition at Freeport put him on the spot.

"To all intents and purposes, gambling has come to the Bahamas to stay," said Hartford. He pointed out that the license for ten years to the Chesler group was issued by the governor and the executive council of the British West Indies, not by parliamentary enactment. Hartford said "they apparently figure the Bahamas will be the Las Vegas of Nassau" and added that "they thought they could do things over there they couldn't do in Nassau." Originally, Hartford had opposed gambling in the Bahamas, but two or three months before the license was issued to his competition, he had decided it would be proper if it were run in a dignified manner.

"Not like Las Vegas," he said.

Hartford offered the government to guarantee 1000 new hotel rooms would be built, and a total new investment of $20,000,000 if he got the license. He would give half the profits to the government for housing, medical care and social welfare, he said.

"I don't know the first thing about running a casino, but I would hire somebody from Europe who knew how to do it," he said. "This puts my position in the open."

In 1949, Wilbur Clark knew how to run the Desert Inn, if only he could get the money to open; he got the money from Cleveland. Then the people with the money took over the place. Maybe Hartford is lucky. His casino manager might have ended up owning Paradise Island. That's the thing about gambling houses — they attract some determined and clever acquisitive people.

After the license went to his competition, Hartford issued a press release which tiptoed around the edges of the main problems inherent in any government going into the gambling business. Said the press release:

As a tourist attraction, gambling probably has no equal. And if it is controlled in Nassau in the manner in which it has been in such places as Monte Carlo, Deauville and Puerto Rico, in the form of dignified casinos, it need not bring an undesirable element into the area. Does Nassau require this attraction as much as Grand Bahama and the other Out Islands? There are two ways of looking at the problem. The Out Islands lack tourists because they lack hotels: Gambling should provide — and is providing — excellent incentive to investors. At the same time Nassau, with a large population and extensive facilities, must depend on tourism as virtually its only industry. A case can be presented on either side concerning the need for gambling in Nassau versus the Out Islands.

But one thing is clear: If gambling comes to Nassau, it will possess other advantages beside that of attracting tourists. The amount of revenue from larger gambling casinos is reputed to be enormous. I have heard of profit figures running into the millions in the case of certain casinos in the hemisphere. If Nassau is to have gambling, into whose pocket is this money going? I believe a good part of it should go to the Bahamian people. Before the era of tourism, the Bahamas possessed little source of revenue, and much of the unemployment and poverty and ill health of earlier days still prevails. Babies are occasionally born blind, and worms, amoebic dysentery, and tuberculosis are prevalent due to poor sanitation and overcrowding. As the owner of Paradise

Island, I have had discussions over a period of years with prospective hotel investors, some interested in gambling, others not. From these talks I believe that I can confidently state that if gambling is permitted in Nassau — including Paradise Island — I can immediately put up at least one thousand first-class hotel rooms and other facilities with an investment of $20,000,000 or more. The resulting employment of thousands of Bahamians goes without saying, and I trust that my past record in giving employment will confirm the responsibility of this statement. Finally, I would like to make an offer: That 50 per cent of the entire net profit of a Paradise Island casino go to the Bahamian government for the specific purpose of improved housing, medical care, social welfare, with which, according to many reports, the government is vitally concerned.

Hartford put many of the classic arguments into that press release. This will bring great returns to Nassau, to the British West Indies, to everybody if only you'll let me open a gambling casino . . . No common people who would lower the standards, certainly not . . . No grifters from the gambling hells of the world, absolutely not . . . Big winnings are possible for us all if only you'll go along, I guarantee it . . . It would even help keep down amoebic dysentery . . . Those are the things he was saying.

Much of what he says is true. Freeport, on the Grand Bahama Island, is some sixty miles east of the Florida coast in the area of Fort Lauderdale and Palm Beach. Certainly the casinos will draw greater and greater crowds who will spend more and more money. But in the vacation market of the United States in these times, the way to make money is to follow the formula of Bill Harrah, the king of the Nevada gamblers — "we want almost everybody." Harrah would leave out the noisy and dirty ones, but everybody else would be welcome. The masses make the business pay. The British in the Bahamas will want all the money they can get, and they will run their gambling bases on the Harrah formula, to the end that the once exclusive vacation spots will be overrun with the crowd that goes on shorter notice to Jones Beach. Will the money be worth it?

It is of interest, incidentally, that the license was issued to Louis Chesler's group because he was a Canadian, not an American. He is associated with Mrs. Wallace Groves, whose Virginia-born husband founded Freeport after World War II.

It was late in January 1964 that the Lucayan Beach Hotel opened its gambling casino for a crowd that tried to be big-time social, but seemed to spend its time wondering in a bored way where the "real action" might be found. There was Fernanda Wanamaker Wetherill, whose party a few months before had turned into an international scandal of juvenile delinquency among the rich, as an entire house was gutted by the guests. Eva Six, the lushly endowed Hungarian actress was there. Mr. and Mrs. Russell Firestone had trouble getting a room when they tired of the gambling, until Mrs. John (Brownie) McLean, the social organizer, insisted that they be registered into a pad.

There were others. But if the idea had been to make the Bahama casino opening an attraction for the jet set, that idea was unfulfilled. After all, why should they go there to gamble when there were better casinos at Las Vegas or at Monte Carlo? Of course, this pseudo society opening fitted into the theme of Chesler and his associates — that only high class gambling was to be done at Lucayan Beach. This of course is ludicrous. A long time ago at Reno Raymond I. Smith showed them all the way to the piles of money — get everybody in who had anything he could lose. That's the way it will turn out sooner or later in the Bahamas, for otherwise the places can't make enough to stay open. The hotels can't survive at the prices they now charge. By Bill Harrah's standards, the casino at Freeport was almost deserted on opening night. There was room to move about, and always a place at the tables.

The croupiers looked like amateurs, too, but maybe this air of innocence is best in the long run, judging from experience elsewhere.

Early in 1963 the authorities on the Isle of Man in the Irish Sea decided to license a casino, too, and naturally they turned to the Americans to run it for them and to help them propagandize the island's three hundred Methodists who raised hell about a gambling joint on the island. The American syndicate was to pay £5000 annually plus 15 percent of the winnings. This was to go to support the costs of government on the Isle of Man. The casino would attract tourists, it was said, and the betting was to be on the "Woolworth principle" of small stakes and large turnover of bettors. Bill Harrah would have loved hearing it called that. No French phrases were used in the gambling places, so that the lower classes expected to pour in from the British Isles would not be uneasy. They even were offered lessons in roulette, chemin de fer, blackjack (which Nevadans called twenty-one) and craps.

In early 1964, when the place had been in operation about seven months, the Manx attorney general moved to prosecute five Americans. He asserted to the magistrates that the Americans had been caught taking it off the top. There was a quiver in his voice as he said that these Americans had a scheme for doing this and "thereby defrauded both the casino company and the government." It must have been a shock. What they did, of course, was just overload the roulette table accounts with paper. It appeared from the accounts that the tables had been losing, for they were forever drawing money to cover losses. This was untrue, of course, for they had been winning, and when the infrequent winners were paid off, their payout slips were altered by increasing them considerably. This kept the table account in an overage position which the Americans were said to have cured by taking off the amount of the overage in cash which was stuffed into a box and locked away in the safe with the name of one of the American executives on it.

Those accused in the fraud charge by Manx authorities were Frank B. O'Neill of Jacksonville Beach, Florida, the casino director; William H. Paris of Las Vegas, the deputy director; and these three members of the casino staff — Raymond Gavilan, James D. Gilson and Arthur P. Anderson. Anderson was identified as a nephew of John D. Hickey of Baltimore, a member of the syndicate which opened the casino. The leader of the syndicate is William A. Albury of Baltimore, and the third member is Mrs. H. McGarvey Saul, a real estate operator in Silver Springs, Maryland, just outside Washington, D.C.

There will be great wailing about the perfidity of it all, and demands that action be taken to prevent any such till-tapping in the future. A few among the Methodists of the Isle of Man may even point to the ultimate truth — when you bring in gamblers, you bring in trained law violators and to expect them not to break the law is to expect the tides not to rise. The odds are that no change — beyond a change in management — will be made. The Manx casino will continue to grind its profits out of the hard-earned money of the people attracted to visit it. The gambling men will continue to run the places, and the methods of taking it off the top of the profits will become more circumspect, more sophisticated and more successful. The method being used in the Manx casino wouldn't have lasted two days in Las Vegas or Reno. These practices will continue for the same reason they do in Nevada — the profits are too great for the gamblers to be able to bear to pay all the taxes on them.

In 1963, the best estimate had the slot machines in Clark County, Nevada, earning $36,000,000 a year. That same day a prominent casino official was giving advice on how to beat the slots, and assuring his hearers that it could be done.

It remains to be seen whether the governments in the islands of the West Indies or the Irish Sea can control the gamblers. After more than thirty years, that same question still is open and unresolved in Nevada. Perhaps the fact is that it can never be resolved. Life is full of such questions. A situation arises in which a new force is created. That force gains power and direction and then becomes a problem for the social order that existed before it was created. Such is the situation with gamblers and gambling wherever the law permits them to exist legally. Most of the states which have pari mutuel betting laws have at one time or another suffered a series of scandals involving the relationships between the track operators and the officials whose duty it was to control them. These scandals run their course; the open wounds they leave in the social order heal; time dulls the livid scars; a new set of scandals connected with the race track stuns the public; the cycle is repeated.

11

GAMBLING —
THE LEGALIZED INFECTION

Is it possible that gambling in Nevada will be voted out by the electorate? Or that the federal government will move to close it down? Or that some other catastrophe will bring to an end this three decades-old experiment in legalized gambling?

There was a time of crisis in the relationship between the gambling empire and the Nevadans who do not own any of the gambling. This came at about the end of World War II, reached its peak with the murder of Benjamin (Bugsy) Siegel, and lasted for several years thereafter. By the middle of the 1950's, gambling might have been voted out if the people of Nevada had been given an opportunity to examine the question in polling booths.

They were not given that opportunity. Most likely they never will be given it.

Repeated scandals connected with the gambling business brought it into ill repute on its home ground. One of the strange things is the revulsion felt by the people of northern Nevada for the high jinks being continually planned and pulled off by the gamblers in Las Vegas. There have been some scandals — rip roaring, succulent scandals — in the Reno area and around Lake Tahoe. But the worst aspects of legalized gambling have been shown in Las Vegas, while the older and more settled residents of Reno shake their heads and suck their teeth over the antics of the people down south.

Never during the years since 1931 have the political figures who ran Nevada shown that they really want to get rid of the gamblers. Control them — yes; there have been many who wanted the gamblers whipped into a straighter line, but to advocate getting rid of the gambling license system — never. It was the politicians, remember, who brought legalized gambling to Nevada in the first place. This was a law that was almost sneaked through the legislature without any great show of support among the voters.

The gamblers have paid and paid and paid over the years for this reluctance of the political figures of Nevada to vote them out of business. Even today the candidates for office call early in the year at the line of casinos down the Strip — or at the office of the man who at that moment is the designated distributor of largess for political campaigns. Some observers in Las Vegas and Reno will explain that it is traditional for a candidate for office to gather much more than he intends to spend. One candidate, widely urged to run a few years ago, finally agreed, but announced that he had to have $50,000 for himself, over and above his campaign expenses, to pay him for his trouble. He got it. In Nevada, the place one gets money of that magnitude is from the gamblers.

Gambling is a great source of public revenues, too, as we have seen. How would the state survive financially if the gambling taxes suddenly disappeared? Nevada would either retrench a state budget already very skinny, or Nevada would go bankrupt. The economy that exists outside the gambling casinos would never support the population that now lives in Nevada. Tourist trade would fall away, and those acres of subdivisions that Moe Dalitz and his playmates built outside Las Vegas would revert to the mortgage holders within a matter of months after the closure of the casinos. Reno would survive, a much constricted place, for Reno had things to offer long before Las Vegas' rapid growth from feeding on the gambling winnings of the casinos.

Most of the big hotels on the Strip would disappear without the profits of the gambling places to keep them going. A strange experiment came about in 1963 with a place in Las Vegas called the Tallyho Hotel. It was a very nice place, with golf, swimming pools, lots of rooms at modest rates, fine dining rooms and entertainment. But it had no casino, and this was the basis of the experiment. The place had cost about $12,000,000 and it closed within the year it was opened. Its new owners applied for a casino license. Reopening awaited state action on the license. People are drawn to Las Vegas by the gambling, and by that alone. The weather is better in La Jolla or northern Mexico, both closer to Los Angeles. Why go across the desert and into Nevada except to gamble? There is no reason. If Las Vegas, with all the attributes of climate that it can muster, were located at about Pittsfield, Massachusetts, the winter run of visitors would swamp the hotels. But Las Vegas is located in an area where its winter climate is no different from that of most of the other towns in the Southwest, and not so good as many.

So they go there to gamble. No gambling; no visitors.

Should the gambling stop, there would yet be a growing attraction in Lake Tahoe, for this is a jewel of a lake in the High Sierra. Without a doubt, a sizeable collection of recreation-supporting facilities such as motels, restaurants, garages and service stations would be supported by the increasing numbers of Californians who would go to Lake Tahoe — gambling or not.

But in the view of the elected leadership, the people who must worry about the state's finances, uprooting gambling would cause the worst depression to hit an American state since the decline of coal mining in West Virginia. The political leaders of Nevada first of all have no predisposition to kill off gambling; secondly, they could never face the complete destruction of their political careers that would follow.

So much for Nevada's possible voluntary ending of the experiment in legalized gambling. It will not be done.

What about the federal government's position in all this? Will some action be taken that will effectively destroy the gambling empires? What chances would such a proposal have in Congress? What would bring it up in Washington? Really, is it any of the business of the other forty-eight states individually, or collectively through their federal government machinery?

These questions have many more subtle "ifs" and "buts" in their answers. To understand one problem, remember that Nevada's first prominence in the Union came as a divorce state; Nevada relied on the "full faith and credit" clause of the United States Constitution to obligate other states to honor the divorce decrees of Nevada courts. Many times, by the light in which divorce is held in other states, those Nevada divorces are nothing more than a conspiracy to commit fraud — a conspiracy in which a state government and its representatives are full partners.

Also remember that in 1931, Nevadans worried about competition for the divorce mills operated in Reno, not about the future that gambling legalization would bring to the state.

These Nevada divorces have been lamented by many a strait-laced judge in other states in the years since they became popular. But the other states have not attacked the Nevada institution. Instead some of them have even adapted the Nevada law to their own uses. So it is with the gambling laws. No other state has tried to move against Nevada's "peculiar institution." Some have even moved a few inches toward copying it a little in state lotteries and legalization of slot machines. So Congress would be reluctant — almost impossibly reluctant — even to hear debate on the subject. It would take an unusual and peculiar and startling set of circumstances to create a situation that would even permit discussion of outlawing Nevada gambling by federal action. So reluctant is Congress — tied as it is to the state's rights views of the Southerners — to limit the rights of the states that such a bill probably would die in committee.

If the bill were to be voted upon, the Nevada senators most

certainly would call in all their political debts, sell their political souls, and do everything within their power to bring about its defeat. The senators from Nevada these days do not have the power that the late Senator Pat McCarran used to be able to wield. Senator Alan Bible of Reno and Senator Howard Cannon of Las Vegas do well for their constituents, but neither of them is able to do it as Senator McCarran once did. While he helped write one of the most reactionary immigration bills in modern American history, Senator McCarran still held himself up as a liberal — because he was "liberal" on matters of conscience that included gambling and prostitution. He used to hold court in the Riverside Hotel in Reno, between bouts in the Senate in Washington. There he would dispense the influence and indulgences that he seemed to think were the things that Nevadans sent him to Washington to bring back.

Perhaps they did.

In the federal system there is little chance that the United States government will ever move to root out the legalized gambling in Nevada. There are just too many troubles in the way — even if Senator McCarran is dead and gone. The federal government may decide some day to root out some of the evils that legalized gambling has brought, however. Take, as an example, the ridiculous situation wherein the State of Nevada can insist that its auditors have full access to the counting rooms of the casinos — and the United States government cannot do that for its internal revenue agents. Of course, there are dangers in such a course, too.

"You ever do that, you just make a lot of rich revenue agents," said one knowledgeable observer. It is significant that when the internal revenue scandals broke during Mr. Truman's second administration, one of the most criticized agents lived and worked in Reno. He specialized in selling worthless mining stock at high prices to gamblers and businessmen whose tax returns failed to meet specifications. When they bought, their tax troubles were over.

There is no reasonable explanation of the failure of the state and United States agents to work together to see that the gamblers pay their full tax load to both governments. There are varying degrees of cooperation on an informal basis, but these things change as administrations change in Carson City and in Washington. They should not change. They should be written into law. That law should expand the areas of cooperation far beyond what they are now informally. From the point of view of the state, this would provide the Gaming Commission with yet another means of holding a choke collar around the gamblers' necks. For the federal treasury, the benefits would be magnificent.

What could the federal government do? What could the state do? What is needed? So many times and so eloquently it has been said that a people cannot legislate morals, that we sometimes act as if we believe it. We should not. We do legislate morals. We have for thousands of years. Sometimes we legislate a brand of morality that the majority disapproves, and then this legislation disappears, and the men who write epigrams cite that disappearance to prove the truth of the saying. What happens generally is that the common morality on a given point will be written into statute, and those who would deviate from it are deterred or punished when caught. Certainly the morality of the run-of-the-mill Nevada gambling operator as we have reviewed it here is not the standard of American morality in the latter part of the twentieth century. Those games played by Bobby Baker and Eddie Levinson are not within the standard of behavior of our time and culture. The contract between the Desert Inn and the Clark County Sanitary District No. 1 does not meet the accepted ethical standards of America of today. None of the nine men who sit on the United States supreme court would have dreamed of issuing a ruling in a case that came as close to his person as did Judge David Zenoff without any showing of serious misgivings. But they sit in Washington; Judge Zenoff sits in Las Vegas.

True enough, the federal government is able to deal with some of the excursions out of the desert against the wealth of the rest of the nation. When the gamblers from the Desert Inn mounted a raid on the stock market, the United States government was equal to the task of capturing them, breaking their wills, and forcing them to serve its purposes in dealing with their associates in the transactions. What of the countless times that these men and their fellows have come out of the desert to work whatever little games went undetected? What of the flow of illicit cash, the "black money," into the American socioeconomic structure? Who is to control that? How will he do it?

There are things that could be done by state law, for the state of Nevada is responsible not only for its own ends in this experiment but for the effect of these things on the rest of the nation. By Gaming Commission regulation or by statute, it could tighten up the bookkeeping still further. Why not sealed meters on the slot machines? Why not some meter arrangement for dispensing and redeeming chips? Is it impossible to devise a system that will give both the state and federal governments access to the fair taxes on the total winnings of the casinos?

Certainly it is possible to establish the winnings. It could be done easily if the state of Nevada pushed hard enough and its officials had stomach for the job. Some of them do now, but others do not. Remember, the gamblers have been an integral part of Nevada life for thirty-odd years, and they have wrapped their fingers around many a heart in those years. Since 1960 the State Gaming Control Board has been struggling to check the flow into the cashboxes of the gambling tables . . . and has failed. It can make estimates; but estimates do not provide evidence sufficient to pass muster in court. In the federal courts, tax agents were able to put Al Capone in jail when they showed that he spent more money than he reasonably could be assumed to have available in light of the income shown in his tax returns. This is called the "net worth" method of prosecution, and has proved to be a potent weapon in the hands of federal agents. But in Nevada, the state courts have not permitted actions against licensees of the Gaming Commission on the same sort of evidence. If an agent can state positively that he saw more money go into a cashbox than the balance sheet at the end of the shift shows was in the box when it was counted, this is not enough to bring about a license revocation. The licensee may claim the boxes were accidentally mixed, or whatever.

The federal government could move against Nevada gambling by completely forbidding the movement of such things as slot machines across state lines, or the moving of gambling equipment across state lines. Perhaps the Congress could ban even travel across state lines when the intent of travel is to be able to gamble. But none of these things will be done, for none of them would solve the problem. The people of Nevada want legalized gambling, and under the federal system, they are entitled to it so long as it does not become burdensome to the other states.

During Governor Grant Sawyer's administration, there have been brightening indications that the state is gradually moving to fulfill the responsibility for control of the monster that it created in 1931. Governor Sawyer's Gaming Control Board is filled with dedicated men, determined to fight the cheaters among the gamblers, and also determined that it will prevail. Governor Sawyer, a Democrat, was elected in 1958, and re-elected in 1962.

"The Black Book" was a product of the Sawyer administration. It was a step in the proper direction. Ten years before, the Kefauver Committee, in hearings in Las Vegas and elsewhere, had shown conclusively that the Las Vegas casinos of that day were the breeding ground for all manner of horrors that were felt across the United States. The then lieutenant governor of Nevada defended his colleagues in the gambling business. But in the decade that followed, until about 1961, there was no serious move by any state administration in Nevada to clean out the thugs who had found refuge there. Today, after all these years, there is still no disposition to run out the men with proved records of thuggery, thieving, prison terms, criminal conspiracy and other acts which point to strong anti-social dispositions. The attitude is more stern, but the stern face is turned toward the newcomer, not toward the old-timer who has been in Las Vegas for a decade or more.

It was all well and good to chase off Frank Sinatra for his association with Sam Giancana. But why the delay in dealing with Allard Roen? He has pleaded guilty to stock market frauds involving millions of dollars, and the record shows conclusively that he was a party to the Guterma operation. What has the state done to unravel the relationship between Moe Dalitz and Sam Garfield? Or between Eddie Levinson and Bobby Baker? What about those gambling houses that borrowed millions from the Teamsters' pension funds? Is that none of the business of the Nevada state authorities? Should not the state of Nevada accept responsibility for the actions and effect on society of those men whose success and power have been created by the state and who learned their ethics in the back alley?

Is it possible for Nevada to control the gamblers who come there to reap the harvests of money from the crap tables and slot machines? Of course it is possible. The state teeters on the edge of doing it right now. But something holds it back. What is it? The state of Nevada is the last refuge of these gamblers and superannuated racketeers. Bill Harrah, that strange man who is the best of all the gamblers, said it so well when he said that giving the gamblers a right to anything was to invite disaster.

Yet the state treats them with as much consideration as the Interstate Commerce Commission treats a collection of railroads. Why? They do not deserve it. Commonly, when a gambler is caught cheating he is asked to surrender his license. The theory is that this method cuts down on extensive legal work and makes things run more smoothly. This is ridiculous. They should put him in jail. If he stuck a gun in a man's ribs and took his money, he would risk being locked up in the little prison that stands on the eastern outskirts of Carson City. But if he cheats at cards while dealing, the state only asks that he give up his license.

Should worst come to worst and the gambler end up in the little penitentiary at Carson City, he would be able to continue gambling, using brass chips issued by the management of the prison. A prison management that operates a gambling game for their inmates! When they win, the winnings are credited to their accounts, and when they lose, their accounts dwindle. No state license, either.

This is Nevada.

Maneuvers in the gamblers' state reverbrate across state lines, too, and in Idaho in 1962's gubernatorial race, the chief platform plank — the only plank — of the Democratic candidate was a campaign to legalize casino gambling on the Nevada pattern. The candidate was a Boise lawyer named Vernon K. Smith, who talked about nothing except the benefits of having gambling casinos. We met in the bar of the Boise Hotel and he waved his arms as he talked about his project, referring frequently to data supplied to him by friends in Nevada.

"Why, this place could have twenty slot machines in it and over there in that part of the dining room you could have your casino," he said. "Idaho's got nothing to sell but scenery, anyway, and look what it did for Nevada."

Smith was no knucklehead. He was a successful lawyer in Boise. Perhaps he really believed what he was saying. I hope not.

Anyway, he was defeated in a year when the Democrats did well in Idaho. He probably will never be heard from again on the political platform. His embracing of the gambling philosophy shows, however, another thing that the Nevada gamblers export. This is the widespread propaganda for gambling as a source of revenue. Certainly they would like to see it in Idaho. The Nevada crowd would control it, whether its names were on the Idaho licenses or not. After all, they became expert in this during the years they dodged around shadowboxing with the state authorities in Nevada. But even though they never managed to get the voters of Idaho to elect a man who spoke the thoughts they liked to have running through a governor's mind, the Nevada gamblers still managed to dip into the Idahoan's pockets. They established open gambling joints at Jackpot on the Idaho border. The Nevada State Gaming Commission abandoned a twenty-eight-year-old policy against stateline casinos with the following reasoning:

> The Gaming Control Board survey on Idaho community opinion centered on Twin Falls, the closest major concentration of population. The feeling toward establishment of non-restricted (casino) gambling generally was favorable. Police officials felt it would cause them no concern and merchants believed that further development would mean business for them, since Twin Falls is the trading center for Jackpot residents. On this point, Jackpot club owners estimated that over 90 per cent of employee salaries was spent in Idaho.

People in Nevada will tell you today that the gamblers live in constant fear of the state authorities. This may be true, but remember that gamblers are not businessmen. Gamblers are never happy except when they have a game with a fixed wheel or fixed dice or some edge that gives them the percentage in the game. One in a hundred would be happy — as Bill Harrah is happy —

with strong state control, with a Nevada Gaming Commission that was full of rugged, tough, hardnosed and suspicious men who distrusted gamblers. The run-of-the-mill gambler becomes as nervous in such a situation as a turkey at Thanksgiving. He tends to twitch and talk to casual acquaintances about how tough it is and that nobody knows how he suffers. This is while he has control of a marvelously productive business that brings him in more money than he can conveniently haul to the bank.

What is happening to the nation under the thrust of power from this new force is comparable in a remote sense to what has been happening to Lake Tahoe's beautiful blue waters as a result of the population growth at the lake's edge. This lake is one of the most beautiful bodies of water in the United States. It fills a huge basin in the summit ranges of the Sierra Nevadas, and served a century ago as a marking point on the boundary between Nevada territory and California. The boundary runs to the northwest from the Colorado River in the desert and through Lake Tahoe, then straight north to Oregon.

For many, many years the lake was a summer vacation place, and was isolated and alone in the winters when the snow piled high, awaiting the melt of spring to feed the lake's volume for the following summer. People who loved the wilderness camped there, hiked there, and enjoyed the majestic beauty of a body of water unsurpassed on the continent.

When the shores were settled by people attracted by the flood of dollars from Nevada's gambling, problems began to arise with the lake's waters. Almost immediately there were indications of stains, of algae, of pollution around the water's edge. Homes and commercial buildings were required to install the best septic tanks that could be had.

The stains of pollution continued to spread toward the deeper waters of the lake.

Then it was discovered that even though the treated sewage

did not drain into the lake, it was causing pollution and gradual increase in algae that eventually would take over the entire lake unless this food supply were shut off. The chemicals of the treated sewage were being washed into the lake after rising to the top of the ground from the septic tank drainage fields. It was said that the only way to protect the lake was to export the sewage out of the Tahoe Valley by a long conduit that would pass through a tunnel piercing the mountains.

Perhaps this will work. Plans to do it are under way.

Nevada also has been exporting the problems that arise from gambling operations. The rest of the nation has been the dumping ground for these. Nevada may have solved some of its problems. The dollars from the gambling tables have provided a tax base that enables the state to survive in good style even though it has an economy based in large part on gambling.

But it is significant that most of the arrests and prosecutions of the gamblers are made by federal agents and in the federal courts. There has been a parade of these Nevada gamblers before the federal judges in the early 1960's as they plead guilty to violating federal laws by using interstate communications to pass betting information. Some of them had top jobs in the casinos; but they were gamblers and the law forbidding what they did had no real meaning to them. Generally, the courts have dealt leniently with them, which perhaps is just as well.

This situation is significant — that the federal government is the only agency able to nail the gamblers for violations of the gambling laws. Can it be true that the state officials actually believe that the gamblers are paying all their taxes? Certainly they do not believe it. But they have been unable to catch them out. This outpouring of "black money" continues to move across the nation, bringing elements of fraud and moral corruption wherever it touches.

The underlying evil of the social and economic impact of the gambling wealth has its roots in the immorality that runs through gambling's entire fabric. We have documented this statement enough in the account leading up to this point. Let us state it clearly: By the social and ethical rules of the American culture, gambling is an immoral business, tainting those who operate it. When it is kept illegal and occasionally is swept under the rug in upheavals of moral reform, this gambling has slight opportunity to work its colors into the permanent pattern of American life. But when given a base of legality, as has happened so spectacularly in Nevada and to a less visible degree elsewhere through the widespread legalization of betting on animal races, the morals and ethics of the gamblers become a part of the accepted pattern of life.

Those who feel compelled to draw absolute judgments may draw their own. This is a fact of sociology — that when gamblers are given a foothold in legality, they rapidly expand it into a permanent bridgehead from which they branch out in all directions. They have a bridgehead in Nevada and from there they are working their changes on the patterns of American life.

Nevada may be able to live with the situation that it has created, a situation which we have described in these pages. But the rest of the nation is not able to endure it. Despite all of those problems of the influence of the Nevada senators and the reluctance of the Southern bloc to move against any state's internal administration, the Congress and the executive branch must move against the evils of gambling in Nevada. At the very least, the gamblers must be contained. They must never be given the feeling that the general morality has been dragged down to their level.

For if they do, they'll move a level lower and tug down on the rest of us from there.

*A Partial Chronology of Some Events
Discussed in this Book*

A List of Persons Mentioned Frequently

A PARTIAL CHRONOLOGY OF SOME EVENTS
DISCUSSED IN THIS BOOK

BECAUSE the events connected with Nevada gambling and its effect on other parts of the United States stretch across so many decades, and because there is a relationship in time between some of these events that would be laborious to point up in the running narrative, it was thought to be helpful to present them in this chronological listing.

1864 — Nevada becomes a state. The mines were producing a flow of wealth valuable to the Union treasury.

1899 — Year of birth of Edward Levinson, M. B. (Moe) Dalitz and Sam Garfield.

1910 — Nevada outlaws gambling, which had been wide open from the earliest times.

1911 — William F. Harrah born in South Pasadena, California.

1920 — The Prohibition Era opens.

The 1930s — Decade when Raymond I. Smith, a former carnival worker, built Harold's Club as the new model for legal gambling houses, directed toward mass appeal.

— M. B. (Moe) Dalitz reportedly associating with such national crime figures as Lucky Luciano, Bugsy Siegel and Meyer Lansky.

1931 — Nevada legalizes the gambling halls which have come back to run openly even though illegally. Divorce laws also are liberalized.

1932 — National Prohibition repealed.

1933-37 — Morris Kleinman in federal prison for violating federal income tax laws.

1937 — William Harrah, successful in a bingo parlor in Reno.

1941 — Edward Levinson, arrested many times for gambling, paid a fine for conducting gambling in Detroit.

1943 — Bugsy Siegel sent to Las Vegas by the national crime organization to open up the Mob's race wire service.

1945 — Nevada levies first state tax on gambling, a 1 percent levy on gross winnings which brings in $100,492.

1946 — Flamingo becomes big money earner after Siegel is killed.

1947 — State tax raised to 2 percent, brings in $518,632.

— Small-time gambler, Wilbur Clark, begins construction on grandiose plan for hotel, casino, golf course, high cost housing development, the future Desert Inn.

1948 — Thunderbird Hotel and casino constructed, partly on money lent secretly by Meyer Lansky and Jake Lansky.

— Reform mayor elected in Portland, Oregon, so that Al F. Winter and his cohorts move bookmaking, gambling and other activities to Las Vegas.

1949 — Moe Dalitz and Cleveland gamblers take over 74 percent of Wilbur Clark's Desert Inn.

1950 — Alexander L. Guterma arrives in the United States from Manila.

— Desert Inn opens with Dalitz crew much in evidence close behind Clark's wide smile.

— On November 15, Kefauver Committee in Las Vegas hearing exposes the criminal backgrounds of many casino operators and the relationship between them and some Nevada political figures.

1951 — Sheriff in Evansville, Indiana, raids offices of Gar-Dan Oil Company as headquarters for national bookmaking operation on sports events. Sam Garfield fined for keeping a gambling house.

1952 — Edward Levinson moves to Las Vegas from Miami, where the Kefauver Committee revelations had shut down gambling.

— Al Winter and the Portland, Oregon, group open the Sahara Hotel. The Sands, with Frank Sinatra, opens this same year.

— Mervyn Adelson and Irwin Molasky arrive in Las Vegas from Los Angeles.

1954 — Edward Levinson appears as owner of 13 percent of the Flamingo hotel, the place the Mob had built.

— Representative George Bender of Ohio elected to finish the term of the late Senator Robert A. Taft.

1955 — Nevada state gambling tax raised again, on sliding scale from 3 to 5.5 percent of gross winnings, produces $5,441,327 that year.

Mid-1950's — Low point of public opinion in Nevada toward the gambling casino owners and system of licensing.

1955 — Alexander Guterma, well known as a high roller in Las Vegas, becomes close associate of various elements in the Desert Inn ownership.
— Edward Levinson shifts to the Fremont Hotel Casino which he has promoted and controls.
— Riviera, Dunes and Royal Nevada casino hotels open.
— Bill Harrah expands from Reno to Lake Tahoe.
— Alexander Guterma buys Garnak Drilling Company from Sam Garfield and Irving Pasternak, giving them Shawano Corporation stock rather than cash.
— Guterma takes Edward T. McCormick, president of the American Stock Exchange, as a yacht guest to Havana, pays off $5000 of McCormick's gambling losses.
— Virgil D. Dardi sells United Dye and Chemical Corporation to Guterma.

1956 — Guterma acquires F. L. Jacobs Company.
— Guterma and Desert Inn group form United Hotels as first step in aborted plan to market public issue controlling physical properties of Desert Inn.
— Royal Nevada closes on New Year's Eve.
— Senator George Bender defeated.

1957 — M. B. (Moe) Dalitz involved in labor payoff by McClellan Committee in its study of James R. Hoffa.
— Ex-Senator Bender turns up on Hoffa payroll.
— Edward Levinson's attorney loses briefcase with interesting papers in Las Vegas airport.
— Nevada supreme court decides in favor of Thunderbird Hotel ownership in concealed interest case, but shakes up gamblers with new law created in the decision.
— Sunrise Hospital deal begins to form; Teamsters lend $1,000,000.
— Tropicana Hotel opens; police find Tropicana casino records on racketeer Frank Costello.
— Lowell M. Birrell leaves United States for Brazil after looting many American companies including United Dye and Chemical Corporation.

1958 — Grant Sawyer, a Democrat, elected governor of Nevada.
— David Zenoff appointed district judge in Las Vegas by lame duck governor, Charles Russell.
— Guterma acquires Scranton Lace, Roach Studios, and Mutual Broadcasting System; the New York *Times* assigns Harrison E. Salisbury to study Guterma.

1959 — Gene Evans and Howard McKissick, Jr., push through Nevada legislature a much strengthened gambling control law.
— Desert Inn owners shed problems of United Hotels by creating United Resort Hotels.
— Guterma falls, indicted in F. L. Jacobs Company violations of securities laws; also indicted in United Dye and Chemical Corporation violations; his former associates at Desert Inn not indicted.
— Roy Cohn buys Lionel Train Corporation.
1960 — Multimillion-dollar convention center built near Strip casinos at Las Vegas with public funds.
— Second indictment brought in on United Dye case.
George Ratterman elected as reform sheriff in Newport, Kentucky, ending long run of illegal gambling there.
1961 — Robert F. Kennedy named Attorney General.
— Third set of indictments in United Dye case, this time by the Democrats headed by Robert Morgenthau as U. S. attorney.
— Star Investment Company gets a loan from the Teamsters Union pension fund to build Stardust Golf Course.
— Allard Roen, Willie Israel Alderman and others get pension fund loan to buy downtown building in Las Vegas.
— Ex-Senator Bender dies while under investigation.
— Edward T. McCormick resigns as president of American Stock Exchange after disclosure of gambling losses paid by Guterma.
1962 — Loan to the Dunes Hotel from Teamsters' pension fund.
— Harold's Club in Reno sold for $16,675,000 in sale and lease-back arrangement.
— Teamster pension fund loan to Riverside Hotel in Reno for $2,750,000.
— Gamblers report gross winnings of $240,000,000 this year, pay taxes to state of $11,263,463.
— Union pension fund lends money to former Teamster official, Homer L. (Dutch) Woxberg, to buy taxicab company in Las Vegas.
— Teamsters make big loan to Desert Inn.
— Judge David Zenoff hears unusual condemnation case.
— Guterma testifies in the United Dye and Chemical trial against his old friends, tells of plan to give $100,000 bribe to Ex-Senator Bender to get S.E.C. investigation stopped.
— Federal grand jury investigation in New York of circumstances of first United Dye and Chemical indictment by 1959 grand jury.
— Grant Sawyer re-elected governor of Nevada.

— Idaho voters turn down Democratic gubernatorial nominee, Vernon K. Smith, who campaigned exclusively for legalized gambling in the Nevada pattern.

1963 — Robert G. Baker, secretary of the Senate majority, makes appointments with John Gates, official of a Pan-American subsidiary, for Edward Levinson and other Nevada gambling figures to attempt to get gambling concessions controlled by Pan-Am in South America; later Baker forced to resign senate job and his association with Levinson becomes known.

— Judge David Zenoff terminates Las Vegas grand jury investigation under circumstances raising questions of conflict of interest.

— Frank Sinatra retires from Nevada gambling after dispute with Licensing Board over his harboring Sam Giancana, notorious Chicago underworld leader.

— All defendants convicted or pleaded guilty in longest criminal trial ever held in a federal court — the United Dye and Chemical Corporation case.

— Roy Cohn and associate, Murray Gottesman, indicted on perjury charges in connection with 1962 grand jury study of 1959 United Dye and Chemical indictments.

— Isle of Man authorities reveal that Americans licensed to conduct gambling as a tourist attraction have been caught "taking it off the top."

— Frank Sinatra, Jr., kidnaped from a motel room while waiting to appear with the reincarnation of the Tommy Dorsey Band at Harrah's Tahoe; released two days later, when father had paid $240,000 ransom; three convicted.

1964 — Legalized gambling begins at Freeport on Grand Bahama Island with big pseudo-society splash.

— Extortion cases in Denver and Los Angeles with Las Vegas backgrounds and involvements create major new problems for gambling control authorities.

— Senate investigation of Robert G. Baker's business activities show them heavily involved with Edward Levinson in a vending machine company, in a Tulsa bank, and in various loans.

— Roy Cohn and Murray Gottesman acquitted. James R. Hoffa convicted of manipulating loans from Teamster Union pension fund.

— Federal authorities attack illegal gambling at Hot Springs, Ark.; state voters refuse to legalize it; casinos close with future in doubt.

— Nevada supreme court overrules Judge Lenoff.

A LIST OF PERSONS
MENTIONED FREQUENTLY

SOME VERY complex relationships are described in this book and it was thought that a short description of some of the frequently mentioned persons would be helpful to the reader. Not all the persons mentioned in the book appear in this list.

MERVYN ADELSON — A partner and co-holder of stock in several enterprises outside the gambling field with gamblers who control the Desert Inn and Stardust casinos in Las Vegas.

WILLIE ISRAEL ALDERMAN — An aging underworld figure who has been connected with various casinos in Las Vegas, and most recently was indicted in an extortion case involving a disbarred Denver attorney as the victim. Known also as Izzy Lump-Lump.

ROBERT G. BAKER — Formerly the secretary to the majority in the United States Senate. A business associate of several Las Vegas gamblers, most notably Edward Levinson, the chief figure at the Fremont Hotel. Baker resigned his Senate staff job in the fall of 1963 and was under intensive investigation as this book was written.

MARSHALL CAIFANO, also known as Johnny Marshall — An underworld figure much feared for many years in Las Vegas, the central figure in litigation over the "Black Book" issued by the State Gaming Control Board in Nevada, and convicted in federal court in Los Angeles in February, 1964, of attempted extortion.

SENATOR HOWARD CANNON — Nevada senator from Las Vegas. Senator Cannon was a member of the Senate Rules Committee which investigated Robert G. Baker.

WILBUR CLARK — The man who dreamed of the Desert Inn, and invested all his money in it, but had to bring in a collection of gamblers and former bootleggers from Cleveland to finance the finish.

M. B. (MOE) DALITZ — The leader of the Cleveland group of gamblers and former bootleggers that went to Las Vegas in 1949 to finance the completion of Wilbur Clark's Desert Inn. Dalitz still makes the major policy decisions for the Inn, and also for a wide spread of non-gambling investments that the same group has made.

NICOLAS DANDOLAS, also known as Nick the Greek — One of the legendary figures in American gambling, now an old man and almost retired, although his name crops up frequently in connection with Nevada gambling.

VIRGIL D. DARDI — A financier intimate with Alexander L. Guterma and others in the stock-rigging scandal involving the United Dye and Chemical Corp. Dardi was convicted of violating federal securities statutes.

JOHN ANDREW DONNELLEY — A San Diego attorney of fine reputation who in 1963 became the executive vice-president of the Desert Inn, replacing Allard Roen who was convicted of Securities Law violations.

BENJAMIN DRANOW — A convict and apparent friend of James R. Hoffa, the Teamster president, who seemed able to arrange loans from the union pension funds to gambling casinos. He and Hoffa were among those convicted in Chicago in 1964 of federal charges of misusing Teamster pension funds.

JOHN DREW — A part owner of the Stardust Casino, whose resort to the Fifth Amendment protection in a Los Angeles extortion trial has raised serious questions for Nevada gambling control authorities.

GENE EVANS — A former Elko newspaper editor and legislator who helped write the 1959 gambling control legislation which has stiffened state control of the casinos. Now he is a press agent for William F. Harrah, the leading gambling operator in Nevada.

SAM GARFIELD — A boyhood friend of Moe Dalitz who has moved with the Desert Inn group in many ventures, including the disastrous one into the stock market with Guterma.

SAM GIANCANA — The leader of the Italian criminal organization in the Chicago area and an associate of Frank Sinatra, the entertainer. This relationship apparently cost Sinatra his right to own gambling casinos in Nevada.

HANK GREENSPUN — Formerly owner of a minor share in the Desert Inn, now the publisher of the Las Vegas *Sun* and bitter enemy of the Dalitz-led group.

ALEXANDER L. GUTERMA — A mysterious White Russian who grew up in China, came to the United States after World War II, and was one of the wolves of Wall Street during the 1950's. He was convicted of violating securities laws, served a penitentiary sentence, and was a witness against his former associates.

WILLIAM F. HARRAH — A Californian who has become the most successful gambling operator in Nevada. The ideal gambling operator in the view of many Nevadans.

MARION B. HICKS — Now dead, Hicks was the controlling personality in the Thunderbird Hotel and casino, and had extensive relationships with underworld figures who helped him build the hotel and bankrolled the casino in its early days.

CLIFFORD A. JONES — A former lieutenant governor who has had extensive gambling interests, and is now involved in several casinos in the West Indies and South America. A partner of Jacob Kozloff.

ROBERT F. KENNEDY — The former Attorney General of the United States and a man greatly feared by the Nevada gamblers. Also the most honorable and militantly dedicated public official I have ever encountered. Now the junior U. S. Senator from New York.

MORRIS KLEINMAN — A member of the Cleveland group, and a major shareholder in the Desert Inn. Served a term in federal prison for income tax evasion, which does not bar him from holding a gambling license.

RUBY KOLOD — A member of the old-time Cleveland underworld group and owner of a major interest in the Desert Inn. Now under indictment, along with Willie Israel Alderman, in Denver, charged with attempted extortion. His case presents serious problems to the Nevada authorities, as does that of Drew.

MEYER and JACK LANSKY — Brothers involved in much of the illegal syndicate gambling in the United States in the past thirty years. They are now located in Miami and have no interests in any Las Vegas or other Nevada casino, as far as the records show, but many observers believe they have concealed interests.

EDWARD LEVINSON — The largest stockholder in the Fremont Hotel, the major downtown casino hotel in Las Vegas. Levinson had gambling interests in Detroit, Cleveland, Newport, Kentucky, and Miami before coming to Las Vegas. He also had extensive business interests with Robert G. Baker, the former secretary to the United States Senate majority. Levinson was called as a witness in the investigation of Baker and took the Fifth Amendment.

PAT McCARRAN — The late senator from Nevada who looked on the gamblers as his special children and protected them in every way he could.

EDWARD T. McCORMICK — The former head of the American Stock Exchange who was forced to resign when it was found that Alexander Guterma had paid gambling debts for him.

THOMAS JEFFERSON McGINTY — Another member of the Cleveland group that controls the Desert Inn.

IRWIN MOLASKY — The other half of the firm of Adelson and Molasky, and a partner in various enterprises with the Desert Inn group.

EDWARD A. OLSEN — The former Associated Press reporter and bureau chief who has been a member and now chairman of Nevada's State Gaming Control Board.

IRVING G. PASTERNAK — A former protégé and partner with Sam Garfield in various oil ventures. Convicted with Garfield, Allard Roen, Virgil Dardi and many others in the United Dye and Chemical Corporation case.

ALLARD ROEN — A protégé of Garfield and Dalitz who was once crown prince of the Desert Inn organization, but now has had to step aside since his federal conviction. A close social friend of Adelson and Molasky.

RAY RYAN — Owner of El Mirador Hotel in Palm Springs, California, and the chief government witness against Marshall Caifano in an extortion trial. Ryan is a high-rolling gambler and wealthy oil and real estate operator.

GRANT SAWYER — Governor of Nevada elected in 1958 and reelected in 1962. He has made many public statements demanding that the gambling laws be tightened and has directed his appointees on the Nevada Gaming Commission and the State Gaming Control Board to enforce the laws strictly.

BENJAMIN (Bugsy) SIEGEL — A paranoiac hoodlum who may have been the most important figure in the history of gambling in Las Vegas. It was Siegel who devised and built the Flamingo Hotel, the pattern for all the other big places on the Strip. Siegel was a murderer, extortionist, sadist, procurer and completely unmanageable psychotic who eventually was slaughtered by a hired killer.

FRANK SINATRA — The entertainer. He was half owner of one casino, and 9 percent owner in another. Had a run-in with state authorities when he refused to stop his long-time association with Sam Giancana, the Chicago underworld leader and sold out shortly thereafter.

RAYMOND I. SMITH — The founder of Harold's Club in Reno, and the inventor of many of the mass advertising, transportation and other sales devices used by Nevada gamblers today.

SAM TUCKER — Another of the Cleveland group that bought into the Desert Inn with Wilbur Clark.

JOE VALACHI — A former member of the Italian underworld who has become a major informer for federal authorities. He had little direct knowledge of Nevada gambling, but insisted that the Cosa Nostra — a name he gave to a group he formerly belonged to — controlled several of the casino-hotels on the Las Vegas Strip.

Index

INDEX